William and Dorothy Killen
1950

T. B. LARIMORE

LETTERS AND SERMONS

OF

T. B. LARIMORE

EDITED BY

F. D. SRYGLEY

AUTHOR OF

Larimore and His Boys,   *Seventy Years in Dixie*
Biographies and Sermons, etc.

VOLUME I

NASHVILLE, TENN.
GOSPEL ADVOCATE PUBLISHING COMPANY
1949

PREFACE TO MARS HILL EDITION

It has now been more than twenty years since the lamented T. B. Larimore died in his eighty-sixth year, in Santa Ana, Calif., and was "gathered to his people," even as Abraham "died in a good old age, an old man, and full of years, and was gathered to his people." Since his death all the so-called "Larimore Books," "Letters and Sermons of T. B. Larimore," Vols. 1, 2, and 3; "Larimore and His Boys" and "Life, Letters and Sermons of T. B. Larimore," have gone out of print.

The demand for the "Larimore Books" continues. It is in response to this prolonged and growing demand that "Letters and Sermons of T. B. Larimore" is being reprinted. If this volume meets with the reception which we expect, it is our purpose to reprint all the "Larimore Books." They will do good—immense, incalculable good. The humility, reverence, love, loyalty and purity of the inimitable Larimore pervade all his books. This generation needs a double portion of his spirit.

This is called the Mars Hill Edition because the school at that place has been revived by Irven Lee and others. The faculty and students of the present Mars Hill School are vitally interested in the publication and distribution of the "Larimore Books."

Nashville, Tenn., October 7, 1949.

B. C. GOODPASTURE

CONTENTS.

EXTRACTS FROM LARIMORE'S SERMONS.

ILLUSTRATIONS.

LETTERS AND SERMONS

OF T. B. LARIMORE.

CHAPTER I.

LETTERS—ORIGIN, CHARACTER, AND DESIGN
OF THE BOOK.

THERE has long been a demand for a book by T. B.
Larimore. Some want a book of sermons; others
want a book of sermons interspersed with other matter of
general interest about the man and his work. A few extracts from private letters will define his feelings about such
a book, explain the origin and purpose of this volume, and
give an outline of the plan on which it is constructed:

" WAYNESBORO, TENN., April 17, 1892.
" Mr. F. D. Srygley.
" Dear Sir: By request I write to find a book of sermons
by T. B. Larimore, if there is such a book or will be soon.
Several parties want such a book. I write this by request
of some young people who heard Brother Larimore in some
of his meetings. T. F. M'ANALLY."

This letter was forwarded to him, with the following note
on the margin:

" I write him no such book is out, and I do not know that anything of the kind is contemplated. Do you think it would be well to bring out a book of sermons?

"SRYGLEY."

He returned the letter and wrote as follows:

"As to bringing out a book of sermons, I think it wise and well to do so if we can get the sermons; but there's the rub. I once thought I could furnish the sermons, but I know a great deal less now than I thought I knew then. Seriously, I do not think my sermons are worth publishing."

This ended the matter for a time; but the question came up again and again in calls for such a book from Alabama, Mississippi, Missouri, Texas, California, and other States where he labored. How he stood against all this pressure, and the conditions on which he finally consented for the book to be brought out, will appear in the following extracts from his letters, covering a period of several years:

Inclosing a letter urging him to let a book be brought out for the good it would do, he wrote:

" Truly I need, desire, and ask for your advice relative to book of sermons referred to in the letter I herewith send you. If, directly or indirectly, anything emanates from my mind, tongue, or pen, worthy of preservation—anything valuable that may be profitable for publication—I want it to be yours, and yours alone, if you want it. This has long been my desire. Now, I request you to tell me plainly—fully, freely, and frankly—what you feel, think, and desire. Please write without reserve. I do not believe my mind is a mine from which much valuable matter can be taken, and I have discouraged the idea of a book of sermons all the time. I think my sermons would not make interesting reading at all. What you think, I do not know. I expect no golden harvest from my literary labors, if there be such labors; but if anything I can say, do, or even write, can bless church or world, I will gladly say, do, or write it."

To this I replied at length, and concluded as follows:

"All this is intended to approve and encourage the idea of bringing out the book, and I will do all I can to assist you or anybody else in such an enterprise; but I cannot give it my personal attention just now, because I already have more work in hand than I can do, in justice to myself."

This caused him to write as follows:

" Of course I would be less than human not to appreciate your suggestions and the anxiety of others relative to a book of my sermons, interspersed with other matter about me and my work; but I think that is of small consequence in comparison with your other work. I think all my friends would heartily approve such a volume if brought out by you, while they would be unwilling to commit the work to other hands. So far as I am concerned, I never approve the thought of entertaining the thought of committing anything along that line to other hands; but whatsoever you may undertake, you may rely on my rendering you all the assistance I can. If good can come of it, I approve it."

This is the shape the matter assumed several years ago. When I took it up with him again, he wrote:

" I am willing to ' preach the word,' but beyond that I

am not willing to trust my own judgment. Do in all things exactly as you deem best, direct me to do whatsoever you wish me to do, and be sure you will please me in full in all respects. I want you to do, always, exactly what you may deem best, regardless of what I may think or say or do. You may always rely on my coöperating with you to the fullest extent of my ability. I have never thought my sermons would be readable. Moreover, I have long wanted you, and you alone, to hold all right to publish anything worth publishing from, of, or about me. If you have any wish in the matter, please express it to me, and as you wish, so shall it be; but, remember, I hold you in honor bound to do nothing because I suggest it, to publish nothing because I write it. You are solemnly and unreservedly committed to this. Remember. When you get manuscript—any and all—from me, always do with it exactly what you deem best, and you will always do exactly as I desire you to do. Never forget that. If you undertake to bring out the book suggested, I will gladly help you all I can; but you can never be under obligation to me—never. In figuring on it, financially or otherwise, always keep free from all thought of obligation to me. There is no such obligation; there never has been such obligation; there never can be such obligation. It will never be necessary to ask me whether anything you wish about the book will please me. Be it what and as it may, if it is what and as you want it, it is what and as I want it; and you may know so. So you are both of us, so far as bringing out the book is concerned. Do as you deem best, and you will please me. This applies to all I have ever sent you and to all I may ever send you. Please remember that. The day may come when it may be of some advantage to you. You owe me nothing; I owe you much. All I have to say on the subject is: Whatsoever you wish to do is what I want you to do, and I am at your service to the extent of my ability. That's all. If you wish to do anything while I live in which I can be of any service to you, I wish to know it and wish to help you all I can. I think, however, my work is almost done. If so, the day is not far distant when all will be in your hands. Then you can do as you wish; it will be nothing to me. The thought that 'I have finished my course' troubles me not. If it were a mere matter of choice with me, I would 'pass over the river' now. I fear nothing beyond—nothing. 'I long to be there.' Now, then, with all the facts and figures before you, you can 'take the case.' 'What I have written, I have written,' and I have nothing more to say. 'Tis all my business here below to cry, 'Behold the Lamb of God, which taketh away the sin of the world,' and I have solemnly resolved to 'preach the word' in love, and to do as much good and as little evil as possible 'while the days are going by.' My work is to work; that's all."

After I had decided to bring out the book and had indicated to him the kind of matter which it would be well to put in it, he wrote:

"900 South College Street,
"Nashville, Tenn., March 2, 1900.

" My Ever Faithful Friend and Brother: For more than thirty years we have known each other intimately and well. Though often separated in space, we have never been separated in spirit. When not constant companions, we have been in constant correspondence with each other. During all these years I have confided in you fully, and have never had cause to regret it—never. I've told you the best, I've told you the worst, I've tried to tell you all I've known or seen or heard about myself. You know me, if any mortal does. You have received from me trunks, and drawers, and boxes full of letters and selections during these thirty years and more—good, bad, and indifferent; wise, other wise, and doubtful; original, picked up, and selected; prose, poetry, and pictures; facts, fiction, and fun—from and about me. You have my permission to use these things as you wish.

"Gratefully, affectionately, and fraternally,
"T. B. LARIMORE."

After I began work on the book, I called to see him about some matters pertaining to it, and by the next mail he wrote:

"Though you tried to be cheerful while with me Friday, there was an indescribable shadow of sadness in your look and language and manner that you could not conceal. Still, you said nothing sad, except: 'I feel like I am preparing to write your obituary.' Well, my beloved brother, that is exactly what you are doing. You are tenderly, tearfully, and prayerfully preparing to make the last book that will ever be made by or about me; a crown for me, woven by willing hands, under the direction of a thoughtful head, in compliance with the demands of a loving heart—a heart always loyal and true. Your work will be bedewed with tears of friends tender-hearted and true when the bodies in which you and I now love and serve the Lord sleep in solemn silence in the bosom of the earth. ' O, why should the spirit of mortal be proud?' ' The time of my departure is at hand.' I am trying to ' fight a good fight.' I have almost ' finished my course.' ' Henceforth there is laid up for me a crown of righteousness '—for you, too. I want no crown if my friends must be crownless; but I rejoice to read, to believe, to know, ' there is laid up for me a crown of righteousness, which the Lord, the righteous judge, shall give me at that day: and not to me only, but unto all them also that love his appearing '—and that includes hosts of friends as faithful, pure, and true as have ever lived and loved and smiled and sighed in this strange world of joy and sorrow, where ' man's inhumanity to man makes countless millions mourn.' I rejoice to know that Heaven knows I am living for the good that I can do; that I am doing all in my power to brighten and bless this world as I pass through it; to add as much to the happiness and as little to the sorrow and sadness of the suffering, sorrowing, sighing sons and daughters of men as possible, as I journey to that land where alone I shall ever find real rest, perfect peace, and unalloyed bliss."

I have quoted thus at great length from his letters to make it entirely clear that, if there is merit in the book, he is entitled to all the honor, for it is his production; if there is no merit in it, I am to blame for putting it upon the public, because I brought it out at the request of others, against his judgment and feelings candidly and frequently expressed.

The design of the book is to do good. He has never consented for it to be published except on condition that " good can come of it." In passing upon everything that is in the book, I have been guided by my own desire as well as by his wish that nothing but that which will do good be allowed to appear in it. Christianity in theory and in practice is what does good. The plan on which the book is arranged is to exhibit the theory of Christianity, as far as he is competent to teach it, in his sermons; the practice, as far as his life exhibits it, in his letters. The clearest revelation of a man's real life and character is his confidential, private correspondence; the best expositions of a preacher's ideals of Christianity are his sermons. This book, then, is the best exposition of Christianity in theory and practice that has been exemplified to the world in the life and sermons of T. B. Larimore. It is not my province to express an opinion as to the merits of either the man or his sermons. I believe they will do good, else I could not publish this book under his instructions; further than this, I venture neither criticism nor eulogy. I have tried to let him fairly represent himself, both in his sermons and in his letters, and I believe he has done it. Whatever estimate a discriminating public may form of him, either as a man or as a preacher, I believe those who study this book carefully will know him exactly as I have known him, both as a confidential friend and as a noted preacher, for more than thirty years. While I had unlimited permission to publish any or all of his private letters which in my judgment would do good, regardless of consequences to himself, I have not used that liberty to gratify the reader's curiosity, or to create sensations, or to make a hero of T. B. Larimore. I have simply tried by quotations from his letters to exemplify in his life, as he has tried to teach in his sermons, that which will help sinners to become Christians, encourage Christians to live godly in Christ Jesus, and stimulate preachers to labor earnestly and abundantly to convert sinners and save souls.

It may be said that the letters quoted in this book do not fairly represent the man, because they all indicate virtues and reveal no faults in him. In some of the letters quoted he frankly admits that his " mistakes have been many and marvelous, " but says he has always done what he believed was right when he did it. This is enough to show that he would not have any one consider him perfect. It is well for every one to remember always that there has been but one perfect life in the whole history of the human race; that was the life of Jesus of Nazareth. All other lives are imperfect. Even when a man's motives are always good and his purpose is always to do right, his judgment is not infallible, and he is liable at any time to do wrong unawares and unintentionally. For this reason every one should take Christ as a model and try to be like him; no one should try to be like any other man. It is well to copy the virtues of all men as far as possible, but it is equally important to remember that every man has faults which ought to be avoided and corrected.

The sermons were delivered during a protracted meeting in Nashville, Tenn., the first weeks of the year 1900, and reported by Miss Emma Page, a competent stenographer. The quotations from his letters are just as he wrote them, barring such corrections as would naturally be necessary to prepare hurried, confidential, private correspondence for publication in a book. The corrections were all made by his permission and with his approval, and the book as a whole was read to him and approved by him in manuscript before it went into the hands of the printers.

I have no financial interest in the book.   Brother J. C. McQuiddy, one of his pupils at Mars' Hill and a lifelong friend, has agreed on behalf of the Gospel Advocate Publishing Company, in which he is a partner and of which he is business manager, to bear all expenses of bringing out the book, and if there is any profit from the sale of it, Larimore will receive it.

CHAPTER II.

SERMON—THE WHOLE DUTY OF MAN.

(Sermon delivered by T. B. Larimore at South College Street Church, Nashville, Tenn.)

R EMEMBER now thy Creator in the days of thy youth, while the evil days come not, nor the years draw nigh, when thou shalt say, I have no pleasure in them [and these dark days are coming to all who do not put their trust in God, and live so as to have the hope of eternal blessings as their light beyond the shadows of time] ; while the sun, or the light, or the moon, or the stars, be not darkened, nor the clouds return after the rain : in the day when the keepers of the house shall tremble, and the strong men shall bow themselves, and the grinders cease because they are few, and those that look out of the windows be darkened, and the doors shall be shut in the streets, when the sound of the grinding is low, and he shall rise up at the voice of the bird, and all the daughters of music shall be brought low ; also when they shall be afraid of that which is high, and fears shall be in the way, and the almond tree shall flourish, and the grasshopper shall be a burden, and desire shall fail : because man goeth to his long home, and the mourners go about the streets : or ever the silver cord be loosed, or the golden bowl be broken, or the pitcher be broken at the fountain, or the wheel broken at the cistern. Then shall the dust return to the earth as it was : and the spirit shall return unto God who gave it.

- 2 -

" Vanity of vanities, saith the preacher; all is vanity. And moreover, because the preacher was wise, he still taught the people knowledge; yea, he gave good heed, and sought out, and set in order many proverbs. The preacher sought to find out acceptable words: and that which was written was upright, even words of truth. The words of the wise are as goads, and as nails fastened by the masters of assemblies, which are given from one shepherd. And further, by these, my son, be admonished: of making many books there is no end; and much study is a weariness of the flesh.

" Let us hear the conclusion of the whole matter: Fear God, and keep his commandments: for this is the whole duty of man. For God shall bring every work into judgment, with every secret thing, whether it be good, or whether it be evil." (Eccles. 12.)

" Let us hear the conclusion of the whole matter: Fear God, and keep his commandments: for this is the whole duty of man. For God shall bring every work into judgment, with every secret thing, whether it be good, or whether it be evil."

The book called " Ecclesiastes " is a very peculiar book. Of course every book has its distinct peculiarities; and if a book should be made not being peculiar in some respects, it would have no special interest to a literary public, from the fact that its field is already occupied. But Ecclesiastes is a *peculiarly* peculiar book. It is so exceedingly peculiar that, unless we are careful to understand the general import of it, we may become very greatly bewildered in reading it.

Of all the books that have ever been written, there are

exceedingly few that are simpler, plainer, or more easily comprehended than the beautiful book called " Ecclesiastes," and yet there are few books that are harder to comprehend. It is so simple that little children can understand it from beginning to end ; it is so hard that sages may read from beginning to end and be worse bewildered when they get through than when they commenced. It depends to a great extent on your general conception of the scope, design, and mission of the work as to whether you understand it immediately, or know scarcely anything about it at the end of a lifetime of study. Unquestionably, Solomon, in writing the book called " Ecclesiastes," was in the hand of Providence as a great actor upon a stage, with the universe for an audience, trying to teach all mankind that this world can never give the bliss for which we sigh ; that it is not the whole of life to live, nor all of death to die. Now, if we will just take that view of it, and understand that Solomon is just a great actor, acting this part now, and not his real self when he is writing this book, just as Booth, the tragedian, on the stage presented "Julius Cæsar," talking as Julius Cæsar, thinking as Julius Cæsar, trying to look like Julius Cæsar, and at the same time being in reality Booth—now, if we can just get this idea, and read the book with that thought before us, we can understand it. If you have never read the book with that key, with that idea, I will feel perfectly safe to say that you, as honest men and women, would say that you have never been able to understand Ecclesiastes ; but if you have read it with that key, that you understand and consider it one of the simplest and sublimest of books.

Man is in quest of happiness in this life. It may be

true that " man is made to mourn," as Burns tells us.   It
is true that " man is born unto trouble, as the sparks fly upward ; " for not Burns, but the Bible, tells us that.   But it
is also true that " man's inhumanity to man makes countless millions mourn," even if Burns, and not the Bible,
tells us that.   But still, man is in quest of happiness from
the cradle to the grave.   So if we can see teeming millions
tending to a certain point, foraging like bees upon a certain field, or going to drink from a certain fountain, then
we can understand that these human beings think that happiness can be found there.   This is based upon the fundamental principle of the philosophy of the human mind,
and is universally true, always has been true, and always
will be true.   Now, remembering this, it will not take us
very long to see from what source people expect to draw
happiness in this life.

There is a widespread, deeply seated, and almost universal impression that knowledge and wisdom can give
happiness ; hence it is there is a general restlessness in the
human family along educational lines.   The fathers and
mothers are willing to wear their lives away to give their
children advantages, many of whom cannot appreciate
these sacrifices until they shed unavailing tears above the
silent dust of those who gave their lives to lift them up
and make them happy.   Hence it is that men will trim
the midnight lamp, and read, and think, and write, until
they sap the very foundation of their physical constitution, and bring themselves to an untimely grave, as Pollock
did, many of whose finest writings are in condemnation of
that very course, when he was, while writing these things,
following that course to a suicide's grave, when otherwise

he would have been in the prime and vigor of young manhood. Hence our restlessness with reference to the news. If it is time for the afternoon paper, and we make a mistake and get the morning paper, we are vexed. We want to keep abreast of the times and keep on learning. Now Solomon was the man to go on the stage and present this to all of us, and to go on before us across the stage and then tell us the result.

The curtain rolls up for the first scene and we behold the wise man, Solomon. Look at him. We see he is a marvelous man—the expression of his countenance, the shape of his head, his whole mortal frame bearing the stamp of wisdom and knowledge. He had divine assurance that he was wiser than any man who had preceded him on the stage of action, and until time's knell should sound no man should come upon the stage of action that could rival him. His wisdom was such that kings and queens and princes came from different parts of the earth to study like little children at his feet and gather wisdom from his lips. Amazed and dazzled at the splendor of his wealth of knowledge, they returned to tell their subjects that the half had never been told. We see Solomon on the stage enjoying all this prominence. Is he happy? We see him thinking deeply. We see him take his pen and write, "How dieth the wise man? as the fool"— one event painful to them both; that increase of wisdom is ever an increase of sorrow, and we realize that he is thinking of the day, not far distant, when the flaming torch of his intellectual superiority is to be dipped in the silent river rolling between the shores of time and eternity; that he himself will be upon a level with any toad that dwells in the land, side by side in the solemn silence of death, nor will he have any superiority over the toad when the end comes.   So, thus writing, he turns and looks out; we see sorrow and sadness and despair depicted on his face; and he turns and writes: " Vanity and vexation of spirit."   In other words, he writes over the fountain of wisdom and knowledge, "All is vanity and vexation of spirit," that the old and young, while time shall last, may read and understand.   It means that if you are not looking beyond this world, if you are not looking beyond the stars, but expect to get happiness from the fountain of wisdom and knowledge, you are doomed to disappointment, and will find, when the solemn hour of death comes, that " all is vanity and vexation of spirit."   And while we see him stand with saddened face, the curtain falls upon the first scene.

There is a widespread impression that wealth can give happiness, that wealth can give the peace for which we sigh.   Hence, from the rivers to the ends of the earth there is a ceaseless struggle—people trying to gather, to hoard up, wealth.   Men will turn from their loved ones; cross rivers, mountains, plains, and seas; and practically bury themselves alive, in their efforts to gain wealth, as was illustrated especially back in the early fifties in this land, when there was a vast army marching from the older States to the Pacific States to hunt gold in those golden sands.   There are hundreds, if not thousands, of lonely graves marking forever the paths that were followed by men in quest of gold.   And people are doing that now. Not many months ago, just after the train left Louisville, I noticed that a man on the seat near me was very restless.

Directly he said something to me and we got into a conversation. He briefly told me his story, and I learned from him that he was then forty-four years old; that he had left his old Kentucky home when he was about twenty-two; that he had gone to the mining district of Mexico, and had spent twenty-two years there. He was returning home then, with two bullets in his body and about twenty thousand dollars in gold in the bank in Louisville for safe-keeping. He asked the conductor repeatedly about what time he would get to a certain station. The conductor could hardly pass without his asking some question. He said to me: " I am going back home. I am expecting my brother to meet me there. Since I left, my father has died, my mother has died, and my sister also. My brother is still living, and I expect him to meet me." I said to him: " Now it is all over, and you have given your twenty-two years of life for twenty thousand dollars in gold, do you think it pays ? " He thought seriously for a second, and he said: " No, it has not paid. I have money enough, if I will be careful of it, to last me the remainder of my days; but things about the old home have changed, so that as I go back now with the twenty thousand dollars in Louisville to my credit, I cannot be happy." The train stopped; he got off within three miles of his country home. The train simply stopped to let him get off, and started on again. I looked back, and the last I saw of him he was in the embrace of a man. I noticed standing near them a boy whom I took to be a nephew. As I went on I thought of the son, that wanderer, going back with his gold, meeting his brother who was left at the old home. He could not ask him: " How is mother ?

and how is father? and how is sister?" He knew all
about that. But he could go back with his brother, and
when he got home there was no father to meet him at the
gate; there was no mother to come with her arms thrown
out to receive him in her fond embrace, to kiss him and
sob and weep, and thank God for his return; no sister in
the home, keeping the house neat and tidy, and making
it a paradise, if possible, because brother was coming home.
He could go into the house and see the vacant seats of the
absent loved ones; he could go out in the orchard back of
it and see the graves of father, mother, and sister, and then
remember that he robbed home of the joy and sunshine and
gladness with which he might have filled it for twenty-two
years. He had left father without a stay and support, mother without his sympathy, and sister without his care, until
all had died and he had returned too late to tell them about
his fortune and divide his gold with them. As I thought,
I did not wonder that the man said, with a sigh: " No, it
did not pay." I felt if I had been that man, and had
that gold in two packages and could have lifted and thrown
them, I would have felt like throwing it all into the depths
of the sea. I could not bear to look upon it and think
what I had lost and what I had deprived others of in my
thirst and search for gold. But this is the history of the
world. People have been doing this through all the ages,
and there are men who will live like paupers for forty years
in order to die rich. Now, then, the race needed some
one upon the stage of action for the purpose of presenting
this to the human race, to tell us the result before it was
too late; for if that man could have looked down the
stream of time to the morning when we met for the first,

and perhaps for the last, time—could have seen the difference between *then* and *now* in his old Kentucky home—
he would not have gone to Mexico; he would have stayed
at home. The race needed some one to present these
things, that we might learn without such bitter experience.
While thinking thus, we notice that the curtain has rolled
up, and we see the same actor. He has retained his knowledge, his wisdom, his experience, but he is just glittering
with radiant gems and jewels rare and with flashing diamonds. As he turns in the light he is perfectly dazzling.
We look around him; we see nothing that is less precious
than gold—gold and pearls and diamonds—things of wondrous commercial value. We look up the great stage; in
the background it seems that the wealth of the universe
has been gathered and heaped. And why? Solomon is
the richest of the earth. Men experienced along that line,
who have made estimates, tell us that Solomon's wealth
was such that Crœsus, whose name has been a synonym for
wealth, was practically a homeless wanderer, a penniless
pauper, in comparison with him. In Solomon's days the
surrounding nations poured their glittering, golden treasures into Palestine, and Solomon had charge of these treasures. Gold and silver were as rocks for abundance about
Jerusalem at that time. He realized that his wealth was
almost boundless; that it was practically impossible for
him, by reckless extravagance, to diminish the wonders of
his wealth. Was he happy with all this wealth, with all
these streams flowing in perpetually—the streams of glittering gold—dwelling in a palace that caught the rays of
the rising sun upon a golden roof? If wealth can make a
man happy, Solomon is happy. But he has sense enough

to know that he can use but little of this wealth; he can
dwell in but one golden palace at a time; he can sleep
upon but one couch, wear only one suit of clothes, eat but
one meal at a time. He can in a lifetime use very little
of his wealth, and he is grieved and burdened and perplexed because of his anxieties with reference to the great
surplus he has. He has sense enough to know that he can
never use it, and beyond what he can use it cannot practically bless—just as if a man were thirsty, and the Pacific
Ocean were the best of water to drink, and he owned it and
had it hedged about so that no bird or man or mouse could
drink of it. He could drink but a little of it at a time,
and all the rest would be practically valueless to him.
Then the thought ought to come to him: " It is cruel to
have all this ocean when I can drink but a little, and let
teeming millions die of thirst in agony." Then Solomon
remembered that he knew not whose these things would
be when he departed, whether this wondrous wealth would
belong to a wise man or a fool. He did not know whether
friends or foes would own it then. He did not know but
that the sons for whom he was hoarding up would butcher
each other, and stain with blood the very treasures he had
spent a lifetime in gathering together. He remembers
that if he had owned the whole earth, and owned it until
he died, there would be but one breath between the millionaire and the pauper; that the hour was coming when
he would die, and one moment after he breathed his last
breath he would be as poor as the poorest beggar in the
land; that his body would sleep in the bosom of the earth,
and that would be all of earth to him; and he turns away
in deepest sadness, and writes over that pool—the glitter-

ing, golden pool of wealth—"Vanity and vexation of spirit," thus saying to the human race: "If you expect wealth to make you happy, you might as well stop now, for at the end of your race it is all vanity and vexation of spirit." The curtain drops, the scene ends, but the lesson is ours.

We have the same evidence that there is a widespread impression, especially among the young, that revelry, rowdyism, dissipation, frolic, frivolity, and fun can give happiness. There are in this town thousands of hopeless, hapless, helpless invalids languishing upon beds of affliction, who would have been happy fathers and mothers now had they learned in early childhood, and reduced to practice, what all of us may learn from the lesson taught us by Solomon, if we will. Their parents warned them, some of them having probably followed the same course and learned from experience the folly of it, but could not teach them. They thought: "You have had your day and do not want others to be happy." So on they went and wrecked themselves, and others are going on the same way, not taking time to heed the words of warning, but hastening on, thinking they will miss the rocks on which others were wrecked, and so the race goes on. Now, God, taking the place of all anxious, careful parents, has put Solomon on the stage to show us the folly of such a course. While we are thinking of this, the curtain rolls up and there is the actor. The stage is glittering with gems, covered with gold. We can see that Solomon is a man of wealth, but his costume is changed, his appearance is changed. He has retained his wealth, his wisdom, his knowledge, but he is dressed like a rowdy. He reels, and every movement

shows that he is just from the giddy dance. The Bible
tells us that he gave himself up to mirth; that he procured
men singers, and women singers, and gave himself up to
the follies of man, and withheld from himself no good
thing—that is, what the rowdy calls good. He "went all
the gaits," went all the way—does that while he is on the
stage before us. Is Solomon happy in the midst of all
this? He thinks for he could not retain his wisdom
and not think—he remembers that this cannot last; he remembers that after a night of revelry there is a day of
headache, a day of utter gloom and misery; he remembers
that after a lifetime of rowdyism there is a night of endless darkness. He remembers that the day is not far distant when the jeweled fingers touching so lightly the harp
strings that vibrate and give forth strains of music almost
divine are to be cold and stiff as icicles; when the eyes that
look tender love into the depths of eyes that look love in return will be closed to earth and all its pleasures; when that
throng of revelers, with their laughter and jest and song,
will be cold and silent in the bosom of the earth, and but
for the oncoming tide of humanity to take the place of the
tide that now is, his royal palace would soon be as silent as
the chambers of death. In deepest sadness he turns and
writes over that whirlpool of pleasure, " Vanity and vexation of spirit; " the curtain falls, and the third scene is
ended.

There is an impression in the world that power can give
happiness. There is not a crime in the long catalogue of
sin too bad for men to commit in order to gain and retain power, as the history of the world clearly shows, reaching down from remotest ages to the present time. The

history of the world shows that men will shed blood; that men will convert happy homes into blazing wrecks; that men will drench fertile, peaceful lands with blood and fill them with moans and shrieks of unavailing sorrow, to gain and retain power. They will sacrifice the truest, fondest friends they have, as did Napoleon, who tore from his embrace the pure, faithful, loving wife, as a farmer would dash from his hand a venomous viper, and left her to die of a broken heart, that he might form a matrimonial alliance that would give him a little more power, or help him retain the power he already held. Now, knowing this, God wanted the sons of men to know before it was too late what would be the result of such ambition; and while we are thinking of this, the curtain rolls up, and again we see Solomon, with his wisdom, his wealth, Solomon relaxed by his revelry, sitting upon an ivory throne, dazzling with radiant splendor, with a crown upon his head such as the world had never seen, with a royal scepter in his hand— Israel's king swaying that scepter over Israel's hosts. In a few seconds of time the space of forty years sweeps by. Solomon is swaying the scepter over proud Israel, a commander in chief, before whose hosts the combined armies of the earth were driven like chaff before the storm king in his fury. Is Solomon happy now? We look and see sadness succeeding the expression of gladness. Solomon is thinking now that this cannot last; that the day is not far distant when the arm that sways that scepter is to be unnerved, and Solomon, the mighty king, will be no more than the beggar in the dust. Like Xerxes, when he looked down upon the marshaled hosts crossing the Hellespont to rob Greece of her glory, and wept to remember that in a hundred years all that host and the sovereign thereof would be silent in the grave, so Solomon knows that a day is coming when Israel's king and Israel's hosts will alike be vanquished by an unseen foe. He turns and writes over that whirlpool of earthly power and glory, "Vanity and vexation of spirit," and the fourth scene is ended forever.

We all know enough of the history of the world to realize something of the vanity and vexation of such ambition. Do we not remember the disappointment of Alexander, who brought himself to a drunkard's grave by debauchery when he was scarcely one-third of a century old, just when he was recognized as the ruler or conqueror of the world? Do we not remember Cæsar, wounded by the very men he had loved and treated as friends; Hannibal, who committed suicide in a foreign land? And do we not know enough of these things to realize that the lesson coming from Solomon is a correct one? But the curtain falls, and that scene is ended.

While we are thinking, it rolls up again, and gives us the fifth and last scene. And now when I am done presenting this lesson, and you are done with your patient, polite listening, then you can go home and study and study until God shall call you hence, but you will not find anything that mortals depend upon for happiness that has not been presented in one of these four pictures—in wisdom, in wealth, in pleasure, or in power. The curtain rises and we can see far down the stage. It is a little gloomy, but the mists clear away, and through the rifted clouds the sun shines down, and we can see, far away on the other side of the stage, Solomon again. What is he doing? Weary of these things, he has retired from the busy haunts of men to commune with nature in fair primeval woods, to find the bliss for which the soul sighs. We see that he is looking at a dewdrop that rests on the cheek of a fragrant flower—the tear of night, but now the radiant gem of the morning, in whose bosom the blazing sun is mirrored, a gem equaling in beauty any gem in his diadem. Something attracts his attention—he hears a bird sing, and looks to see it, but the bird is gone. He turns again to the dewdrop, but at the first kiss of morning it has dropped from the cheek of the flower and it is gone. Something attracts his attention—he looks around, and, looking back again, he sees the flower itself is faded; too sensitive and delicate to bear the sunshine upon it, it falls to the earth and the dust has hidden its sweetness and its beauty. He looks again; years have flown by like moments. He sees the tall trees, that stood like bannered hosts in battle array, tottering; the cedars fall—the tall cedars of Lebanon. The hills are crumbling, the mountains are fallen. The nations of the earth sink down into the bosom of death. He turns to the heavens; he sees the stars falling from the withered vault above, it being night because the sun has been suddenly extinguished. The time for the crash of matter and the wreck of worlds is come. He sees the elements melt like wax before the flame. The right arm of Jehovah is bared; he shakes the earth and folds up the firmament like a scroll. The whole world is ablaze, lighting up with fearful splendor the eternal city of our God. It is all gone, and Solomon turns and writes back over the flame: " Vanity and vexation of spirit."

He comes to the front and stands before us. He tells us that he appreciates the privilege and opportunity that

God has given him to show the value of earthly things, if we look to them for happiness; and then dipping his pen in the living light of God, he brings it down upon the waiting scroll, and as he writes he breathes it out to all the listening earth: " Let us hear the conclusion of the whole matter: Fear God, and keep his commandments; for this is the whole duty of man.   For God shall bring every work into judgment, with every secret thing, whether it be good, or whether it be evil."   And having thus written the conclusion of the whole matter, the pen drops from his weary fingers, the curtain falls, the picture is complete, the play is ended.

This is Ecclesiastes.   Only in the gift of his Son to save a ruined and recreant race has God manifested more clearly his love for the sons and daughters of men than in placing Solomon upon the stage to teach us these wonderful lessons.

I am here to-night to try in a feeble way to bring these lessons before you.   I rejoice that it is my privilege to encourage you, men and women, boys and girls, to come out on the Lord's side.   Remember that we are drifting to eternity's sea; that our hearts

> " Still, like muffled drums, are beating
> Funeral marches to the grave."

Remember, there is no more solemn truth than " man no sooner begins to live than he begins to die."   Remember that we are dying perpetually, but while we are dying the Lord Jesus Christ practically stands before us, in God's eternal truth, wiser than Solomon, and says to all of you that are subjects of the gospel call: " Come unto me, all ye that labor and are heavy laden, and I will give you rest.'

Take my yoke upon you, and learn of me; for I am meek and lowly in heart: and ye shall find rest unto your souls. For my yoke is easy, and my burden is light." Jesus practically says: " Poor dying sons and daughters of men, I am your Savior; I, by the grace of God, am your only Savior. I came from the courts of glory to these low grounds of sorrow, lived a life of poverty and pain, and died on the cross, and now I call you to me. If you will live in harmony with my will, my God shall be your God, he will be your shield and exceeding great reward; you shall be holy and happy here and blessed in that deathless land forever." If you believe these things; if you believe the Bible; if you believe the Savior tells you the truth; if you believe the Savior does actually say to you, " Come unto me, all ye that labor and are heavy laden, and I will give you rest; " that he says, " I, Jesus, have sent mine angels to declare unto you that I am the root and offspring of David, the bright and morning star "—if so, may the Lord bless every one of you in rising and coming to Jesus to be saved, while we wait to lovingly welcome you and pray that you may come.

-3-

CHAPTER III.

LETTERS—ABUNDANT LABORS.

A DISTINGUISHED American has defined genius as " an infinite capacity for painstaking, hard work." All great men have been great workers, and no great worker in any line of human endeavor has failed to make himself felt as a factor in the affairs of men. The divine decree is: " In the sweat of thy face shalt thou eat bread, till thou return unto the ground." (Gen. 3: 19.) The law of God, as well as the experience and observation of all mankind, is aptly expressed in the old proverb: " There is no excellence without labor." The great apostle to the Gentiles said: " His grace which was bestowed upon me was not in vain; but I labored more abundantly than they all: yet not I, but the grace of God which was with me." (1 Cor. 15: 10.) His idea evidently was that the grace of God abundantly and freely bestowed was an incentive and an inspiration to abundant labor, and that it would have been bestowed in vain had not he who received it labored abundantly. So closely does he connect great grace with abundant labors that, as he sees it, 'twas not he that labored, " but the grace of God which was with " him. The life and teaching of Christ among men were little else than a series of lessons on abundant labors. From his baptism till his crucifixion he was probably the hardest and most constant worker the world has ever known. He was often weary, but never idle. In one of his parables he says: " Why stand ye here all the day idle?" (Matt. 20: 6.) When they said, "Because no man hath hired us," he said: "Go ye also into the vineyard; and whatsoever is right, that shall ye receive." (Matt. 20: 7.) The Bible furnishes neither justification nor excuse for idleness. There is always demand for labor, and employment for laborers, in the service of the Lord. When the world was full of idlers and idleness, Jesus said: "The harvest truly is plenteous, but the laborers are few; pray ye therefore the Lord of the harvest, that he will send forth laborers into his harvest." (Matt. 9: 37, 38.) Quotations from letters showing abundant labors in the Lord will be a timely sermon on an important subject always, everywhere, and under all circumstances. A few years ago he wrote:

"Always poor, I have been busy fully fifty years. I am fifty-five years old now, and if I ever knew what real rest—freedom from toil and care—is, I have forgotten. My rest is all beyond the river. 'So mote it be.' I believe I have neither time nor inclination to rest here. My favorite programme for preaching is: Twice every day and three times every Sunday when days are short; three times every day when days are long. I am at home now, but not to rest. I am taking an old-time remedy—getting back to first principles—to get my constitution in first-class condition for work. I am working between meals. The boys and I are clearing a piece of ground. Briers, bushes, vines, and trees of all sorts and ages! I have a brand-new ax—four pounds—and handle. We work, and no mistake about it. It tells, too, on me as well as on the woods. It is worth two drug stores to me."

The world is slow to learn that Christianity is a working-man's religion. Most of the apostles were fishermen, Paul was a tentmaker, and Jesus was a carpenter. No man can walk in "the footsteps" of Jesus without making a few tracks in a carpenter shop or some other place of honest labor. Of all the men Jesus selected for special work and important positions in the kingdom of heaven, he never chose a gentleman of wealth and leisure for anything. The following newspaper clipping inclosed in one of his letters is in point in this connection:

"Ralph Waldo Emerson once said: 'The men in cities who are the centers of energy, the driving wheels of trade, politics, or practical arts, and the women of beauty and genius, are the children or grandchildren of farmers, and are spending the energies which their fathers' hardy, silent life accumulated in frosty furrows, in poverty, necessity, and darkness.'"

There is no idle time in the life that is photographed by private letters in this volume. When he closes a meeting at one place, he begins another one immediately somewhere else; when he goes home to rest, he preaches day and night "to the home folks" and works "between meals;" when too sick to work or preach, he writes encouraging letters to other workers every moment he is able to sit up between spells of "heart failure" and "extreme weakness." Several years ago he wrote from home as follows:

"My work is to 'preach the word;' the wide, wide world is my field. My commission from Jesus reads: 'Go ye into all the world, and preach the gospel to every creature.'

(Mark 16: 15.) How I have endured what I have endured, I do not know. I have worked constantly, under heavy pressure, with all my might all my life, a very few years, beginning with the cradle, excepted. People think I come home to rest when I leave some distant field—well, I am going home to rest by and by. For weeks we have scarcely seen the sun here. Rain, rain, rain! During all this time I have preached two sermons per day in Florence, four miles from home, and gone into the water to baptize, usually, once per day. We leave home, rain or no rain, but nearly always rain, at 9 A.M. and 7 P.M.; return at 1 and 11 P.M. After we get home at night, we sit up and talk about what we have done, and said, and heard, and seen, and thought, and felt, till about midnight. Thus far the Lord has sustained me. I am driving four times four miles through the rain, preaching twice and baptizing once every day; but so far as I can see, I am holding up in all respects as well as usual. Health good, voice perfect, no cold, never hoarse; always happy in the work. I hope they will let me quit this week. Other places are pressing me for meetings."

At another time, while at home resting and preaching twice every day in Florence, he wrote:

"I am gaining strength every day; preaching day and night, and driving four miles every night after preaching. I thought I was sick when I came home, but I believe I simply needed the remedy I am taking in this meeting. Weather cloudy and rainy much of the time. I am certainly testing my powers of endurance in this meeting. Voice good. 'Bless the Lord, O my soul: and all that is within me, bless his holy name.' "

Once, when he was ready to leave home, he wrote:

" I expect to be gone nine months on this trip, and do my very best all the time.   Nothing suits me, nothing is endurable for me, but constant work for the Lord."

Every preacher, and especially every preacher's wife, will know what burdens weary hearts had to bear during these long trips from home.   Others besides preachers, whose duties demand long periods from home, will read between the lines here their own experience in homesick longings for the dear ones far away.   On the principle that " misery loves company," there will be consolation to many readers in the following scrap of poetry inclosed in one of his letters while he was in a meeting in the far West on a long trip from home:

WHEN YOU COME HOME AGAIN.

It comes to me often in silence,
  When the firelight sputters low,
When the black, uncertain shadows
  Seem wreaths of the long ago;
Ever with a throb of heartache
  That thrills each pulsing vein
Comes the old, unquiet longing
  To have you home again.

I feel that you are sick of the cities
  And of faces cold and strange;
But you know where there is ever a welcome
  So allow your yearning fancies range
Back to the dear old homestead
  Without an aching sense of pain,
For there'll be joy in the coming
  When you come home again.

MRS. T. B. LARIMORE.

When you come home—why, there's music
  That may never die away;
And it seems the hands of angels
  On a mystic harp at play
Have touched with a yearning sadness
  On a beautiful, broken strain,
To which my fond heart is wording,
  " When you come home again."

Outside of your darkened windows
  Is the great world's crash and din,
And slowly the autumn shadows
  Will come drifting, drifting in;
Slowly and sobbing, the night winds murmur
  To the splash of the summer rain,
While I dream of the glorious greeting
  When you come home again.

On the margin of this clipping he wrote:

" Mrs. Larimore sends this to me."

One of the hardest parts a preacher has to play is to be
cheerful in his work, entertain and be entertained, visit and
be visited, take an interest in everything and everybody
around him, nor show by word, look, laugh, or melancholy
abstraction any sign of the burden on his heart he cannot
help but feel, if he is any part of a man, for the loved ones
in loneliness at home. O yes, " preachers **have a good
time**," if it is " a good time " to play a part in home pleasures and enjoyments, and then hide away in hearing of
music and laughter to read a letter from a wife and mother
who tries to be brave and cheerful and encouraging, but
breaks down in the effort and lets her heart talk in a waif of
poetry clipped from a newspaper. Others besides preachers have the same kind of good times. Many a soul in this
world has mastered the art of manufacturing pleasure for

others out of its own sorrows as raw material. Whoever can do this is a philosopher and philanthropist, and whoever tries to do it is a hero, whether he succeeds or fails in the effort.

Inclosed in one of his letters, a clipping from a local paper in Arkansas was introduced with the following words by the editor:

" The two pretty stanzas below are from the pen of our friend, L. Stevens, of Mill Creek, a gentleman whose sparkling wit, expressed in rhyme, has created so much merriment around Pope County firesides."

The two stanzas are as follows:

TROUBLE'S WINE.

At trouble's table I have dined,
And drank the dregs of trouble's wine;
Misfortune held it to my lips
Until I sipped it sip by sip;
And when I think the glass to drain,
It seems some power hidden
Does replenish it again,
As though I am forbidden
To empty it, and thus I find
Another cup of trouble's wine.

And thus it's been my whole life through:
My troubles great, my pleasures few;
With all mankind I laugh and jest,
And none of them have ever guessed
That, with all my mirth, I hide a heart
That's filled with deepest sorrow;
That in this life I act a part,
My mirth I only borrow;
Nor have they ever yet divined
That I am drunk on trouble's wine.

His idea of " the best things " is expressed in the following newspaper clipping which he inclosed in one of his letters:

" The best law is the Golden Rule; the best philosophy,
a contented mind; the best statesmanship, self-government;
the best war, that against one's weaknesses; the best medicine, cheerfulness and temperance in all things; the best
music, the laughter of an innocent soul; the best science, the
extracting of sunshine from gloom; the best art, painting a
smile upon the brow of childhood; the best biography, the
life which writes charity in the largest letters; the best tele-
graphing, flashing a ray of light into a gloomy heart; the
best engineering, building a bridge of faith over the river
of death; the best diplomacy, effecting a treaty of peace
with one's own conscience; the best journalism, printing
only the good and the true; the best navigation, steering
clear of the rocks of personal contention; the best mathe-
matics, that which doubles the most joys, subtracts the most
sorrows, divides the gulf of misery, adds to the sum of human pleasure, and cancels all selfishness."

His caution, discretion, and tenderness in dealing with
the prejudices of people are proverbial and thoroughly
characteristic. In one of his meetings where prejudice
was high and opposition to him and his work was strong,
he wrote:

" I am well and working well, the load and the team considered. I am patiently doing what duty demands, without imprudently antagonizing prejudices and exciting opposition that might defeat the purpose I have in view in all
my work—viz., to win souls to Christ."

No matter how much work he does, or what success attends his labors, he is never satisfied. He wants to do more every year than he has ever done in one year before. There is a uniformity in his letters at the close of one year and the beginning of another, during his whole life as a preacher, which would be monotonous to the reader. It will save space to publish the following letter and ask the readers to read it one time for the beginning of each year he has been preaching, if they want a complete record of his correspondence on that subject:

"I am exceedingly anxious to do more for Christ this year than I have ever done in one year; but I have scarcely begun yet. My vow for this year is: Be better—do more, pray and labor for better results—than in any previous year of my life. So far as work and results are concerned, I have only eleven months in which to break my record for any previous year. Well, beginning, ' the Lord willing,' January 31, I am determined to try."

Whatever else may be thought of him or said about him, no one can successfully deny that he works. It is doubtful whether any man, living or dead, has preached more sermons under more different circumstances in more different places than T. B. Larimore during the same number of years he has been preaching. Preaching twice every day and three times every Sunday, besides business cares, correspondence, baptizing, visiting, attending weddings and funerals, and worrying over other people's troubles, can hardly be counted the hardest part of his work. Perhaps his hardest labors are the discomforts, exposures, loss of sleep, irregular meals, excitement, dangers, and general inconveniences of travel in long trips on scant time between meetings.

When in a Western city, ready to begin a meeting, he wrote:

"Just reached here this morning. From Monday noon till Sunday morning coming from Florence, Ala. Worn out. Wrecks, washouts, bad connections, etc. Hope to be in good shape for work to-morrow. Sorry I cannot write you to-day."

Think of going into a city Sunday morning on a belated train after such a trip, and then undertake to preach three times to a strange audience that day, and still " hope to be in good fix for work to-morrow." Think, also, of keeping this up continuously, without a break, for more than thirty years.

CHAPTER IV.

SERMON——REST FOR THE SOUL.

(Sermon delivered by T. B. Larimore at South College Street Church, Nashville, Tenn., on the evening of January 31, 1900.)

THEN began he to upbraid the cities wherein most of his mighty works were done, because they repented not: Woe unto thee, Chorazin! woe unto thee, Bethsaida! for if the mighty works, which were done in you, had been done in Tyre and Sidon, they would have repented long ago in sackcloth and ashes. But I say unto you, It shall be more tolerable for Tyre and Sidon at the day of judgment, than for you. And thou, Capernaum, which art exalted unto heaven, shalt be brought down to hell: for if the mighty works, which have been done in thee, had been done in Sodom, it would have remained until this day. But I say unto you, That it shall be more tolerable for the land of Sodom in the day of judgment, than for thee.

"At that time Jesus answered and said, I thank thee, O Father, Lord of heaven and earth, because thou hast hid these things from the wise and prudent, and hast revealed them unto babes. Even so, Father: for so it seemed good in thy sight. All things are delivered unto me of my Father: and no man knoweth the Son, but the Father; neither knoweth any man the Father, save the Son, and he to whomsoever the Son will reveal him.

" Come unto me, all ye that labor and are heavy laden, and I will give you rest. Take my yoke upon you, and

learn of me; for I am meek and lowly in heart: and ye
shall find rest unto your souls.   For my yoke is easy, and
my burden is light."   (Matt. 11: 20-30.)

In the Isle of Wight there is a beautiful and costly
monument erected by the sympathy and liberality of
Queen Victoria to perpetuate the memory of a pure, sweet
girl of beauty and intelligence, who lived and loved, and
sorrowed and died, in the long, long ago.   That monument represents a young lady in a reclining position, her
cheek resting upon the marble page of an open Bible, on
which page is the language: " Come unto me, all ye that
labor and are heavy laden, and I will give you rest."

That beautiful girl was the daughter of Charles I., of
England, and she was arrested because she was the daughter of a king, of such sweetness of spirit as to give her
wonderful influence among the people of the realm in
which and over which her father reigned.   She was kept
in prison; news in reference to her father was kept from
her; nothing in the world was done or said to give her
comfort; she was anxious to hear and afraid to hear the
news; the heartless spirit of that age had no sympathy for
her; and, finally, one morning the keeper of the prison
found her in the prison lying lifeless, with her Bible open,
and her cheek resting upon the page which says: " Come
unto me, all ye that labor and are heavy laden, and I will
give you rest."

Queen Victoria thought it proper to perpetuate the
memory of that sweet girl and at the same time to erect a
monument that would preach—a monument that, in a
very important sense, will represent the Savior himself.
That monument is ever solemnly saying, in the language of

Jesus, to every passer-by, weary and heavy laden: " Come unto me, all ye that labor and are heavy laden, and I will give you rest. Take my yoke upon you, and learn of me; for I am meek and lowly in heart: and ye shall find rest unto your souls. For my yoke is easy, and my burden is light."

We ought not only to appreciate the spirit of the good sovereign who erected that monument, but we ought to go beyond the monument, and beyond the thought that prompted the sovereign to erect that monument, and see the Savior—a staid, sorrowful man, divine here upon the earth—and hear him saying to the toiling millions of all time, weary and heavy laden, burdened with sin: " Come unto me, all ye that labor and are heavy laden, and I will give you rest. Take my yoke upon you, and learn of me; for I am meek and lowly in heart: and ye shall find rest unto your souls. For my yoke is easy, and my burden is light."

Then, if we have heeded that language; if we have yielded to the persuasive power of the blessed Savior as set forth in this precious invitation, we ought to rejoice that we are saved, that we have been freed from our sins, that we are on our journey home, that we are in Christ, and in the enjoyment of that sweet rest and perfect peace, passing all understanding, that Heaven guarantees to every faithful soul in the service of God from the rivers to the ends of the earth. And if we are enjoying that rest, and thus having only a taste of the rest that remains to the people of God in that brighter and better world, we certainly ought to sympathize enough with suffering humanity to extend this call to all that need it; to impress it with all the power of earnestness that we possess upon the minds of those that are subject to the call; to do our very best to lead the lost to the Lamb of God that taketh away the sins of the world.

I trust all of us appreciate the spirit that prompted Queen Victoria to erect the monument to which I have alluded.

There is not a Christian man, woman, or child in this audience, in this community, or on this earth, that may not invite and persuade people to come to Jesus and find rest for their weary souls. There is not a Christian man, woman, or child upon the earth that may not in some way call the living to the Lord, which will be better than simply perpetuating the memory of the dead. And while little boys and little girls old enough and intelligent enough to be responsible in the sight of God should love Queen Victoria all the more because of the spirit she manifested in perpetuating the memory of that sweet girl, they ought to look far beyond the power and presence of Queen Victoria; far beyond all pageantry, pride, power, wealth, glory, and sinfulness of the world, to Jesus, the Man of sorrows; to the immaculate glory of a life in God, the guaranteed King of kings and Lord of lords, and love him more, appreciate him more, and be more devoted to his service and consecrated to his will, because he is saying to all the sinful, toiling, weary, and heavy-laden sons and daughters of men: "Come unto me, all ye that labor and are heavy laden, and I will give you rest. Take my yoke upon you, and learn of me; for I am meek and lowly in heart: and ye shall find rest unto your souls. For my yoke is easy, and my burden is light."

Do we, all of us, realize now that this is the Savior's language?

When I told you of that beautiful monument, and of the spirit that erected it, and of the lines which are inscribed upon it, I think you believed that. I think that you believe that it is a reality, and that you appreciate it, and that you would be glad to see it, and if you were traveling to where it would be convenient for you to do so, that you would turn aside and stand at the foot of that monument and read that impressive language, and look at that reclining marble figure. If you should ever see that monument, you would think of the sweet girl which it represents; of the bloody, tearful period that swept her into eternity and beheaded her father; and then think of this night, and of the nights that you sat here, and of the opportunity that you embraced or slighted; and in all your thoughts you would realize that Queen Victoria did one of the many thousands of good and great things she has done when she erected that monument.

Why not, then, go beyond that and above that to the source from which that language, spirit, and thought emanated, and realize that Jesus is a sublime and blessed reality, and that the language is the language of the Man of sorrows who died upon Calvary's cross to save you and me, and save all we love and all that love us? Jesus bled and died upon the cross to ransom the lost; to lift us up from our fallen condition; to roll back the tide of sin and sorrow threatening to engulf the human race and envelop the globe; to set our souls free to float above the sorrows and sighs of this world, that we may nestle in the bosom of the love of God, and be with the angels and archangels while eternal ages roll on.

If we have a feeling of admiration for, and appreciation of, the good queen who erected that monument to perpetuate the memory of that sweet girl, and to breathe this sweet sentiment on and on and on until time's knell shall be sounded, then why not have a feeling of admiration for, and appreciation of, and sympathy with, and purest and truest love for, the Man of sorrows, who uttered that language when he himself was here upon the earth? And why not show that appreciation, show that sympathy, show that admiration, by submitting to his will? Shall we feel, and think, and talk, and act in reference to Queen Victoria and her work in a way that will convince the world that we believe these things are real, and then feel, and believe, and talk, and act in reference to Jesus and his life and his language as if we believe all these things belong to the shades of the mythological ages of long, long ago? Unless we watch ourselves, there is danger that we will do exactly that way. And surely when sinners hear this invitation and turn away without any emotion, and without any manifestation of appreciation go their way as if Jesus had never given this invitation, they fail to show that they believe these things are real, and their conduct might be interpreted to mean that there is no reality in the story of the cross and in this manifestation of the Savior's love going out to the lost.

Now we who claim to be Christians think it is strange that intelligent men, women, and children responsible, out of Christ, will act that way. It may seem to them far more unreasonable and much stranger that we, claiming to believe these things, and claiming to be on our journey through this world of sorrow to the land of eternal blessedness, should be careless and indifferent in reference to the work before us. It may seem to them one of the strangest of all strange things that we claim to believe these things, and at the same time will mix and mingle with them socially from day to day, week to week, month to month, and year to year, without trying to induce them to cease their sins and their wanderings and come to Jesus, that they may be saved. If we believe the Bible, we believe that practically, in the love light of God's eternal truth, the Savior stands before us and says: "Come unto me, and you shall have rest." We believe that he is saying right now to each and every one of us: "Come unto me, all ye that labor and are heavy laden, and I will give you rest. Take my yoke upon you, and learn of me; for I am meek and lowly in heart: and ye shall find rest unto your souls. For my yoke is easy, and my burden is light."

Do we, all of us, believe the Bible? I deem it safe to say we do, at least safe to say we think we do. Then, that being true, we believe that Jesus is calling to him every sinner in this audience. Now, do you that are subjects of the gospel call believe that he is calling you to come to him? If you believe the Bible, you not only believe that, but you believe he is making you a promise: "Come unto me, and I will give you rest."

Do you want that rest of body, soul, and spirit for all the days you have to live upon the earth, and then throughout the never-ending eternity? I trust that you do. You know how to get that rest. It is an insult to the Lord

Jesus Christ, an insult to Jehovah, an insult to high
Heaven for us, in view of this language, to claim that we
can get that rest without yielding to the invitation and
coming to the Savior as he demands. Why beg us? Why
persuade us? Why implore, entreat, beseech us to come
to him that we may find that rest, if we can find this rest
away from him? The very language itself practically
says: "Unless you come, you cannot receive that rest."
For us to say, then, we can receive that rest without coming, just as if we had come, is equivalent to challenging
the veracity of Jesus. He gives us a positive promise, but
we have to come in order that we may receive that rest.
We are not to merit the rest, but we are to come to Jesus
that we may receive it, because he himself, who knows what
is best for us, invites us to come, and the promise that we
shall receive that rest is based upon the demand that we
come. Of course, now, the Savior does not mean in this
that we are to come through space, as we measure space
upon the earth, to him; we could not do that. But we
are separated from him spiritually; we are away from
him; sin hath separated us from Christ; and now he calls
us back to him that we may find this rest. This call does
not include the righteous, for the Savior says: "I came
not to call the righteous, but sinners to repentance."
(Mark 2 : 17.) So this call is for sinners. If you do not
realize that you are a sinner, then you do not realize that
this call includes you. This call does not include Christians, of course, for the apostle Paul teaches us that Christians are in Christ—that is, in his spiritual body, which
is the church. "And hath raised us up together, and made
us sit together in heavenly places in Christ Jesus." (Eph.

2: 6.) It simply includes all the weary and heavy laden, and that is what it says—those who are burdened by sin, those who are exposed to eternal death, those who are living without God and in danger of dying without a promise of the glorious immortality. Now, if we do not belong to that class that is far away from Jesus, then we ought to rejoice that we are not away from him. If we do belong to that far-away class, then we ought to rejoice that Jesus loves us, that Jesus sympathizes with us, that Jesus gave his life for us, and now he tenderly begs us to come to him. Give how many of the weary and heavy laden rest? All of them that come to him. How can we come? Jesus says: "No man can come to me, except the Father which hath sent me draw him: and I will raise him up at the last day." (John 6: 44.) He immediately explains how the Father draws: "It is written in the prophets, And they shall be all taught of God. Every man therefore that hath heard, and hath learned of the Father, cometh unto me." (John 6: 45.) The terms "heard" and "learn" are used in the sense of obedient or submissive hearing and learning—hearing in order to learn, and learning in order to live according to the will of God.

Now that is the way God draws us to Christ, and that is God's work. God's power, through the truth, draws every wanderer that will heed it, listen to it, and appreciate it, toward and to Jesus of Nazareth, who stands pledged to give the rest. We may resist that power, stay away from Jesus, and never receive the rest; or we may yield to it and come to Jesus, obey the gospel, walk in the footsteps of our Savior, and reign and rejoice with him in glory forever. And that choice is before every sinner in this house to-night. You have the option between the two, and you do not know but that the decision you make in a few moments now is to be the decision that will settle that question forever. It is a very important question before us, then, to decide. You have to decide the question as to whether you will or will not heed this divine invitation to-night. To decide you will not is to reject the Savior for this time; to decide that you will is to accept the Savior now. To decide that you will not come to him to-night is to decide to still be burdened by sin and exposed to eternal death; to decide to come to Jesus to-night, and come, is to come to the one who promises you rest, and his promise can never fail. It follows, therefore, to decide to come, and come, is to secure peace, pardon, and rest—rest for body, soul, and spirit; rest for conscience, rest for mind; rest for evermore.

Of course all of us understand, or should understand, that the word " yoke " is used here in a metaphorical sense; that it does not mean literally a yoke; but we understand it in that figurative sense just as well as we do in the literal sense. When we speak of the yoke of Great Britain, all of us understand that means the government of Great Britain. When Christ says, " Take my yoke upon you," he means his authority. To be under the British yoke is to be under the British law, or government. To be under the yoke of Christ is to be under the law and government of Christ, for Christ is the King over his own kingdom, he is the Head of his own army. He rules or governs his own church, and none other; and, therefore, to take his yoke upon us is to obey the gospel and enter into his kingdom, his army, or his church. But, remember, we have no assurance of this rest unless we take the yoke. So there is no promise of peace, pardon, and rest—the rest that Jesus promises—outside of the covenanted relationship with God in Christ, or in the divine institution of which Jesus is the head. We ought to appreciate this invitation because it comes from the loving Lord who died to redeem us; we ought to appreciate it because there is connected with it the precious promise of rest, if we will only heed the invitation and do what heaven demands. And just to the extent that we appreciate rest of the very highest character, we certainly ought to appreciate the promise of the Savior: "And I will give you rest." There is no perfect rest out of Christ. We can have rest to a limited extent, but when it comes to absolutely perfect rest, that is found only in the service of him who so loved the world as to give his Son to die that we might live forever.

Rest is sweet to all the toiling millions of earth. Rest gives the opportunity for exhausted powers to recuperate so that they may go on with the toil until they are bound to have rest again; but if we come to Jesus and obey the gospel and live right, we have all the time the rest that he promises—rest from every fear of eternal destruction; rest from the pressure of sin that drags us down and destroys us; rest that comes with eternal blessedness in the presence of our God; and this rest stays with us all the time.

Rest is sweet to the farmer who has toiled from the rising to the setting of the sun, as he turns his face toward his home. The thought comes to him that loved ones are waiting and watching to welcome him. The very thought of the rest that is there with the loved ones by him is sweet to him, and yet he knows that he has to return to the field of his labor to-morrow; and on and on with his toil, and rest and toil, until life shall cease within him.

We, if we are Christians, are laborers in the vineyard of the Lord; and when the sun of the day of our mortal life shall set, and that night shall come, as the Savior says, " when no man can work " (John 9: 4), we shall enter into a rest sweet and perfect; a rest with the angels, with loved ones not lost, but gone before; a rest that shall never end.

Rest! The very thought of rest is sweet to the soldier who has been far away from home on bloody fields, and has faithfully done the duty of a soldier. When the war is over, the last battle is fought, the last victories are won, and the cannon is allowed to cool, and the sword is sheathed and hung on the wall, and the muskets are stacked, and the bayonets are allowed to rust, he is honorably discharged and turns his face homeward, ever thinking of the love and peace and rest awaiting him there.

We, if we are Christians, are soldiers of the cross, clad in the panoply of heaven, armed with the sword of the Spirit, and filled with the love of God and sympathy for poor lost and suffering humanity, marching beneath the fluttering folds of the banner of Prince Immanuel, who died to redeem us; battling with the world for the glory of God and the salvation of souls. But the day is not far distant when our warfare shall be ended, when our last battle shall have been fought and our last victory shall have been won. Then we can lay down the sword and the cross, and be borne by angels to the land of eternal light, and receive the crown, and enter into the enjoyment of that perfect rest that shall be ours while the eternal ages shall last.

The thought of rest is sweet to the sailor who has been tossed upon the restless, storm-swept bosom of the sighing sea, far away from home and loved ones, rocked upon the billows, but never to rest. When the time comes for the ship to return home, and he realizes that he is homeward bound, his soul leaps for joy within him at the thought that the day is not far distant when the ship is to be anchored in sight of home, and he is to be conveyed to the shore in a little boat and permitted to plant his feet upon the solid land, and be taken into the arms and fond embrace of the mother, the wife, or the sister. He is going to his home and sit down there where he can be quiet and still, with the smiles of joy and tears of gratitude manifesting an appreciation of his loved ones on his return home, and then realize what rest is.

We are sailors upon the storm-swept bosom of the sea of life. If we are Christians, we are aboard the good old ship of Zion, that has borne to the bright port of eternal bliss many millions, and can bear as many millions more to that happy land. If we are living in harmony with God's law, we are aboard that blessed ship, and Jesus is our Captain. The hand of Omnipotence is upon the helm, and we are driven by the strong breath of Jehovah through the storms, defying the lightning's livid flash and the thunder's awful roar, defying all the storms of sin and Satan that may sweep the seas around us. The day is not far distant when the eternal shore shall be in view and we shall see the glittering gates and gorgeous walls of the New Jerusalem and that Happy Land, as the good old ship casts anchor in the laughing waters of the pearly port of endless peace. Then we shall be conveyed to the shore and be permitted to walk the streets of the New Jerusalem rejoicing in that peace and rest purchased by the blood of Jesus. While the eternal ages come and go our bliss shall be endless, our rest shall be perfect; there we are to spend eternity in that blessed land where hearts neither can bleed nor break, where life is eternal and a treasure sublime; but, remember, we must be in Christ Jesus and live in harmony with his law, that these blessed results may flow to our souls like rivers of bliss while time and eternity shall last. The sweetest rest that earth knows for responsible human beings here can be found in a mother's fond embrace. Strangely cold-spirited, and heartless, and false must be the boy, it matters not what position of honor and power he may fill on earth, who can forget the sweetness and preciousness of rest in a mother's arms.

A sweet, Christian girl, living not many miles from my humble Alabama home, married and went far away toward the western verge of the United States, stayed there a few years, and consumption commenced doing its deadly work, slowly, but surely. The roses faded from her cheeks; she grew paler and weaker and thinner as the days went by, until at last she realized fully that the grave was not far away from her, that the day was at hand when she should cease her sighing and sorrowing and enter into that rest that remains to the people of God. She feared no danger, and she dreaded no death, because she had gone to Christ for rest, and was securely and safely sheltered from all storms in the bosom of the Rock of Ages; but yet she was not willing to die then and there. She wanted to be brought back home, and wanted her mother to get into the old family rocking-chair and take her upon her lap and let her lean back upon her bosom, and wanted the mother to put her arms around her and kiss her, and rock her in the old rocking-chair; " and then," she said, " from that sweet rest I am willing for angels to bear me home to the rest that earth can never give." The loving husband and other friends managed to bring that sweet, Christian woman home. The rocking-chair was prepared just as she wanted it. The mother, tears blinding her, took her seat in the rocking-chair; the sweet woman, that was almost a skeleton and almost in the grave, was helped to her mother; she took her seat upon her lap and leaned back and nestled on her bosom as she did in the long, long ago, when she was a sweet little child. The mother, sobbing and trying to talk, put her arms around her and pressed her close to her warm, sorrowing heart and kissed her. The daughter laid her head down upon the mother's shoulder, drew as close to her as she could, and said: " Rock me now, mamma." Her mother rocked her for a long time. She said: " You can take me to the bed now. You will be tired, mamma. I don't want you to rock me too long." She was taken to the bed and placed upon it, and expressed herself as being perfectly satisfied—not another wish, not another request; that was all for her in this world—but one more step, and that was to the only rest that is sweeter than the rest that can be found upon a mother's bosom and in a mother's arms. The day was then not far distant when she was released; but a few days came and went; and when the sweet spirit left the crumbling clay, to be buried in the little family graveyard, that spirit went home to God to nestle forever in the bosom of the love of him who said in person here when he was upon the earth: " Come unto me, all ye that labor and are heavy laden, and I will give you rest. Take my yoke upon you, and learn of me; for I am meek and lowly in heart: and ye shall find rest unto your souls. For my yoke is easy, and my burden is light."

May the Lord bless every soul in this audience subject to the gospel call, and help you to fly like a bird to the sheltering rock, and be folded like a child to its mother's arms, so that the peace that passeth all understanding may be yours while living, perfect contentment be yours in the hour of death.

" Come unto me, all ye that labor and are heavy laden, and I will give you rest. Take my yoke upon you, and learn of me; for I am meek and lowly in heart: and ye shall find rest unto your souls. For my yoke is easy, and my burden is light."

Will you come? If so, we wait to lovingly welcome you.

CHAPTER V.

LETTERS——WORK IN HARD PLACES.

THE correct measure of a preacher's consecration is not the great work he does in strong churches under favorable circumstances at liberal rates of remuneration for his services, but the self-sacrificing work he does in hard places for the love of the Lord.   It is to the credit of Paul not only that he labored more abundantly than all the other apostles, but that he " strived to preach the gospel, not where Christ was named," lest he " should build upon another man's foundation," but to preach to those who had "not heard" and "to whom he was not spoken of." (Rom. 15: 20, 21.)   His reputation as a consecrated preacher rests very largely on the fact that he was, of all men, " in labors more abundant, in stripes above measure, in prisons more frequent, in deaths oft."   The pathos of facts in his life is a strong indorsement of his earnestness: " Of the Jews five times received I forty stripes save one.   Thrice was I beaten with rods, once was I stoned, thrice I suffered shipwreck, a night and a day I have been in the deep; in journeyings often, in perils of waters, in perils of robbers, in perils by mine own countrymen, in perils by the heathen, in perils in the city, in perils in the wilderness, in perils in the sea, in perils among false brethren; in weariness and painfulness, in watchings often, in hunger and thirst, in fastings often, in cold and nakedness.   Beside those things that are without, that

which cometh upon me daily, the care of all the churches."
(2 Cor. 11 : 24-28.)   In all this he had no sinister motives.
" I have coveted no man's silver, or gold, or apparel.   Yea,
ye yourselves know, that these hands have ministered unto
my necessities, and to them that were with me."   (Acts
20 : 33, 34.)

A great victory usually, if not always, comes after a
hard fight. Inclosing a photograph of a ten-acre field
which nestles in the mountains of East Tennessee:

" THE TEN-ACRE FIELD.

" I am in the ' ten-acre field ' to-day, and my mind is
scanning pages and pictures of the past.

" ' The ten-acre field ' is on ' the ridge,' about one mile
nearly due south from Dunlap, the capital of Sequatchie
County, Tenn.   The beautiful Sequatchie flows along the
eastern foot of ' the ridge.'

" ' The ridge ' would be a mountain in Kansas or Texas,
but in East Tennessee, shadowed by rock-ribbed chains of
towering mountains that bound Sequatchie Valley on the
east and on the west, it is only a baby asleep on the bosom
of the beautiful valley, and we simply call it ' the ridge.'

" The mountains, the valley, the river, and the ridge
are parallel—approximately so, at least.   The river, about
seventy to one hundred miles long, runs from north to
south.

" The field and I are about the same age, and both of us
are older than we were when we were chums three and
thirty years ago.   I feel like a boy to-day, however, and
the field is not worn out.   The soil on the surface of the

"THE TEN-ACRE FIELD."

field is thinner than it was long ago, and I am somewhat thinner on top, too.

" When I was in the middle of my teens, and the field was comparatively ' new,' two negroes and I cultivated ' the ten-acre field ' and other fields. The doctor inherited ' Samps ' and Tamar, and brought them from Currituck County, N. C., when he came to Tennessee. He hired me ' for six months, includin' crop time,' for thirty-six dollars, which was more than the market price of boys of my age and size and strength in ' the valley ' then. The *reason* the doctor rendered for voluntarily paying me such an exorbitant price was that he expected me to somewhat oversee and manage matters in my sphere, while he practiced medicine.

" The natural tendency of the doctor's kindness and confidence and of my financial boom, all coming upon me suddenly and at the same time, was to make me very vain and very grateful, of course, and I resolved then and there that the doctor should never be disappointed in *me*.

" That spring was *very* favorable for ' pitching crops,' and we succeeded splendidly.

" When the time for ' laying off ' ' the ten-acre field ' came, the doctor sent me alone to do that. I was to go alone and ' lay it off ' one way. Then, as I ' laid it off ' the other way, Tamar was to ' drop ' the corn and ' Samps ' was to ' cover ' it. The field was a lonely spot in the woods. There was not a house in it or in sight of it then, nor was there another field near. I was afraid of wild cats, witches, and things; but a boy who was valued at six dollars a month could not afford to be otherwise than brave, so I went without a murmur. I waited at ' the gap' till day dawned and brightened sufficiently for me to see to 'run a row.' Then that day's work began. A big battle was before me. My heart was set on getting ready to begin planting that field at the dawning of the next day. My honor and reputation were at stake. I resolved to do my very best, and I did.

"The moon, almost full, was hanging low over the brow of the mountain to the east, and I could see my shadow distinctly, when I finished my task. I never entertained the thought of quitting till my task was done. Nothing short of the scream of a panther or the cry of a wild cat could have driven me from that field till the victory was complete. Years have come and gone since then, and many battles I have fought; but I am not sure I have ever been more elated over any victory I have won than over that. My task was done, the victory won, and I was happy.

"The doctor was delighted. He said: 'Make a hurry, "Samps"—make a hurry! Theophilus has laid off the ten-acre field to-day. I thought it would take him two days, but he has done it in one. Make a hurry, now—make a hurry! Get the seed corn ready. That field must be planted to-morrow. Make a hurry—make a hurry!'

"How real sometimes seem things trivial and tame that transpired almost a lifetime ago! I can almost see 'Samps' now, and hear the doctor's voice as he says: 'Make a hurry, "Samps"—make a hurry!' That was the way he talked to 'Samps,' but he never did tell *me* to make a hurry. He encouraged me, praised me, and paid me— paid me all he promised—and *gave* me twenty-five cents.

"I worked for the doctor six months, lost only one half

day—one afternoon—and worked till midnight of that day. I thought if George Washington was the first man, Dr. Bell was the second.

"The day his firstborn was born and buried, and his right arm was broken, was a dark and dreadful day to me.

"The doctor died long ago, leaving a worthy wife and intelligent children to fight the battle of life without him. I pray that they may all prosper and always be happy—in time and in eternity. I *believe* ' Samps ' and Tamar ' went away wid de Yankees endu'in' de wah.' "

As a preacher, he has not always worked in easy places. He has held many meetings in strong churches where he had every convenience, comfort, and advantage money could procure, large audiences could provide, or the love and thoughtfulness of a host of friends could devise; he has also done much work without any financial remuneration in hard places and against many discouragements. From a country place where the population was dense, but the people were poor and the land was poorer, he wrote:

" Our meeting is progressing very nicely. Thirty-three added to the Lord the last three days—thirteen yesterday. I baptized seventeen yesterday in a creek as clear as crystal. When I commenced work here, four members—two men and two women, husbands and wives—were all I could find in this country. Now, at the appointed time for work, they come up to the house of the Lord in encouraging numbers. The saints can possess this land, if they will. Preaching every day at 10: 30 A.M., 1: 30 and 7: 30 P.M.; dinner—basket dinner—at noon; and baptizing at 3 P.M."

At a time when he was more than five hundred miles

from home, hard at work, and many people no doubt thought he was preaching for money and faring " sumptuously every day," he wrote:

" House small—exceedingly so. Very little, if any, over half the space in the diminutive auditorium occupied by seats. Just about half the seats occupied by people last night. In addition to the almost ludicrous diminutiveness of the house, with small inside and here and there a seat, with broad spaces and spacious aisles, the walls are cracked from foundation to roof. The opinion is said to prevail that it is perilous for any one whose life is worth preserving to enter the little, old, shabby, tumble-down building.

" Brother —— explains that he did not, and does not, expect to carry on the meeting in this house very long. The programme is to get up an interest here, and then move the meeting to a commodious hall. Now, the question is: How are we to get up an interest ? The preaching in this little, empty house cannot do it unless we can preach the house down. Of course there is a reason for all these things. What the reason is I do not know. The preaching is not to blame, for nobody has heard it, a few of the faithful and visitors from a distance excepted. Well, the preacher must just simply do his best and be satisfied with results. That is exactly what he proposes to do."

His determination to " just simply do his best and be satisfied with results " turned defeat into victory against all these discouragements. Later in the meeting he wrote:

" We are all right now. House packed, interest good, success assured."

After the meeting closed he wrote:

" Meeting closed last night. Every inch of available space occupied, from pulpit to door, and I know not how many outside. Nobody moved, and many stood from start to finish of services, which lasted, including baptism, more than two hours. Ninety added to the Lord. Seventeen added yesterday, thirteen of them at the close of the last sermon of the meeting last night."

How preachers who labor in such places are to be supported is a difficult question. I know of no better way than to go and do the work, and look to the people who are benefited by the preaching for support. An effort to raise money at that place to support the meeting before the work was done would have been a very moderate success, if not, indeed, a complete failure. It would have been easier to raise a thousand dollars for the preacher the night the meeting closed than to have raised one hundred the day it began. Even a panic in the preacher about his support after the meeting began would have been disastrous to both the financial interests of the preacher and the spiritual welfare of the town. When a preacher goes to such a place and wins a victory under such circumstances and against such discouragements, I am not disposed to censure him or criticise the people if, after the work is done, the laborer is rewarded in a measure which many good people would consider extravagant liberality. However, preachers who work faithfully, but fail to move the people—as every preacher does in some cases—should not be allowed to suffer want or go unrewarded.

From a place where " the pastor " privately, cautiously,

T. B. LARIMORE AND HIS MOTHER AT MARS' HILL.

(69)

and courteously suggested that he adhered too closely to
the Bible in his preaching, and quoted too much scripture
in every sermon, to the neglect of originality and intellec-
tuality, he sent the following joke, clipped from a political
paper:

"A Kansas Legislator has introduced a bill to enact the
Ten Commandments into a law, and his party has sat
down on him and flattened him out like a postage stamp
for running off after heresies."

There is always demand for his labor, because he creates
a demand by constant, hard work.   In every line of human
endeavor there is always a demand for men who are constantly employed.   Men who will not be idle are in demand when workers are wanted for anything.   Preachers
are no exception to the rule.   It is hard to get work and
places for " unemployed preachers " because people who
want a preacher prefer one who will not be " unemployed."
This thought is well expressed in the following stanzas,
clipped from a paper and inclosed in one of his letters:

I OFTEN WONDER WHY 'TIS SO.

Some find work where some find rest,
  And so the weary world goes on;
I sometimes wonder which is best;
  The answer comes when life is gone.

Some eyes sleep when some eyes wake,
  And so the dreary night hours go;
Some hearts beat where some hearts break;
  I often wonder why 'tis so.

Some wills faint where some wills fight,
  Some love the tent, and some the field;
I often wonder who are right,
  The ones who strive or those who yield.

Some hands fold where other hands
  Are lifted bravely in the strife,
And so through ages and through lands
  Move on the two extremes of life.

Some feet halt where some feet tread
  In tireless march a thorny way;
Some struggle on where some have fled;
  Some seek when others shun the fray.

Some swords rust where others clash,
  Some fall back where some move on;
Some flags furl where others flash
  Until the battle has been won.

Some sleep on, while others keep
  The vigils of the true and brave;
They will not rest till roses creep
  Around their name above a grave.

Several years ago he wrote:

" Brother —— is kindly calling in the papers for work for me to do. Well, I am much obliged; but I already have calls enough from one State alone to keep me busy as a bee can be five long years. That's all right. Brother —— is earnestly doing his very best for all concerned, I doubt not."

No small part of his labor is answering letters and worrying over work he cannot do. To lighten this labor as much as possible, he had the following typewritten letter prepared in large numbers, which he mailed in many cases where nothing else was necessary in answer to calls for meetings which he could not hold:

" FLORENCE, ALA., January 7, 1898.

" My Dear Friend and Brother: The time has come when I must say ' Yes ' or ' No ' to your appreciated call question—request; and, absolutely forced to forego the pleasure of saying ' Yes,' I reluctantly and regretfully say ' No '—I cannot be with you this year. This is my reply to nine-tenths of the calls before me now. I am sure it is safe to say more work is pressing me now than it is possible for me to do in seven years. May the Lord always abundantly bless you and yours, graciously granting you all the desires of your hearts, and love and lead and save us all, now, henceforth, and for evermore.

" Gratefully, affectionately, and fraternally,

" T. B. LARIMORE."

This was the year of his long and serious sickness, which kept him at home, unable to work, from May till September. Nevertheless, the few months he was able to preach that year he did much preaching in country places among very poor people, where his remuneration was exceedingly meager. Less than two months before the date of this circular letter he wrote:

" I am pleasantly and delightfully situated here, in a beautiful little city in glorious old Kentucky, in the best room in the best hotel in the town, in the bright blaze by night of brilliant, artistic, electric lights that look like brilliant buds from the burning bush and blazing blossoms from the bosom of the sun. I am surrounded by all the comforts, conveniences, and luxuries of modern civilization and of this luxurious age and country. Moreover, my audiences are fine, fashionable, attentive, attractive, polite, patient, intelligent, intellectual, considerate, courteous, and kind—just such audiences as I always expect to find in respectable towns and cities everywhere; but if you suppose that I feel more at home here than I feel among poor people in the country, that I appreciate and enjoy these city comforts and conveniences more than I enjoy the accommodations in Christian homes in the country, while you may be correct in everything else, you are as far as possible from correct in this. I am here because I considered it my duty to come, and I will stay till I consider it my duty to leave. Style is all right in its proper place and sphere, but it is very light diet. I love flowers— am passionately and childishly fond of them. 'A thing of beauty,' they are ' a joy forever; ' but fruits are far more nourishing. Peach blossoms are beautiful, exquisitely so to me—my favorite flower. To my eye, a peach orchard in full bloom is the most beautiful thing in inanimate nature; but, to satisfy the appetite and gratify the inner man, as well as nourish the body and keep body, soul, and spirit in good preaching trim, I'd rather rely on one can of a good old country sister's peaches than a big basketful of blossoms."

While at home for a few days after a long trip, he wrote:

" My health seems to be perfect, as is also the weather; but I am so pressed with work, and it is so hard for me to say ' No,' that I am not enjoying either health or weather. I think it is perfectly safe to say more work is pressing me now than I could do in seven years."

It is thought by some that a demand is created for a preacher by the prominence that is given him in newspapers. This is no doubt true to some extent, but hard and constant work will soon bring a preacher into prominence in the newspapers. It is as difficult for a preacher who works hard and constantly to keep out of the papers as for one who is ' unemployed ' to get any newspaper notoriety. As a rule, a preacher who publishes himself in the papers as ' unemployed ' and open for engagements simply advertises his own inefficiency. When a preacher begins to advertise for work, the people very properly begin to lay plans to get rid of him and steer clear of all his sort. There are very few things the world has less use for than an ' unemployed ' preacher. Soon after he recovered from the long spell of sickness referred to in another place in this book, he wrote:

" You can imagine—only imagine—how sorely I am perplexed, how I am worried. At least twenty places are pressing me to come, so that it truly grieves me to postpone going to any one of them, even for one day. Now, knowing me as you alone know me, consider the pressure from one source, and then multiply that by twenty, and you can imagine how I am distressed. I have not kept count of calls this year, but I believe I have been urged to go to one thousand different places. What to do I know not. Well, I'll continue to try to do all that duty demands."

On reaching home, after a long absence, he wrote:

" I am overwhelmed with work; weak, weary, and worn; yet not one day can I rest—not one."

At the beginning of a dull meeting in a hard place he wrote:

" I am doing my very best all the time. No two places alike. I expect to go into this meeting full of hope, without doubt or fear, and preach the word to the close. If, as you say, I am always at my best when under pressure of the greatest disadvantages, and if this field is what I think it is, I will be better than my best in this meeting. We nearly froze in the meetinghouse Sunday night. They put up a stove on Monday, after they had frozen the meeting. The clock pointed to twelve—midnight—before we dismissed Monday night, but no one could tell what time it was by that clock. We couldn't even tell by the clock whether it was to-night or to-morrow night. We had no clock last night. The pastor said he supposed it had been taken to the shop. Don't know why they didn't take the pastor and the church to the shop, too. House scarcely lighted at all. They talk of putting in electric lights. Had they had all things ready to begin, the meeting had been a success; but—well, I'll do the best I can."

When he goes into a hard place, he spends money, if he has it, as freely as he gives time and labor to make the meeting a success and establish the church. While working at such a place, he wrote:

" Please send me, by express, two dozen song books. Please charge them to me, send me the bill, and I will pay it right away. We ought to have six dozen, but two dozen will do to begin with. I intend to give the books to these people. They have four song books in this neighborhood already—two of a sort—but they are badly worn. I am trying to give them a little lift. They are good people."

Referring to a matter of business in which we were both trying to help a mutual friend, he wrote:

" Please do not depend too much on me in this matter this time. I am trying to do my very best, but I have thirty days' work to do in three days, and I am so rushed and bothered that I am heartily ashamed of the very best work I can do. I am well, but worried—that's all. I am anxious as possible to help, and would cheerfully give one solid week's work now, if I could; but I really cannot conveniently do that and do thirty days' other work that just simply must be done—all in seventy hours."

Men who propose to form big combinations backed by ample capital to establish great institutions have made liberal and tempting propositions to control his name and influence to help boost their schemes, but he has been singularly fortunate in keeping out of all such enterprises. One of many letters on this point will be sufficient. While he was in a meeting in a Western city, when town booming was the ruling passion with speculators all over the country, he wrote:

" They think they can locate me here permanently. Town-booming scheme is on foot, I think. Suburb laid off; lots of lots going and lots of money coming, they say. The scheme is to get me to take hold—be president—build up a big school, big church, big town, etc. They tell me I can get my own salary—money is no object with them;

BACK VIEW, EAST VERANDA, LARIMORE'S HOME, MARS' HILL.

(77)

they guarantee everything, pay everything, do everything, boom everything, etc.   Of course I listen politely and say nothing.   They evidently think ' money makes the mare go,' but—well, my duty is to ' preach the word ' and do as much good and as little evil as I can.   ' The Lord willing,' that is what I will do, and all I will try to do, as long as I live."

I select this letter from many others of the same kind referring to similar schemes in different places, because this enterprise, though speculative and inflated, was backed by men—some of them members of the church—who were worth, in the aggregate, more than a million, and who had been singularly fortunate in former years of successful business.   He could have made sure of several thousand dollars in this scheme at the first venture, with a chance of a fortune in a few years.   From this meeting he went home, and in a few weeks he was out of money, as usual, and preaching in the woods near home to large audiences of poor, but honest, country people—three times and baptizing once—every day.

Strong churches at different places have made very liberal propositions to locate him as " pastor," but he has declined all overtures of that kind and kept steadily to the idea that " the wide, wide world is my field."   Soon after he recovered from his long sickness, which threw him " behind, financially and otherwise," he wrote from a country meeting:

" I am away out here in the country, among good people, where I see but one paper and hear but little of what is going on in the world—preaching twice every day and three times every Sunday, and hunting ' scaly-bark hickory nuts ' between sermons. I hope to be able to keep up till Christmas and be in good condition for work next year. I am getting old now, but I may have reserve force enough to enable me to rally for a few more campaigns for Christ before I ' go hence.' I have several liberal propositions and strong appeals to locate in easy places with good churches. I would willingly go to any good church to preach twice every day and three times every Sunday as long as I can do more good there than anywhere else, if they would consent for me to go anywhere else at any time and stay as long as I thought I could do more good. I might compromise on a proposition to preach one time— at night—every day in the week, except Saturday, and twice every Sunday, making seven sermons every week, or an average of one sermon every day."

He has never been a member of anything but the body of Christ, which is the church, and of which every Christian is a member because he is a Christian; nor has he ever been employed on a salary by any organization, or directed and controlled in his work by any kind of a board or committee.

Speaking of work in hard places, the following letter, which he received from a young preacher and sent to me some years after he had written the young preacher some wholesome advice and timely encouragement, will illustrate both the kind of work he has done himself and has advised and encouraged others to do:

" You wrote me that you had done much good by preaching at such places as ' Lickskillet ' and ' Raccoon Hollow,' and you encouraged and advised me to go to such places

and ' preach the word.'   I now see that I had wrong ideas
then, and that your advice was wise and best.   Anyway,
you have the love, respect, and confidence of ' us all ' here.
    " Truly and fraternally,   JOHN HAYES."

It is not the purpose of this volume to give the estimate
which people who have heard Larimore preach have formed
of his gifts as a speaker and of his power over an audience,
but to furnish data in his sermons and private letters, from
which people who have never heard him and who do not
know him may form their own opinion of him, both as a
man and as a preacher.   I have enough flattering eulogies
of him to fill several volumes like this, but I shall not publish them.   His voice and personality, however, which cannot be put in a book, are potent elements of his popularity
as a speaker and of his mastery over an audience.   As
readers of this book who have never seen him nor heard
him will be dependent upon the testimony of others as to
his gifts in these things, it will not be improper to publish
the following clipping from the Madisonville (Ky.) Mail:

    " T. B. Larimore has been with us, to ' preach the word,'
to build us up, to make us one, to make us better, to make
us happier, to strengthen saints, to save souls, and has
gone to other fields to sow the seeds of righteousness, unity,
and peace.

    " The seeds he has sown here are sure to germinate and
produce an abundance of fruit to the glory of God, the
honor of Christ, and the salvation of souls, having been
warmed by the love light of God's eternal truth and watered
by the tears of sympathy and love.

    " I have heard Gov. ' Bob ' Taylor in his happiest moods,

and have followed him in his loftiest flights of fancy and dream. I have heard him on ' The Fiddle and the Bow,' when he touched every chord in the soul that can be touched by all that is pathetic and tender, sweet and soul-inspiring. I have heard him on ' Paradise of Fools,' as he talked thrillingly of ' God's first thought for the happiness of man; ' and he filled my heart with gentleness, kindness, and love —sweetest sentiments of the soul. I have heard him on ' Visions and Dreams,' when he so eloquently and tenderly told of his return to the dear old home of the ' long, long ago; ' and he filled my mind with sweet, sad memories of the delightful days, forever gone, when I dwelt with father, mother, sisters, and brothers in the dear home that can never be home again.

" I have heard Ditzler on ' The Judgment Day,' and he held me fixed to my seat and overwhelmed with horror as he depicted the tortures of torment and told of the shrieks of the doomed banished into outer darkness forever because of sin. I have heard him in his ' Halleluiah Sermon,' and he pictured so beautifully and vividly the beauty and grandeur and glory of heaven that the flame of love and reverence for heaven and heavenly things he kindled in my breast has never been extinguished, though long, eventful years have come and gone since last I heard him speak.

" These are but samples of men and things I have heard and seen; yet, as I sat, last Sunday, and listened to T. B. Larimore as he reasoned of the ' vanity of vanities ' in wisdom, wealth, pleasure, power, and the alluring beauties of nature—beautiful words of wisdom pouring in torrents and bursting like flames from his lips, and sparkling and scintillating as purest gems of reason in brightest light of

-6

thought, filling and flooding every mind present with light almost divine—I involuntarily said, ' Never man spake like this man; ' and this was the unanimous verdict of one of the largest and most intelligent audiences ever assembled in the city of Madisonville."

CHAPTER VI.

SERMON——CONSEQUENCES OF SIN AND RIGHT-
EOUSNESS.

A ND God spake all these words, saying, I am the Lord
thy God, which have brought thee out of the land
of Egypt, out of the house of bondage. Thou shalt have
no other gods before me. Thou shalt not make unto thee
any graven image, or any likeness of anything that is in
heaven above, or that is in the earth beneath, or that is in
the water under the earth: thou shalt not bow down thyself to them, nor serve them: for I the Lord thy God am a
jealous God, visiting the iniquity of the fathers upon the
children unto the third and fourth generation of them that
hate me; and showing mercy unto thousands of them that
love me, and keep my commandments." (Ex. 20: 1-6.)

" Thou shalt not bow down thyself to them, nor serve
them: for I the Lord thy God am a jealous God, visiting
the iniquity of the fathers upon the children unto the third
and fourth generation of them that hate me; and showing
mercy unto thousands of them that love me, and keep my
commandments."

" Know therefore that the Lord thy God, he is God, the
faithful God, which keepeth covenant and mercy with
them that love him and keep his commandments to a thousand generations." (Deut. 7: 9.)

Taking these three verses together, we learn what we all
ought to consider seriously: that God visits the iniquities

and righteousness of the wicked and righteous, respectively, upon their posterity to the thousandth generation. Is not that a wonderful thought? Is it not a fearful thing to stand before an audience of intelligent men, women, and children, and undertake to speak to that audience upon such a theme as this, and feel the wondrous pressure of the wondrous weight of the wondrous responsibility resting upon you? If not, you are a strange son of Adam, to say the least of it. I am standing before an audience of people interested in Bible themes. I am standing before people who believe the Bible, and hence believe, as the Bible teaches it, that God visits the iniquities and the righteousness of the wicked and righteous, respectively, upon their posterity to the thousandth generation. Do I stand before a man believing the Bible, and hence believing this wondrous declaration, who is careless and indifferent in reference to the manner in which he lives? If so, a strangely unfortunate man indeed is he, and fearfully unfortunate must be his posterity. There are other passages of scripture that seem to contradict this passage, and yet there are no real contradictions in God's Book. The language of Ezekiel (18: 19-30, and 33: 1, 2) seems to directly antagonize, or contradict, the language I have just read. I will not take time to quote these passages, but will quote you a sample from them: "The soul that sinneth, it shall die. The son shall not bear the iniquity of the father, neither shall the father bear the iniquity of the son: the righteousness of the righteous shall be upon him, and the wickedness of the wicked shall be upon him." This is a sample of the two chapters, and especially of the two lengthy paragraphs to which I have just referred. Coming down to the New

Testament, we find multitudes of passages of scripture seeming to be in line with these two chapters in Ezekiel, and to directly antagonize the scripture I have read. " Of a truth I perceive that God is no respecter of persons: but in every nation he that feareth him, and worketh righteousness, is accepted with him." (Acts 10: 34, 35.) That makes it an individual and personal matter. A man is not accepted or rejected upon the merits or demerits of his great-great-grandfather, but is accepted or rejected upon the merits or demerits of his own conduct. Of course there is a higher and holier sense in which the man is accepted by merit; that is the merit of the blood Jesus shed for a lost and ruined race; but this is the language of inspiration, and it places the responsibility upon a man himself. " Of a truth I perceive that God is no respecter of persons: but in every nation he that feareth him, and worketh righteousness, is accepted with him." He will render unto every man according to his deeds—not according to the deeds of his great-great-grandfather, or according to Adam's deeds, but to every man according to his own deeds. " Who will render to every man according to his deeds: to them who by patient continuance in welldoing seek for glory and honor and immortality, eternal life: but unto them that are contentious, and do not obey the truth, but obey unrighteousness, indignation and wrath, tribulation and anguish, upon every soul of man that doeth evil, of the Jew first, and also of the Gentile; but glory, honor, and peace, to every man that worketh good, to the Jew first, and also to the Gentile: for there is no respect of persons with God." (Rom. 2: 6-11.)

" For we must all appear before the judgment seat of

Christ; that every one may receive the things done in his body, according to that he hath done, whether it be good or bad." (2 Cor. 5: 10.)

"And, behold, I come quickly; and my reward is with me, to give every man according as his work shall be. I am Alpha and Omega, the beginning and the end, the first and the last. Blessed are they that do his commandments, that they may have right to the tree of life, and may enter in through the gates into the city." (Rev. 22: 12-14.)

" Marvel not at this: for the hour is coming, in the which all that are in the graves shall hear his voice, and shall come forth; they that have done good, unto the resurrection of life; and they that have done evil, unto the resurrection of damnation." (John 5: 28, 29.)

" Let us hear the conclusion of the whole matter: Fear God, and keep his commandments: for this is the whole duty of man. For God shall bring every work into judgment, with every secret thing, whether it be good, or whether it be evil." (Eccles. 12: 13, 14.)

" Who in the days of his flesh, when he had offered up prayers and supplications with strong crying and tears unto him that was able to save him from death, and was heard in that he feared; though he were a Son, yet learned he obedience by the things which he suffered; and being made perfect, he became the author of eternal salvation unto all them that obey him." (Heb. 5: 7-9.)

" For the mystery of iniquity doth already work: only he who now letteth will let, until he be taken out of the way. And then shall that Wicked be revealed, whom the Lord shall consume with the spirit of his mouth, and shall destroy with the brightness of his coming: even him, whose

coming is after the working of Satan with all power and
signs and lying wonders." (2 Thess. 2: 7-9.)

" Go ye into all the world, and preach the gospel to every
creature. He that believeth and is baptized shall be saved;
but he that believeth not shall be damned." (Mark 16:
15, 16.)

" He that believeth and is baptized shall be saved." It
does not say that the son or grandson of the man who believes and is baptized shall be saved, and it does not say that
the grandson or the great-great-grandson of the man who
believes not shall be damned.

Now this is a fair sample of what some people call the
contradictions of the Bible. There are things along here
that are supposed to be insurmountable difficulties. A
very old man, whose head is covered with the snows that
never melt, whose natural force is abated, whose eye is
dim, whose body is bent, who is almost in sight of his open
grave, said to me once—not so very long ago, either:
" There is one thing in the Bible especially that troubles
me more than anything else. I can get around everything
in the Bible but that." (Now, why he should try to get
around anything in the Bible, I cannot tell you. None of
us should want to get around anything in the Bible.) He
said: " I can get around everything else but where it is
taught that God shall visit the iniquities of the fathers
upon the children to the third and fourth generation.
That bothers me; that troubles me; I can't get around
that. That being true, I do not know, and I never can
know, whose sins I have to answer for. If my father was
a bad man and went to perdition, or if my grandfather was
a bad man and went to perdition, or if my great-grand-

father or my great-great-great-great-grandfather lived and died in rebellion against God and went to perdition, then I have to bear his sins; and if his sins were heavy enough to sink him to perdition, they are heavy enough to sink me down; so I am necessarily lost, and it is impossible for me to know whether there is any chance for me to be saved. According to that, a man is not rewarded or punished according to his own sins, but according to the sins of his ancestors. There is no personal reward or punishment for deeds done in the flesh, and that relieves us of personal responsibility, and leaves us in darkness, and we must grope our way to the grave, and then wake up and see what kind of man our great-great-great-grandfather was before we will know whether we are saved or not." I rather think that unfortunate man intended his talk to appear irreverent. There was something about his appearance, in the very sound of his voice, indicating that he intended that I should understand that he meant to say by this: "I have no use for your Bible, no use for your religion, and no use for your God." I could not wonder so very greatly, after it was all over, that he should feel this way, reasoning from effect to cause, reasoning from what he said back to what caused him to say it. Well, is there any difficulty here? None in the world. God uttered a solemn truth, a truth that ought to make us shudder at the thought of doing wrong, when he declared that he would visit the iniquities of the fathers upon the children to the third and fourth generation, a truth that should make us glad when he declared he would visit the righteousness of the righteous to the thousandth generation to them that fear him and keep his commandments. God breathes a truth as immutable as himself in all the passages we quoted showing that we are individually responsible; that "the soul that sinneth, it shall die. The son shall not bear the iniquity of the father, neither shall the father bear the iniquity of the son: the righteousness of the righteous shall be upon him, and the wickedness of the wicked shall be upon him." There are two distinct lines under consideration here. In the passages I read, God has under consideration what he visits upon posterity through the established, fixed, and unchangeable laws of nature; in the other passages that seem to antagonize this, he has under consideration his dealing with the human race through the laws of grace; and whenever that thought takes possession of our hearts in connection with these things, the shadow vanishes, the mists are cleared away, and we see that there is no inconsistency in these things. Well, but does God do what is done by and through the laws of nature? Yes, he does, in the sense that he is the author of the laws of nature. God is the author of the laws of nature, just as he is the author of the laws of grace. "Ye have heard that it hath been said, Thou shalt love thy neighbor, and hate thine enemy. But I say unto you, Love your enemies, bless them that curse you, do good to them that hate you, and pray for them which despitefully use you, and persecute you; that ye may be the children of your Father which is in heaven: for he maketh his sun to rise on the evil and on the good, and sendeth rain on the just and on the unjust." (Matt. 5: 43-45.) Does he do this through the laws of grace, or does he do these things through the laws of nature? Through the laws of nature. The power being his that brings about this result, in that sense he does everything that is done by and through the laws of nature; and it is in this sense, and in this sense only, that he visits the iniquities and the righteousness of the wicked and righteous, respectively, to the thousandth generation—not only to the third and fourth, but to the thousandth generation.   But, then, to stem the tide of iniquity and eternal destruction, he sent his Son by grace to this world to suffer, bleed, and die to redeem us, and in him he gave us a system of grace.   Now this is personal, God regarding us individually when it comes to this, to spiritual blessings. "The soul that sinneth, it shall die.   The son shall not bear the iniquity of the father, neither shall the father bear the iniquity of the son: the righteousness of the righteous shall be upon him, and the wickedness of the wicked shall be upon him."

Here are a father and mother caring for their firstborn. It is but a few brief weeks old, very young and very tender.   It is summer time, a leisure time with them, and they go fishing.   They are not in all respects what parents should be.   They make preparations for the babe before they start, and take it along with them.   They fix a nice pallet in the shade of a tree—the surroundings seem to be safe—and they put the little one, who is sleeping, flat of its back upon the pallet.   They go off fishing, and they sample the contents of a bottle that ought to have been left at home, because it is filled with something very bad for people to drink.   They get thirsty again directly, and they again sample the contents of that bottle.   They get a little vexed because the fish seem not to be hungry, and they sample the bottle again.   Then they forget the babe. Hours afterwards they go back to the tree.   Now God causeth the "sun to rise on the evil and on the good, and sendeth rain on the just and on the unjust," through the laws of nature, and as the hours have gone by the shade has moved, so that the sun shines full down into the face of the innocent, tender little babe. It cries, and the tears are made to blister its cheek as the pitiless rays of the sun pour down upon its face. Its life is almost destroyed, but it is cared for tenderly and nursed back to something like the health it had before; but its vision is destroyed, it is blind the balance of its days. Did God do that? Yes, through the laws of nature; and precisely in that sense the Bible teaches that he visits the iniquities of the fathers upon the children unto the third and fourth generation. Its children are born blind, and from that blind family come other blind children, and the blindness is handed down through the laws of heredity to the third and fourth generation. And thus God visits the wickedness of that father and mother upon their posterity to the third and fourth generation, and yet this is through, and only through, the established laws of nature, without which man could not live.

A man is a drunkard; he bequeaths an appetite for strong drink to his boys, and they yield to the pressure of that demand and become drunkards; and their boys are drunkards; and this drunkenness is handed down to the third and fourth generation, and maybe to the thousandth generation. The iniquity of that father is visited upon his posterity. God does that, but only through the established laws of nature. Nothing in this for which we can censure God. Who shall be censured? Those who do the wrong. On the other hand, the righteousness of the righteous may be visited upon posterity to the thousandth generation; so certainly there is no wrong here for which we can censure God. How careful parents should be as to how they live!

All parents, and all who contemplate being parents, should understand, not so much for themselves as for their posterity, that they are under the most solemn obligation to be as nearly absolutely perfect and pure as it is possible for them to be. We are trifling with the rights of our posterity when we are living bad lives—not only with the few, but with a countless host, even millions. We ought to remember that the results of our living will be visited upon our posterity to the thousandth generation. It is a fearful thing for either father or mother to live contrary to the principles of right; it is fearful in the extreme for both to do so. What chance have children of parents who habitually live, before the birth of their children and afterwards, so that through the established laws of nature the iniquities of the parents shall be visited upon their posterity to the thousandth generation? Some one asked a physician of world-wide reputation once: " Doctor, how early in life do you think the education of a child should begin?" He answered: " Madam, a hundred years before it is born." Mortal man, without the inspiration of the Holy Spirit, never uttered a truer truth than that; and not only did he utter the truth when he said the education of children should begin a hundred years before they are born, but if he had said, " Madam, the education of children *does* begin a hundred years before they are born," he would have uttered the truth—yea, if he had said the education of children begins a thousand years before they are born, he would have uttered the truth. The influences that tend to make a child what he is begin long, long before he is born.

The greatest highway robber that ever lived in Tennessee said, between the time he spent in the Nashville penitentiary and the day when his body was put away in the silent spot near the head of the Sequatchie River, shadowed now by the towering peaks of glorious old East Tennessee: "My father was an honest man, but my mother was ' true grit.' My mother was all right; she backed me; but my father was an honest man." It is a fearful thing for a boy's mother to be wrong, and there is not a mother in all this land who ought not to shudder at the thought that she was not a Christian, and as nearly perfect as such as it was possible for her to be, before the birth of her firstborn. If she is still away from God and out of Christ, and serving Satan and going to perdition, she ought to shudder at the thought. She ought to rise and rush to Jesus, grasp the cross, and hold to it until she dies. But would you see the saddest sight that ever shocked the sensibilities of sensitive souls upon the storm-swept shores of this sad world of sickness, sorrow, pain, and death? Go not to the city of the dead, where mourners weep about the open grave that waits for what was dearer than life; go not to the lunatic asylum and view the thrones once occupied by brilliant minds long since wrecked by sorrows worse than death; go not to the sorrow-shrouded home where a faithful Christian wife or husband tenderly presses the hand of the loving companion, unconscious and speechless in the silent shadow of the valley of death. Would you see a sadder scene than any or all of these, go to that home that ought to be a paradise of prosperity, purity, and happiness; a bright, blooming oasis in the dark, dreary desert of life; where a pure, chaste, Christian wife is doing all in her power to train her precious treasures—her boys and girls—for usefulness, honor, and happiness in this world, and glory, and honor, and immortality in a world that is better and brighter than this; while a dissolute, dissipated, reckless husband is dragging those same priceless jewels, for whose very existence he is responsible, down to the eternal depths of everlasting despair, over her aching, bleeding, breaking heart. Look at the withered lilies that rest upon the cheeks where roses once in beauty bloomed; look at the snow upon the tresses prematurely gray; look at the blinding tears that should never have been shed that are washing the luster from her eyes; hear the sorrowful sigh that makes your own soul sick, and then know you have found the sad, sad scene you have sought. May the Lord bless you and yours in so living as never to be responsible for such a scene.

It is a blessing that our posterity shall inherit our propensities and the result of the manner in which we live here, provided we live as we ought to live. Would we bless posterity to the thousandth generation, then we ought to live righteous, godly lives. But—O!—it is a fearful thing that posterity shall feel the pressure of the evil that we do through a thousand generations just as much as we do. I believe—however, I may be wrong in this—that there is not a responsible father or husband, or prospective father or husband, one that contemplates being a husband or father, in this audience at this moment who can fully realize the wondrous importance of this line of thought that I am trying to present to you, and that is presented upon the bright pages of God's eternal truth, and be a bad man. No father or prospective father can practice one bad habit without trifling with the dearest interest of his own posterity. Yea, I believe that if I had the power to properly impress upon your minds the wonderful, solemn, fearful, and infinite importance of this train of thought, so as to make you feel and comprehend it in all its glory, grandeur, and beauty, on the one hand, and all that is terrible and dreadful, on the other hand; that if there were a hundred of you husbands and fathers, or prospective husbands and fathers, living in the service of Satan, who understand duty's demands, you would all make a sublime rush for Jesus, confess your faith to the Savior, bow in meek submission to his will, and the remainder of your days live as God would have you live, as you are going to wish you had lived when you reach the brink of the deep, dark river. May God bless you and your posterity to the thousandth generation, through your sublime devotion to the eternal truth, in your submission to God's will, until life's fitful dream is over and he shall call you home.

Now, if I have made any declaration that you consider reckless, please remember that I have been pleading for the pure wives and helpless children of this community; I have been pleading for the sorrow-shrouded, sin-cursed homes of the land; and, remember, I have been pleading for generations that are to come upon the stage of action long centuries after these hands are still, this tongue is silent, these lips have returned to the dust from which man originally sprang—yea, I have been pleading for the rights and happiness of billions of people yet unborn. May the Lord bless all of you and help you take these thoughts home with you and ponder them in your hearts, and then do all that you can do to swell the tide of zeal and enthusiasm and spiritual reformation and revolution in this land, for the glory of God, the honor of Christ, and the eternal salvation of precious souls.

CHAPTER VII.

LETTERS——HUMILITY.

HUMILITY is a token of true greatness and an essential element of Christian character. Solomon said: " Pride goeth before destruction, and a haughty spirit before a fall." (Prov. 16: 18.) Paul said " to every man that is among you, not to think of himself more highly than he ought to think." (Rom. 12: 3.) A greater than Solomon or Paul said: " Except ye be converted, and become as little children, ye shall not enter into the kingdom of heaven. Whosoever therefore shall humble himself as this little child, the same is greatest in the kingdom of heaven." (Matt. 18: 3, 4.) " When thou art bidden of any man to a wedding, sit not down in the highest room; lest a more honorable man than thou be bidden of him; and he that bade thee and him come and say to thee, Give this man place; and thou begin with shame to take the lowest room. But when thou art bidden, go and sit down in the lowest room; that when he that bade thee cometh, he may say unto thee, Friend, go up higher: then shalt thou have worship in the presence of them that sit at meat with thee. For whosoever exalteth himself shall be abased; and he that humbleth himself shall be exalted." (Luke 14: 8-11.) Much, if not most, of the strife and animosity in the church and in the world comes from unholy love of high places and great honors. " Only by pride cometh contention; but with the well advised is wisdom." (Prov. 13: 10.)

- 7 -

The spirit of rivalry for high places cropped out among the disciples in the presence of the Lord himself. " Then came to him the mother of Zebedee's children with her sons, worshiping him, and desiring a certain thing of him. . . . Grant that these my two sins may sit, the one on thy right hand, and the other on thy left, in thy kingdom." (Matt. 20: 20, 21.) This spirit caused trouble then, as it has caused trouble many times since then. "And when the ten heard it, they were moved with indignation against the two brethren." (Matt. 20: 24.) The purpose of Christianity is to destroy this love of high places and great honors, and make men great by making them humble. "Jesus called them unto him, and said, Ye know that the princes of the Gentiles exercise dominion over them, and they that are great exercise authority upon them. But it shall not be so among you: but whosoever will be great among you, let him be your minister; and whosoever will be chief among you, let him be your servant: even as the Son of man came not to be ministered unto, but to minister, and to give his life a ransom for many." (Matt. 20: 25-28.)

T. B. Larimore is an exponent of a cardinal principle of Christianity to the extent people see in his life and sermons the grace of humility. After hearing him in several sermons, the editor of a daily paper referred to him in an editorial paragraph as a " consecrated man," and in the news columns of the same paper a very complimentary notice of his preaching contained the following words:

" If he is a great man, he is not aware of it; and if he were told so, he would not believe it."

Referring in one of his letters to very flattering compliments from an unexpected source, he wrote:

" What I have ever thought, said, done, or been to justify or cause anything of the kind, I do not know."

Inclosing a letter filled with extravagant eulogies, he wrote:

" Inclosed is a sample of letters I have received from various sources, an occasional sample of which I have sent to you, but never to any other, as you are the only one to whom I tell all. I have never seen anything remarkable in myself—never. I do my very best to be perfect for Christ's sake, but never succeed in being more than barely passable and endurable in my own estimation. Of course I appreciate friends and admiration, but some esteem me too highly."

It is to the credit of his modesty and humility that he carefully avoids the use or approval of all honorary titles. In his fraternal association with people, he is " Brother Larimore " to everybody, and by letter he prefers to be addressed as simply " T. B. Larimore."

On an envelope addressed, " Mr. T. B. Larimore, Christian Minister," he has written:

"A new one on me, sure. Wonder if that's the way big preachers do. Truly, ' the world do move.' "

On another envelope addressed, " T. B. Larimore, Pastor Christian Church," he has written:

" That settles it."

Answering a request to write a sermon to be published in a book, entitled " Biographies and Sermons," consisting of twenty sermons by twenty different men, he wrote:

"Of course you knew when you saw me a few days ago that I ought to be at home in bed. Well, I am in the same condition still. Utterly unable to preach, I have decided to stay at home and do my best to get well. No man knows better than you know how hard it is for me to say, 'I can't.' I want to live no longer than I can work, and I want to work as long as I can. Well, I must submit to the inevitable and try to make the best of the situation. It is scarcely possible that a sick man, in no way related to Solomon, save 'in Adam,' is a very safe man to write a sermon, especially a man who has never tried to write a sermon and who has absolutely no confidence in himself as to his ability to do such a thing; but, as you want me to try, and as this is my only time, I will try."

Every man's ability is the measure of his duty in the service of God. No one should cultivate, or yield to, the grace of humility and modesty so far as to decline to do the best he can from fear that the best he can do may not meet the approval or elicit the applause of men. Somewhere in his travels he found an old copy of a license to preach which so comically expresses this thought, while intending to be perfectly serious, that he sent me a photograph of it, with the remark:

"Everybody ought 'to preach the gospel to the best of his ability,' and no man can preach it any better than that."

Preachers who have the Christian virtues of modesty and humility will resort to no sensational tricks or catch-notice formalities in their work.

When on the ground ready to begin a protracted meeting, he wrote:

Lureangrove
Church
of Christ
This is to certify that
Bro E. B. Jones Liberated
to Preach the Gosple
to the best of his ability

D. M. Jones
J. H. Webster
Elders

"LICENSE TO PREACH."

" We meet to-night—Saturday—at 7: 30, sharp or flat, not sure which, to dedicate the new meetinghouse. We could wait till to-morrow, but somebody might be there, and as I am a green hand at the business and might make a botch of it, I think it best to do the thing Saturday night. Bell not to be rung; simply for the saints. If we can get the house dedicated Saturday night, we will be ready to preach the gospel to the people Sunday when they come."

After a very successful meeting in a city church, he wrote:

" They press me for another long meeting. I argue that I am not the man for the place, but they argue that facts and figures prove that I am the man they need and want. They say the results of my work there heretofore are permanent and exceedingly beneficial. Really, I do not know what is my duty in this case; but I will try to do my duty, if I can ever decide clearly what it is."

Inclosing a circular which announced that a certain church proposed " to hold a grand fair to raise money for the benefit of the church," he wrote:

" You know how hard it is for me to antagonize people who, as I believe, mean well; but I do sometimes speak plainly from the pulpit against tricks and traps—oyster eating, ice cream feasting, fairs and fandangos—to raise money for the Lord, thus advertising him as a vagabond, a bankrupt, and a beggar. I cannot well avoid that."

Speaking of unchaste language and vulgar witticisms in the pulpit, which sometimes attract attention, create a sensation, and draw a crowd, he wrote:

"An elegant and refined lady and gentleman were conversing yesterday, when the gentleman, who is almost as chaste in conversation as a lady, declared something to be ' hot as hell.' The lady, who herself related the circumstance to me this morning, looked at him with such astonishment that he, greatly confused and mortified, said: ' I do hope you will pardon me. I heard Evangelist —— preach last night, and it always takes me about a week to get over my profanity after hearing him preach.' Such preachers and preaching no doubt do some good, but they unquestionably do much harm."

Referring to a style of evangelists that was very popular in many places a few years ago, he wrote:

" I believe I sent you a clipping from the Courier-Journal stating that Evangelist —— has become skeptical. Well, that seems to me to be a move in the right direction. I well remember that my deliberate conclusion was, when reading accounts of his marvelous meetings a few years ago, that he was then an atheist. I am of ' the same opinion still.' I do not believe—have never believed—a man of his sense, believing in the existence of Jehovah, would do and preach as he did and preached. I believe I have never doubted but that he was an atheist. If he has advanced so far as to be simply ' skeptical,' he may yet see and embrace the truth. Moreover, if he can ' come to a knowledge of the truth,' there is hope—reason or ground of hope —that some other evangelists may some time see the light. Reason revolts at the thought that any man who believes in God, Christ, and the Bible will make a joke of the interests of the soul. The work of the preacher is too solemnly sacred for that; the pulpit and the grave are too close together. The preacher whose 'stock in trade' consists of jokes, yarns, fun, frolic, and profanity, is not a child of faith. A child of faith never thus prostitutes the pulpit—never. He would as readily ridicule the features of his own dear mother."

His idea of a consecrated preacher and his preparation for pulpit work is expressed in the following poetry, clipped from a paper and inclosed in one of his letters:

THE VALLEY OF SILENCE.

I walk down the Valley of Silence,
　Down the dim, voiceless valley alone;
And I hear not the fall of a footstep
　Around me, save God's and my own;
And the hush of my heart is as holy
　As houses where angels have flown.

Long ago was I weary of voices
　Whose music my heart could not win;
Long ago was I weary of noises
　That fretted my soul with their din;
Long ago was I weary of places
　Where I met but the human and sin.

I walked in the world with the worldly;
　I craved what the world never gave;
And I said: "In the world each ideal
　That shines like a star on life's wave
Is wrecked on the shores of the real,
　And sleeps like a dream in the grave."

And still did I pine for the perfect,
　And still found the false with the true;
I sought 'mid the human for heaven,
　But caught a mere glimpse of its blue;
And I wept when the clouds of the mortal
　Veiled even that glimpse from my view.

And I toiled, heart tired of the human;
   And I moaned 'mid the mazes of men,
Till I knelt long ago at an altar
   And heard a voice call me. Since then
I walk down the Valley of Silence
   That lies far beyond mortal ken.

Do you ask what I found in the valley?
   'Tis my trysting place with the Divine,
And I fell at the feet of the Holy,
   And above me a voice said: " Be mine! "
And there rose from the depths of my spirit
   An echo: " My heart shall be thine."

Do you ask how I live in the valley?
   I weep, and I dream, and I pray;
But my tears are as sweet as the dewdrops
   That fall on the roses in May;
And my prayer, like a perfume from censers,
   Ascendeth to God night and day.

In the hush of the Valley of Silence
   I dream all the songs that I sing;
And the music floats down the dim valley
   Till each finds a word for a wing,
That to hearts, like the dove of the deluge,
   A message of peace they may bring.

But far on the deep there are billows
   That never shall break on the beach,
And I have heard songs in the silence
   That never shall float into speech,
And I have had dreams in the valley
   Too lofty for language to reach.

And I have seen thoughts in the valley—
   Ah me, how my spirit was stirred!
And they wear holy veils on their faces;
   Their footsteps can scarcely be heard;
They pass through the valley, like virgins,
   Too pure for the touch of a word.

Do you ask me the place of that valley,
    Ye hearts that are harrowed by care?
It lieth afar between mountains,
    And God and his angels are there;
And one is the dark mount of sorrow,
    And one the bright mountain of prayer.

Without a word of comment or explanation, but probably to show that in politics as well as in religion people
are sometimes moved by sound instead of sense, he inclosed
the following newspaper clipping in a letter:

" When Major Botts lived in Tennessee, about 1855, he
had in his household, members of his family, two young
law students—one named Stanton, the other named Talbott. The former was a young man of wealth and a college graduate. He was a very bright young fellow and
gave promise of a brilliant career, which promise was fulfilled; for he became a Congressman before he was thirty,
and would have been a man of national reputation had he
survived the war, in one of the battles of which he was
killed at the head of his regiment. Talbott was of the
rough-diamond order, without education, but with plenty
of practical sense. Both were barely eligible to the State
Legislature when the Whigs nominated Stanton for Representative, and the Democrats nominated Talbott. Botts
was equally fond of both, and, though he was a Democrat,
he resolved not to take part in the contest, thinking Talbott's chances hopeless, as the Whigs had a majority in the
county of nearly one thousand. In those days it was cus-
tomary for candidates for the Legislature in Tennessee to
make two speaking canvasses of the county, speaking each
time at every town, village, hamlet, church, and school-
house. After the candidates returned from the first tour

PRESENT HOME OF T. B. LARIMORE'S MOTHER—EAST TENNESSEE.

the Whigs were jubilant.   It was evident that Talbott was no match for Stanton on the stump.   This aroused Botts' party spirit; besides, he began to sympathize with the ' under dog ' in the fight.   He took Talbott aside and said to him: 'John, let me advise you.   When you start out next time, speak loud and long.   It doesn't make any difference what you say; utter the first words that occur to you, but on no account halt or hesitate; and occasionally turn round to him and say: " I want you to answer that when you follow me." '   The young men started on their second round, and in less than two days reports came to town that such eloquence as dropped from the lips of Talbott had never been heard in Tennessee; he was literally tearing Stanton all to pieces.   Confirmation of this report followed fast and followed faster.   When the boys came home, Botts asked Stanton how he was getting on.   ' Badly,' was the response.   ' I believe he will beat me.   You might take the dictionary and cut out of it five thousand words, and put them in a basket and shake it, and then draw out word by word and set them in a row, and you would about have Talbott's speech; and, what is the worst of it, every five minutes he turns to me and says, " I want you to answer that," when there is nothing to answer.'   At the election Stanton had less than one hundred majority, when he ought to have had one thousand."

He has never adopted the modern evangelistic fad of preaching to " men only," or to " women only," or to " children only," or to anybody else " only," except to whomsoever will come.   I have never known him to do anything of the kind but once, and then he inclosed a circular announcing that he would preach to " men only," and wrote:

"As to this ' men only ' business, I simply preached the gospel, at the time and place appointed, to all who came. I had nothing to do with getting it up."

CHAPTER VIII.

SERMON—REASONS FOR NOT PREACHING ON BAPTISM.

AS I have delivered about ninety and nine discourses in this meeting and have not preached on the subject of baptism, there may be some of the audience who wonder why I have preached on so many subjects and have not preached on baptism at all. Well, there is a reason for that, and it is not improper that people should at least ask what that reason is. I have preached on other things than baptism thus far not because I was either afraid or ashamed to preach on baptism, I am sure. I would be afraid to be ashamed, and ashamed to be afraid, to preach or practice anything that my Savior preached and practiced personally or by proxy; I would be afraid to be ashamed, and ashamed to be afraid, to preach on anything that is a part of the divine message that Jesus has commissioned his apostles to preach to every creature in all the world; I would be afraid to be ashamed, and ashamed to be afraid, to preach on anything that constitutes clearly an important part of the great commission under which all gospel preachers have labored in the cause of Christ from the establishment of the church of Christ unto the present day; I would be afraid to be ashamed, and ashamed to be afraid, to preach to patient, polite people about anything that human beings practice by divine authority; I would be afraid to be ashamed, and ashamed to be afraid, to preach about anything that I dare to do in the name of the Lord

Jesus Christ. And whenever you find that I am afraid or ashamed to preach on baptism; and whenever you hear me say one slighting, contemptuous, or disrespectful thing of baptism; or whenever you hear me say it is not necessary for people to be baptized, then you may say, "We will never see Brother Larimore perform the ordinance of baptism in the name of Jesus Christ again;" for I am, and certainly ought to be, afraid to be ashamed, and ashamed to be afraid, to follow the instructions of the Lord Jesus Christ in anything, and I should certainly shudder at the thought of doing anything by his authority in reference to which I would utter one disrespectful, slighting syllable. I would be afraid to be ashamed, and ashamed to be afraid, to preach about anything that I endeavored to perform in the name of the Lord Jesus Christ—perform in connection with the solemn ceremony where the name of the Father, Son, and Holy Ghost are used—remembering that that is the only ordinance or the only work in connection with which high Heaven grants to mortal man the privilege of calling on the name of Father, Son, and Holy Ghost; I would be afraid to be ashamed, and ashamed to be afraid, to preach on any ordinance to which the Savior himself in person submitted, or which he, in connection with his submission to it, called a part of all righteousness; I would be afraid to be ashamed, and ashamed to be afraid, and certainly ought to be, to preach about anything, and especially about the only thing that represents the burial and resurrection of the Savior, the Lord Jesus Christ, just as the Supper represents his death; I would be afraid to be ashamed, and ashamed to be afraid, to preach anything the Bible teaches is for the remission of sins. So certainly, if

I have anything like a just conception of the situation, it is not because I am either afraid or ashamed to preach on baptism that I was willing to preach ninety and nine discourses to you, and the one hundredth one, and still not preach on that subject. There are reasons, however, and good reasons, why I have devoted all this time and thought and labor to other subjects, but have not preached on the subject of baptism. I think it has not been necessary. I really do not know, because the Bible does not tell me, why God has made the subject of baptism so exceedingly simple and plain; why the Holy Spirit has taken pains to make it clearer and simpler and plainer, perhaps, than anything that comes by God's revelation to man. It may be because God knew that there would be wrangling and disputing over it; that people would make various substitutes for it; that people would do their very best to keep others from submitting to it; that theologians would do their very best to keep people from understanding it; and, therefore, it was made by the Holy Spirit, the apostles, and the evangelists so plain that there never could be, while time lasts, any real reason why any responsible soul could not understand everything connected with it. I am not sure that that is why it is made plainer than anything else in the Book, but that may be why. If we will just believe the Bible, turn to the book, and read and study it with an earnest, prayerful desire to understand it, we can understand what the Bible teaches on that subject, if we are intelligent enough to be responsible for what we do. Does some one say, "We cannot understand it alike"—that one may understand it one way, and one another way? That cannot be. One may misunderstand it, and another may understand it. You may understand it, and I may misunderstand it; but if we understand it, we understand it, and this is all there is of that. Are we going to claim to be responsible in the sight of God and acknowledge that we have not intelligence enough to understand the plainest thing in the Bible? But others say: "There are so many different phases of it." It does not matter what you may think or say about the different phases of it. If we are responsible in the sight of God, we can, if we will, by reading what the Bible says, understand all that Heaven would have us understand with reference to the action, subject, and design of baptism. Really, it is not a question of understanding; it is a question of faith. We can understand what the Bible says on the subject. The question is: Do we believe it? I am not saying the question is: Do you believe it? The question is: Do we believe it? I never try to separate myself from my hearers and act in a I-am-holier-than-thou spirit, I-am-wise-and-thou-art-otherwise spirit. Not that. But just as sure as thought exists upon the earth, so certainly this is not a question of understanding, but of belief. And now, while I am not expecting to preach on baptism, and may not preach on it during this meeting, I am willing, conceding that you wish me to do so, to just quote what the Bible says on this subject, and see if you are willing to concede that you have not intelligence enough to understand it. I would defend you against that insult, if any man should say you have not sense enough to understand what the Bible says on that subject; but if you want to say it, I have nothing to say. I would not like for any man to say that of you. I will just quote what the Bible says on the subject, giving you chapter and verse, leaving you to believe it or not believe it; but I am not going to believe that you believe that I can believe that you have not sense enough to understand it.

And now when I am about to quote what the Bible says on the subject of baptism, of course all of you who have read the Bible on the subject and understand it thoroughly will know that I am not going to quote from the Old Testament. And why not quote from the Old Testament? Why not go to the Old Testament to find what Heaven teaches on the subject of baptism? Just for the very same reason precisely that I would not go to the North Pole to hunt June berries in January. One would be just as reasonable as the other, and I would find a bushel of June berries clustering about the North Pole in January for every passage I would find in the Old Testament on the subject of baptism; and of course, unless I want to lead you away from the subject, keep you in darkness, away from the light, I am not going to quote anything from the Old Testament. Well, you ask me: "Is baptism not mentioned in the Old Testament?" No, not that I know of; but I am not reckless enough to assume that I know everything, and I am not sure that the Old Testament does not speak on the ordinance of baptism. So far as I know, the word "baptism" does not occur in any English translation of the Old Testament in existence, and I usually preach in English when I preach to people who understand the English language. I am not saying positively that it is not there, but I will appreciate it very greatly if you will direct my mind to the passage where it can be found in the Old Testament. So far as I know, there is not one single word about baptism in any English translation of the Old Testament in existence. We, that are men and women, learned when we were children, and now these children are learning or have already learned, that words are the signs of ideas; and since there is not one word about baptism found in any translation of the Old Testament, it is safe to say in the presence of any intelligent audience that from the beginning of Genesis to the end of Malachi there is no intimation of the idea of baptism as a religious ordinance. Do you ask why the doctors of divinity go back to the Old Testament for baptism? Well, you just ask them. I am not here to represent other folks; I might misrepresent them. You can just tell them I never tried to represent them, and, therefore, that I never misrepresented them. I might edify you on other subjects by taking you through the Old Testament; but as there is not even the shadow of a shade of an intimation of the sign of an idea on the subject of baptism to be found in it, I would not expect to give you much light on that subject. Well, where does the subject begin in the Bible? It is mentioned first in the third chapter of Matthew. You can start there and go back to the beginning of Genesis, and you will not find baptism mentioned. It is not there. You ask me if this is the reason the theologians go back to the Old Testament and preach more about Moab and Joab and Judah than about the New Testament. You ask them.

But I am ready now to give you some quotations from the Scriptures on the subject; and remember that I have already assumed that it would be an insult to my audience to think that there is one ten years old that cannot understand the action, subject, and design of baptism by just reading and studying carefully and prayerfully what the

Bible says on the subject.   Now this is not assuming anything, of course, that can be offensive to anybody.   I am
just assuming that you have intelligence enough to understand what is exceedingly simple.   I want to quote—and,
remember, I want to quote without comment, and do not
want to give you my exegesis or my idea or my understanding of the Scriptures, but simply to quote the scripture and tell you where to find it, and let you accept it or
reject it as you will.   Now, I have confidence enough in
all of you to believe that you have moral courage enough
to throw aside any prejudice or hobby and look at the scripture—just look at the scripture as you go along, and see
whether you can understand the action, subject, and design
of baptism.   I may find it necessary in going along to
quote a few passages where baptism is not mentioned, because they may be connected with other passages, to show
the meaning of some terms.   But I want to go straight
along; I don't want to stop to talk, because you might get
to thinking about what I say, and not about what the Bible
says.

  " Then cometh Jesus from Galilee to Jordan unto John,
to be baptized of him.   But John forbade him, saying, I
have need to be baptized of thee, and comest thou to me?
And Jesus answering said unto him, Suffer it to be so now:
for thus it becometh us to fulfill all righteousness.   Then
he suffered him.   And Jesus, when he was baptized, went
up straightway out of the water: and, lo, the heavens were
opened unto him, and he saw the Spirit of God descending
like a dove, and lighting upon him: and lo a voice from
heaven, saying, This is my beloved Son, in whom I am well
pleased."   (Matt. 3: 13-17.)

" Go ye therefore, and teach all nations, baptizing them in the name of the Father, and of the Son, and of the Holy Ghost: teaching them to observe all things whatsoever I have commanded you: and, lo, I am with you alway, even unto the end of the world.   Amen."   (Matt. 28: 19, 20.)

"John did baptize in the wilderness, and preach the baptism of repentance for the remission of sins.   And there went out unto him all the land of Judea, and they of Jerusalem, and were all baptized of him in the river of Jordan, confessing their sins."   (Mark 1: 4, 5.)

" For this is my blood of the new testament, which is shed for many for the remission of sins."   (Matt. 26: 28.)

"And he said unto them, Go ye into all the world, and preach the gospel to every creature.   He that believeth and is baptized shall be saved; but he that believeth not shall be damned."   (Mark 16: 15, 16.)

"And he came into all the country about Jordan, preaching the baptism of repentance for the remission of sins.' (Luke 3: 3.)

"And all the people that heard him, and the publicans, justified God, being baptized with the baptism of John. But the Pharisees and lawyers rejected the counsel of God against themselves, being not baptized of him."   (Luke 7: 29, 30.)

"After these things came Jesus and his disciples into the land of Judea: and there he tarried with them, and baptized.   And John also was baptizing in Ænon, near to Salim, because there was much water there: and they came, and were baptized.   For John was not yet cast into prison." (John 3: 22-24.)

" Now when they heard this, they were pricked in their

heart, and said unto Peter and to the rest of the apostles, Men and brethren, what shall we do? Then Peter said unto them, Repent, and be baptized every one of you in the name of Jesus Christ for the remission of sins, and ye shall receive the gift of the Holy Ghost. For the promise is unto you, and to your children, and to all that are afar off, even as many as the Lord our God shall call. And with many other words did he testify and exhort, saying, Save yourselves from this untoward generation. Then they that gladly received his word were baptized: and the same day there were added unto them about three thousand souls." (Acts 2: 37-41.)

" But when they believed Philip preaching the things concerning the kingdom of God, and the name of Jesus Christ, they were baptized, both men and women." (Acts 8: 12.)

"And the angel of the Lord spake unto Philip, saying, Arise, and go toward the south unto the way that goeth down from Jerusalem unto Gaza, which is desert. And he arose and went: and, behold, a man of Ethiopia, a eunuch of great authority under Candace queen of the Ethiopians, who had the charge of all her treasure, and had come to Jerusalem for to worship, was returning, and sitting in his chariot read Esaias the prophet. Then the Spirit said unto Philip, Go near, and join thyself to this chariot. And Philip ran thither to him, and heard him read the prophet Esaias, and said, Understandest thou what thou readest? And he said, How can I, except some man should guide me? And he desired Philip that he would come up and sit with him. The place of the scripture which he read was this, He was led as a sheep to the slaughter; and like a lamb dumb before his shearer, so opened he not his mouth: in his humiliation his judgment was taken away: and who shall declare his generation? for his life is taken from the earth. And the eunuch answered Philip, and said, I pray thee, of whom speaketh the prophet this? of himself, or of some other man? Then Philip opened his mouth, and began at the same scripture, and preached unto him Jesus. And as they went on their way, they came unto a certain water: and the eunuch said, See, here is water; what doth hinder me to be baptized? And Philip said, If thou believest with all thine heart, thou mayest. And he answered and said, I believe that Jesus Christ is the Son of God. And he commanded the chariot to stand still: and they went down both into the water, both Philip and the eunuch; and he baptized him. And when they were come up out of the water, the Spirit of the Lord caught away Philip, that the eunuch saw him no more: and he went on his way rejoicing." (Acts 8: 26-39.)

"And at midnight Paul and Silas prayed, and sang praises unto God: and the prisoners heard them. And suddenly there was a great earthquake, so that the foundations of the prison were shaken: and immediately all the doors were opened, and every one's bands were loosed. And the keeper of the prison awaking out of his sleep, and seeing the prison doors open, he drew out his sword, and would have killed himself, supposing that the prisoners had been fled. But Paul cried with a loud voice, saying, Do thyself no harm: for we are all here. Then he called for a light, and sprang in, and came trembling, and fell down before Paul and Silas, and brought them out, and said, Sirs, what must I do to be saved? And they said, Believe on the Lord

Jesus Christ, and thou shalt be saved, and thy house. And they spake unto him the word of the Lord, and to all that were in his house. And he took them the same hour of the night, and washed their stripes; and was baptized, he and all his, straightway. And when he had brought them into his house, he set meat before them, and rejoiced, believing in God with all his house." (Acts 16: 25-34.)

"And Crispus, the chief ruler of the synagogue, believed on the Lord with all his house; and many of the Corinthians hearing believed, and were baptized." (Acts 18: 8.)

"And now why tarriest thou? Arise, and be baptized, and wash away thy sins, calling on the name of the Lord." (Acts 22: 16.)

"Know ye not, that so many of us as were baptized into Jesus Christ were baptized into his death?" (Rom. 6: 3.)

"For as many of you as have been baptized into Christ have put on Christ." (Gal. 3: 27.)

"Giving thanks unto the Father, which hath made us meet to be partakers of the inheritance of the saints in light: who hath delivered us from the power of darkness, and hath translated us into the kingdom of his dear Son: in whom we have redemption through his blood, even the forgiveness of sins." (Col. 1: 12-14.)

"Beware lest any man spoil you through philosophy and vain deceit, after the tradition of men, after the rudiments of the world, and not after Christ. For in him dwelleth all the fullness of the Godhead bodily. And ye are complete in him, which is the head of all principality and power: in whom also ye are circumcised with the circumcision made without hands, in putting off the body of the sins of the flesh by the circumcision of Christ: buried with him in baptism, wherein. also ye are risen with him through the faith of the operation of God, who hath raised him from the dead." (Col. 2: 8-12.)

" If ye then be risen with Christ, seek those things which are above, where Christ sitteth on the right hand of God. Set your affection on things above, not on things on the earth. For ye are dead, and your life is hid with Christ in God. When Christ, who is our life, shall appear, then shall ye also appear with him in glory. Mortify therefore your members which are upon the earth; fornication, uncleanness, inordinate affection, evil concupiscence, and covetousness, which is idolatry: for which things' sake the wrath of God cometh on the children of disobedience: in the which ye also walked some time, when ye lived in them. But now ye also put off all these; anger, wrath, malice, blasphemy, filthy communication out of your mouth. Lie not one to another, seeing that ye have put off the old man with his deeds; and have put on the new man, which is renewed in knowledge after the image of him that created him: where there is neither Greek nor Jew, circumcision nor uncircumcision, Barbarian, Scythian, bond nor free: but Christ is all, and in all. Put on therefore, as the elect of God, holy and beloved, bowels of mercies, kindness, humbleness of mind, meekness, long-suffering; forbearing one another, and forgiving one another, if any man have a quarrel against any: even as Christ forgave you, so also do ye. And above all these things put on charity, which is the bond of perfectness. And let the peace of God rule in your hearts, to the which also ye are called in one body; and be ye thankful. Let the word of Christ dwell in you richly in all wisdom; teaching and admonishing one another in psalms and hymns and spiritual songs, singing with grace in your hearts to the Lord. And whatsoever ye do in word or deed, do all in the name of the Lord Jesus, giving thanks to God and the Father by him." (Col. 3: 1-17.) This is to be taken in connection with the quotation from Col. 2: 1, giving rules for our guidance after we are risen with Christ, the other showing how we are risen with him.

" Which sometime were disobedient, when once the long-suffering of God waited in the days of Noah, while the ark was a preparing, wherein few, that is, eight souls were saved by water. The like figure whereunto even baptism doth also now save us (not the putting away of the filth of the flesh, but the answer of a good conscience toward God,) by the resurrection of Jesus Christ." (1 Pet. 3: 20, 21.)

Now, this is all I know about it, and I have nothing to say about it—not a thing. This is what the Bible says about it, and we either believe or we do not believe, and hence we are on the Lord's side or on the other side; and we ought never to forget that glory, honor, and immortality, heaven and all that heaven means, are on the Lord's side. Do you say, " On which side are you? " You go and read the scripture—I have given you the references —that is the Lord's side. If, after reading, you are still undecided, you just read them again, and as you go along say: " This is the side he is on." This is a serious matter. It is a fundamental principle. The world is confused on the subject, and they say it is only a difference of opinion. It is not a question of opinion; it is not a question of intelligence beyond simple intelligence enough to be responsible; it is not a question of understanding. It is a question of faith. If we have not intelligence enough to under-

stand the Scriptures, we are not responsible in the sight of
God; and if we are responsible in the sight of God, we can
understand these things. It is simply a question of faith.
We believe them or we do not believe them, and this settles
all that, and may the Lord bless and help you to show that
you believe them by acting accordingly.

Now, if you want my apology for delivering ninety and
nine discourses in this meeting without preaching on baptism, you have it. This is my apology. I want you to
take it home with you and study it seriously. Never forget that I have not given you my interpretation, have not
given you my application, have not expressed an opinion
as to what they mean. It is not necessary, never has been
necessary. If theologians through the ages had just allowed people to read the Scriptures and interpret them for
themselves, they would never have been mixed up as they
are. This is a sample of the simplicity of God's eternal
truth, and if we go according to our theories, our personal
prejudices, our fancies, or our fads, instead of taking God's
eternal truth as our guide, and find ourselves lost at last, it
will not be because God did not give us intelligence enough
to understand his word.

We are going to give all in this audience who are in any
sense subjects of the gospel call an opportunity, not to
accept my hobby, or my theory, or my personal preference,
but simply to accept Jesus—to accept God as your Father,
Jesus as your Savior, the Holy Spirit as your Comforter,
the Bible as the lamp to your feet and the light to your
pathway, Christians as your religious associates, the church
of God as your abiding place, Christianity as your life work,
and heaven as your home.

And now, if it be the will of any of you who are in any
sense subjects of the gospel call, we beg you to come out on
the Lord's side now, thus saying to heaven, earth, and the
under world that you are determined to follow Jesus, if
need be, through floods and flames, and we wait to lovingly
welcome you and pray that you may come.

CHAPTER IX.

LETTERS——PURE IN HEART.

ONE of the first things Jesus taught his disciples in the famous Sermon on the Mount, which has been aptly styled " the constitution of the Christian religion," was: " Blessed are the pure in heart: for they shall see God." (Matt. 5: 8.)   Long before Jesus appeared among men Solomon taught: " Keep thy heart with all diligence; for out of it are the issues of life."   (Prov. 4: 23.)   Men have always been great with God in proportion as they have been pure in heart: " The effectual fervent prayer of a righteous man availeth much."   (James 5: 16.)   Righteousness has in all ages been a passport to the favor of God: " The eyes of the Lord are upon the righteous, and his ears are open unto their cry."   (Ps. 34: 15.)   From the beginning to the end of his life and teaching among men, Jesus indorsed and encouraged righteousness and purity in life and heart every way he could.   " Beware of false prophets, which come to you in sheep's clothing, but inwardly they are ravening wolves.   Ye shall know them by their fruits. Do men gather grapes of thorns, or figs of thistles?   Even so every good tree bringeth forth good fruit; but a corrupt tree bringeth forth evil fruit.   A good tree cannot bring forth evil fruit, neither can a corrupt tree bring forth good fruit.   Every tree that bringeth not forth good fruit is hewn down, and cast into the fire.   Wherefore by their fruits ye shall know them."   (Matt. 7: 15-20.)   A righteous life springs from a pure heart as naturally and as philosophically as a clear stream flows from a clean fountain.

The letters and sermons in this book will be a blessing to the world in so far as they encourage and inspire people, by precept and example, to strive earnestly for pure hearts and righteous lives. No man knows better than T. B. Larimore that many people form their opinions of Christianity from the lives and sermons of preachers, rather than from the life and teaching of Christ, and for this reason, as well as from a desire to be saved himself, he is always anxious lest something he may do or say will not correctly represent the holy life and sound doctrine which the Bible teaches. Speaking of mistakes men sometimes make in the frailty of old age, after a long and exemplary life in the service of God, he wrote:

" —— said things and did things, after he began to ' die at the top,' which have been used against Christianity; —— did likewise. Small as I am and little as I have done, I fear the same with regard to myself. When we begin to fail, about the first thing we lose is the power to perceive we are fallible and failing. There's the trouble."

From a Western city, in the midst of a great revival, with the burden of labor and cares heavy on his heart, he wrote, several years ago:

" ' Some sweet day ' I'll breathe my last. When you tell the world I am gone, please tell them I was ready, willing, and anxious to go; that I dreaded not death; that I fought and fell believing I was on my journey to the best and brightest place. I never doubt that. I hope it is not egotism, for I feel small as an atom. I hope it is simply faith sublime, but I no more doubt that I am to be eternally as happy as any angel existence than I doubt the existence of Jehovah himself. That, in my mind, is eternally settled. Conscious of my own littleness, I do my very best, always, everywhere, and under all circumstances, to do all that duty demands—do it with all my might—and do nothing else. So shall it ever be. I want you to know that. My conscience is clear always—never an exception. While I have often come short of duty's demands, and frequently gone beyond the limits of right, I have never done so intentionally. I believe I tell ' the truth, the whole truth, and nothing but the truth,' when I say I have never done what I believed to be wrong, never refused to do what I believed duty demanded. My conscience is as clear tonight as when I slept in my mother's arms. I am sure that is true. Without a clear conscience I could not endure to live, I could not dare to die. Every day of my life is a day of solemn endeavor with me to keep my heart pure and my conscience clear, to be and to do good. I am living for the good that I can do. If the Lord should say to me, ' Die to-night, or live to-morrow and forty more years with an impure heart and defiled conscience,' I know I would say: ' Lord, please take me now.' You may often blush, as many times no doubt you have blushed, because of my egregious mistakes and ignorance; but when this head and heart and hand ' lie silent in the grave,' you will not have to apologize because of any intentional evil I have done. I live to love and to be loved, to be good and to do good. To this end I eat, sleep, walk, work—do everything I do and refuse to do everything I refuse to do. To this there is no exception—absolutely none—even down to the minutest details of my life."

At the beginning of another meeting he wrote:

" I am trying to ' clear the way ' to-day so as to get down to solid work to-morrow. You may know I am always doing my very best. I have solemnly resolved to always do what I believe duty demands, and do it as nearly to perfection as I can. Knowing that all I am and all I have belong to Him from whom all blessings flow, I have solemnly resolved to do all that I can do to contribute to the success of this meeting. Knowing this may be my last opportunity to lead loved ones now lost to ' the Lamb of God for sinners slain,' I vow to do all that circumstances may permit or duty may demand to bring as many souls as possible into the fold of Christ in this meeting. I am to reach home not later than December 24, spend the rest of December there, and begin the new year with the determination, by God's help, to deliver more sermons, add more souls to Christ, be better, and do more good and less evil than in any previous year of my life."

He rarely failed to write what he called a " new-year letter " about the beginning of the year. These letters always contained an expression of his desire and determination to be better and do more good and less evil than in any previous year of his life, and he rarely failed to do so. From time to time during the year he would refer to these letters and ask me to take them as a basis for calculations, and keep count while he worked and reported results, to see how faithful he was in living up to them. Once he departed from his custom and wrote as follows:

" Columbia, Tenn., December 31, 1895.

" Instead of writing you a new-year letter, as I have so often done, I write you, as follows, a few of my life rules, as they occur to me in the light of the last day of 1895—rules which I hope to strictly observe, both in letter and spirit, till God shall call me home:

"(1) Be kind; (2) be meek; (3) be true; (4) be humble; (5) be gentle; (6) be polite; (7) be patient; (8) be earnest; (9) be careful; (10) be hopeful; (11) be faithful; (12) be cheerful; (13) be grateful; (14) be generous; (15) be prayerful; (16) be courteous; (17) be unselfish; (18) be thoughtful; (19) be industrious; (20) be consecrated; (21) be conscientious; (22) always ' do the right; ' (23) do as much good as possible; (24) do as little evil as possible; (25) eat to live, not live to eat; (26) if possible, be perfectly pure; (27) if not, be pure as possible; (28) always make the best of the situation; (29) be clean—body, soul, and spirit—clean in thought, in word, in deed—always clean; (30) conscientiously consecrate all to Christ—head, hand, heart—body, soul, spirit—time, tongue, talent—mind, muscle, money—consecrate all to Him who gave his very life to ransom a recreant, lost, and ruined race."

The first marriage in his family occurred on December 30, 1897. His present to the bride—his oldest daughter— was a Bible he had used in evangelistic meetings. The inscription was as follows:

MARY D. LARIMORE,	MARY L. GEORGE,
December 30, 1897, 2 P.M.	December 30, 1897, 4 P.M.

My Daughter: Friends and loved ones excepted, this " blessed Bible," that has been my constant companion so long, is the dearest thing on earth to me, " more precious than gold; " and now I sadly and gladly give it to you, my precious daughter, praying that you may always lovingly "walk in the light" of this precious book—walk in the love light of God's eternal truth—and that the Lord Almighty may graciously grant and give you all the desires of your pure heart till, at the peaceful close of a long and useful life, he shall call you home to reign and rejoice in glory with Jesus our Savior forever. Your father,

T. B. LARIMORE.

On the margin of the typewritten copy of this inscription which he inclosed to me the following paragraph was written in his own hand:

"Our family circle was first broken at 3 P.M. to-day. May the Lord grant and give us an eternal reunion.

"T. B. LARIMORE."

From May till September, 1898, he was at home sick. Many feared and he believed that he was liable to die any day for several weeks.   As this is probably the last message in permanent form the world will ever receive from, of, or about him, letters he wrote while facing death, as he believed, during that long spell of serious sickness, will be of special interest to his friends as long as his memory is cherished.   He stopped with me one night on his way home at the beginning of that sickness, and in a few days wrote as follows:

"Sick when I saw you, sick ever since.   As usual, when I cannot work I think my life work is about done.   I do not want to live, but I do want to work while I do live. I am in no condition for work now.   I began this letter Monday, but had to quit and go to bed.   This is Wednesday, 9 A.M.   I was not up yesterday at all, except a few

THE FAMILY UNBROKEN.

seconds twice.   Could not sit up; may not sit up many
moments now.   Do not be uneasy about me.   I will come
out all right if I live, I think; if I die, I will come out all
right, I know.   So, then, whether I live or die, it is all
right."

A few days later he wrote:

"Well, it's all right—all, all right.   Of course I am
willing to get well, but I am no less willing to die.   Why
should I be?   All that I dread is the grave, if I die; all I
dread is being a burden to others, if I live.   If I could be
healthy, helpful, and useful, I would neither murmur nor
complain, though I had to live as long as Moses lived.   I
rally and relapse.   I was able to sit up nearly all day yesterday.   I have neither been nor done so well to-day, and
the day is only half gone.   Constant cough, slight fever,
extreme weakness, sore throat, sore chest, no appetite, in-
ability to sleep soundly or sufficiently—these are some of
the symptoms.   Do you say they are alarming?   I really
do not know.   One thing I know: they have not alarmed
me.   Why should they?   In the long ago we sometimes
sang by an open grave:

> "'Why should we mourn departed friends,
>   Or quake at death's alarms?'

We have all sung many times:

> "'I would not live alway, I ask not to stay,
>   Where storm after storm rises dark o'er the way.'

Did we mean it?   I believe I did.   I know I mean it
now."

I feared the worst, but wrote him as cheerfully as I

could, and begged him especially not to abandon all hope
of recovery, but to get well, if he could, and live as long as
he could for the good he could do. I also inclosed him a
letter from a sister expressing her fears that he would not
be with us long and speaking of his work and worth in a
way that I thought would be encouraging to him, provided
he would not attach too much importance to her " fears of
his early death." To this he replied as follows:

" You say: ' Do not get scared at the sister's fears of your
early death.' Scared! I do not understand myself. One
thing I do know: instead of being afraid of ' early death,'
a feeling of disappointment possesses—overwhelms—me
whenever I think of not having died long ago. There is
not a squirrel that plays, or a bird that sings, or a flower
that blooms, that I fear less than I fear death. I want you
to remember that when I am gone. I am not worrying.
A few more days or years at most and this life will be over
with me, but I want to do all the good I can before I go
hence and as long as my influence may last—for evermore.
What this world has in store for me, I do not know. I
have hopes, but no fears, of the eternal future. In other
words, I know not whether this world hath weal or woe,
pain or pleasure, in store for me; but no fear of pain beyond the tomb ever disturbs my mind. As you know, I
long neither expected nor desired to live here beyond fifty.
Somehow I have felt disappointed ever since I passed that
point. I tried to do a hundred years' work in fifty, and
then I wanted to go home. I am here yet, and that feeling
of disappointment overwhelms me to-day. However, I
may be permitted to go as Jesse Sewell went, though not

"ON THE WEST VERANDA WITH A LITTLE CLOCK BEFORE ME."

Many have been my mistakes, &, to _me_, some of them seem _marvelous_; but I am not conscious of having _ever_ done anything that I believed to be wrong. To this, there is _no_ exception. As I approach the tomb, I fear _no_ danger, I dread _no_ death. Not death, but _dying_; Not the _Judgement_, but the _grave_ — the lonely, gloomy _grave_ — do I dread. I fear not the eternal future. Why should I fear?

"The Lord is my shepherd."

The Lord is my shield.

The Lord is my strength & my Saviour.

M[y] title is _perfectly_ _clear_.

Gratefully, Affectionately & Fraternally,

        T. B. Larimore.

worthy to be compared with him. For such a sunset I
would be willing to linger here another fifty years. Well,
I'll wait as patiently as I can. While waiting I want to
be working—working for the weal of all, the woe of none.
I am sitting on the west veranda with a little clock before
me. My thoughts are running like music in the air, howsoever little music there may be in what I write. The long
ago sweeps down upon me, and my soul is strangely sad.
I almost see the other shore, and then my soul is glad. I've
tried to do the best I could. No mortal lives that I would
harm. Whether many or few be the days or the years
allotted me here to live, as pure and free from all sin as I
can, by his grace, I shall spend them all. The Lord grant
that I may bless, and not blight, as long as he letteth me
live. If convenient, come to see me. Of course you understand me. Do not come unless it is entirely convenient.
If it is convenient, however, of course we will all appreciate
it and try to make it as pleasant for you as we can. Birds
and squirrels are all around me. I must quit this and give
my thoughts to them. Good-by."

The reference to the death of Jesse Sewell would be in-
complete in this letter without the following extract from
" The Life and Sermons of Jesse Sewell," by D. Lipscomb:

" He began his married life in a log house with one room
and a ' lean-to ' as a cookroom. After over fifty years of
labor and toil, he closed that life in a cheaply built frame
house with two rooms and a ' lean-to ' for a cookroom.
Yet he was comfortable and perfectly contented with his
outward surroundings. For months he had anticipated his

end was near. A few months before his death, he told his wife he was satisfied he would not remain with her long; told her, while they had accumulated but little, there was enough to keep her in comfort as long as she might live, and he wished her to so use it; advised her to remain at her own home. Her son, William, lives next door, and some of the grandchildren are much with her. The day of his death he attended church at Philadelphia meeting-house in the morning. A young brother preached a little lengthy. He kindly and meekly warned him against this habit; presided at the Lord's table, making an unusually earnest and impressive exhortation to his brethren; took dinner with his daughter; attended the burial of a little child at three o'clock, where he made another short, but earnest and affecting, discourse. He went home, some three miles, unharnessed and fed his horse, did a few necessary chores, fixed the stove wood for his wife to get breakfast in the morning, and went and seated himself on the porch to rest. His wife, soon passing by, noticed his head dropped to one side; went to him, and found his body still warm, but he was dead. He never breathed again. He had died without a struggle. He was sitting in a common split-bottom chair just on the edge of the porch. His legs were crossed and his arms folded across his lap, his head leaning to one side on one shoulder. Who doubts that he was carried by the angels to Abraham's bosom?

"His life, uneventful and unambitious, yet full of the true and genuine virtues, was wholly given for the good of his fellow-man and to the service of his Maker and Redeemer. He rests from his labors, but the fruits remain to bless man and honor God."

A few days later he wrote:

" If you decide that you can be with us soon, please tell
me so and we will expect you.   If you can, that's what I
want.   I had a spell of heart failure yesterday morning—
was dead I know not how long.   I am weak this morning,
but feel better.   I think ' the time of my departure is at
hand.'   I hope so, if it be the Lord's will.   I have lived
long enough in this world.   Mars' Hill is pretty now.
The whole land is green and flowery; chickens, birds,
squirrels, etc., in abundance.   I still hope you will be with
us soon.   Young squirrels in both verandas.   One mother
on east veranda has six.   We have never known her to
have more than four at once before.   Of course I appreciate all the expressions of love, confidence, and sympathy
that I receive; but I hope I shall be beyond the reach of
care, or want, or pain, or trouble, in a few days.   The great
change is all I greatly desire now.   For more than thirty
years I have been preaching the gospel, working for the
glory of God, honor of Christ, and salvation of souls to the
utmost of my ability three hundred and sixty-five days in
the year.   Thus I expect to do just as long as I live—not
long now—a few more years at most.   Well, so let it be;
I am ready, I am willing; earth charms me not.   I dread
not death, but it is my duty to live as long as I can.   I
love and live for the Lord.   If I could live life over again,
seeing from the beginning as now I see, I would flee from
the shadow of the slightest semblance of sin as from the
most venomous viper that lives.   There is no real happiness, ' in this world or in the world to come,' without holiness—purity of purpose and purity of life.   ' Follow peace

with all men, and holiness, without which no man shall see the Lord.' (Heb. 12: 14.) Heaven gives no better advice than: ' Keep thyself pure.' (1 Tim. 5: 22.) I am scarcely able to sit up, but I cannot consent to do nothing, so I am trying to write. I have been broken down so long now I am becoming discouraged. I may never leave home again till I go home, but that is all right. ' There is no place like home.' Do not be uneasy about me; I am not uneasy about myself. If I live, it's all right; if I die, it's all right. If I live, therefore, or die, it's all, all right. Be these things as they may, one thing is sure: if possible, I will practice what I preach, and never do or say anything of even doubtful propriety while life shall last. That much is settled."

The very first letter that reported any improvement in his health, after this long spell of serious sickness, told me he was preaching again:

" I am trying to preach some, and hope to be able to resume my life work soon. Yesterday, however, was a hard day on me, and, as a result, I have fever to-day and am scarcely able to sit up. I expect to be better to-morrow. I tried to preach to the home folks yesterday here at Mars' Hill. The day being pleasant, we had a good audience. The house would not hold the women. Had our house been four times as large, I am sure it had been packed. I think there is no reason why you should be uneasy about me. While I have fever and am scarcely able to sit up now, I fully expect to be better to-morrow. I am feeling very much depressed to-day, but I believe all unfavorable symptoms to be simply results of reaction from yesterday."

Throughout this long and serious sickness the perfect freedom from anxiety with which he wrote about death and the great hereafter, when he could " almost see the other shore," was both astonishing and gratifying to me, and it is still marvelous in my eyes.   He talked about this life and the life to come in the same letters, and so blended them as to show clearly that he regarded death as a mere dividing line between here and hereafter which was of too little consequence to demand much attention.   To him, earth and heaven were so close together that death was not " a long journey " at all, but merely a short step.   Soon after he entirely regained his health and resumed his evangelistic work, he wrote as follows:

" My faith has never been stronger; my hope has never been brighter; my head has never been clearer; my heart has never been calmer; my life has never been purer.   I love all; I hate none.   My love for some lifts my soul into the realm of the sublime.   I am willing to die to-day; I am willing to live a thousand years, to tell the old, old story of Jesus and his love.   My friends are dearer to me; association with them is sweeter to me; my sympathy for suffering souls is stronger; my love for all the pure, the true, the beautiful, the good, and the sublime—from the bud, the blossom, the babe, up to Him from whom all blessings flow—is truer, tenderer, sweeter, than ever before. Not a mist floats between me and the land of love and life divine.   I'll never turn back.   I'll never stop to consider what the enemy may think, or say, or do.   I shall simply do as much good and as little evil as possible all the remnant of my days, and gladly leave all results with God.   I

LARIMORE'S RESIDENCE AND DORMITORIES, SOUTH YARD, MARS' HILL.

have crossed the river; the bridge has been washed away. People everywhere treat me with encouraging kindness, courtesy, and sweetness. Truly, I am debtor to all. I sleep soundly, dream sweetly, and 'rejoice evermore.' ' The word ' is sweeter and stronger to me than ever before. O, it is delightful to love and be loved, and to do whatsoever duty demands! My vanity is all gone. What the people say does not bother me. I'll never waver, but always to the right be true. May the Lord always abundantly bless you and yours."

The following " flight of fancy " from Exgovernor Robert L. Taylor on the death of Ingersoll he considers worthy of a place and preservation in this volume:

" I sat in the great theater in the national capital. It was thronged with youth and beauty, old age and wisdom. I saw a man, the image of his God, stand upon the stage, and I heard him speak.

" His gestures were the perfection of grace, his voice was music, and his language was more beautiful than any I had ever heard from mortal lips.

" He painted picture after picture of the pleasures and joys and sympathies of home. He enthroned love and preached the gospel of humanity like an angel. Then I saw him dip his brush in the ink of mortal blackness and blot out the beautiful picture he had painted. I saw him stab love dead at his feet. I saw him blot out the stars and the sun and leave humanity and the earth in eternal darkness and eternal death.

" I saw him, like the serpent of old, worm himself into the paradise of human hearts, and by his seductive elo

quence and subtle devices of sophistry inject his fatal
venom, under whose blight its flowers faded, its music was
hushed, its sunshine was darkened, and its soul was left a
desert waste with the new-made graves of faith and hope.

" I saw him, like a lawless and erratic meteor without
orbit, sweep across the intellectual sky, brilliant only in its
self-consuming fire, generated by friction with the inde-
structible and eternal truths of God.

" That man was the archangel of modern infidelity, and
I said: How true is holy writ, which declares that the fool
has said in his heart: ' There is no God! '

" Tell me not, O infidel, there is no God, no heaven, no
hell!   Tell me not, O infidel, there is no risen Christ!

" What intelligence less than God's could fashion the
human body?   What motive power is it, if not God, that
drives those throbbing engines of the human heart, sending the crimson stream of life bounding through every vein
and artery?

" Whence and what, if not God, is this mystery we call
' mind?'   What is it that thinks, and feels, and plans,
and acts?   O, who can deny the divinity that stirs within
us?

" God is everywhere and is in everything.   His mystery
is in every bud, and blossom, and leaf, and tree; in every
rock, and hill, and mountain; in every spring, and rivulet,
and river.

" The rustle of his wings is in every zephyr; his might is
in every tempest.   He dwells in the dark pavilion of every
storm cloud.   The lightning is his messenger, and the thunder is his voice.   His awful tread is in every earthquake
and on every angry ocean.   The heavens above us teem

with his myriads of shining witnesses—the universe of solar systems whose wheeling orbs course the crystal dread halls of eternity, the glory and power and dominion of the all-wise, omnipotent, and eternal God."

I come now to a letter in which he, perhaps without thinking of it at the time, sets forth in a very striking way the philosophy of Christianity as an uplifting force in human character. His great desire to be good and to do good, and his abundant labors in the Lord, are but expressions of his gratitude for blessings he has received. Every blessing he receives from the Lord and every kindness he enjoys at the hands of men are to him an inspiration to be good and to do good. Probably without thinking of it in this light, and certainly without saying anything about it, he wrote:

"—— is every inch a man. He has just sent me a check for —— dollars. He believed he owed it to me. Really, as I see it, it is a gracious gift—purely. Well, I shall always so consider it, anyway. This is not the first time he has been guilty of such a thing. The Lord will reward him, and I will try to do so, too, all my days. He is a sublime friend. How can I ever fall, sustained as I am by such friends and by all the Lord has done for me? I could deliberately starve to death in the midst of plenty as easily as I could intentionally and willfully do anything wrong, anything I believed to be wrong, anything I would be ashamed or afraid to face at the judgment bar of God. Never can I wreck the hopes of friends so firm and true, and grieve the Lord who has done so much for me. Sustained by an everlasting arm that I can almost see and feel, and loved and blessed and guarded by friends than whom man has never dreamed of truer, I have solemnly resolved to be just as pure, just as faithful, just as useful, just as righteous, just as true—true to God and true to man—as possible, 'every day and every hour,' as long as he prolongs my days, doing just as much good and as little evil as possible ' while the days are going by.' This solemn resolve is due, not to my goodness or greatness, but to the devotion of my friends and to the love of the Lord. I cannot disappoint Jesus and such friends among men."

That is the whole thing in few words. The love of God makes us good, because we are too grateful to him for all his blessings to grieve and disappoint him by transgression; the love of friends helps us to be good, because we cannot wreck the faith they have in us. "The goodness of God leadeth thee to repentance." (Rom. 2: 4.)

- 10 -

CHAPTER X.

SERMON——CHRIST AND CHRISTIANS.

(Sermon delivered by T. B. Larimore at South College Street Church, Nashville, Tenn., at 3 o'clock, Sunday afternoon, January 28, 1900.)

I AM the true vine, and my Father is the husbandman. Every branch in me that beareth not fruit he taketh away: and every branch that beareth fruit, he purgeth it, that it may bring forth more fruit. Now ye are clean through the word which I have spoken unto you. Abide in me, and I in you. As the branch cannot bear fruit of itself, except it abide in the vine; no more can ye, except ye abide in me. I am the vine, ye are the branches: He that abideth in me, and I in him, the same bringeth forth much fruit: for without me ye can do nothing. If a man abide not in me, he is cast forth as a branch, and is withered; and men gather them, and cast them into the fire, and they are burned. If ye abide in me, and my words abide in you, ye shall ask what ye will, and it shall be done unto you. Herein is my Father glorified, that ye bear much fruit; so shall ye be my disciples. As the Father hath loved me, so have I loved you: continue ye in my love. If ye keep my commandments, ye shall abide in my love; even as I have kept my Father's commandments, and abide in his love." (John 15: 1-10.)

To the husband nothing is half so sweet when enjoyed alone as if shared with the wife that he loves. Jesus is the Bridegroom: his church, the bride—the Lamb's wife. W should not be surprised, then, when we find, by study of God's word, that Jesus jealously guards the reputation, the interests, and the feelings of the church and the members thereof, dividing voluntarily the glory and honor that are his with all those who constitute that spirit body, to establish which he shed his precious blood. Jesus is the Savior, and he said to his disciples: " Ye are the salt of the earth." (Matt. 5: 13.) That property in salt which gives it its intrinsic as well as its commercial value is its saving quality. So Jesus teaches that his church saves with him, thus dividing the honor with his bride.

Jesus is the light of the world. "As long as I am in the world, I am the light of the world." (John 9: 5.) To his disciples he said: " Ye are the light of the world." (Matt. 5: 14.) He says in the lesson just read: " I am the true vine, and my Father is the husbandman. Every branch in me that beareth not fruit he taketh away: and every branch that beareth fruit, he purgeth it, that it may bring forth more fruit. Now ye are clean through the word which I have spoken unto you. Abide in me, and I in you. As the branch cannot bear fruit of itself, except it abide in the vine; no more can ye, except ye abide in me. I am the vine, ye are the branches: He that abideth in me, and I in him, the same bringeth forth much fruit: for without me ye can do nothing." (John 15: 1-5.) Jesus is the Vine, but his disciples are the branches; the vine sustaining the branches, the branches coöperating with the vine in bearing fruit to bless the world. The vine supports the branches, while the branches bear the buds and blossoms, produce the fruit and foliage. The vine and the branches, thus coöperating, bless those who come in contact therewith in a way to be blessed. The branches share with the vine whatsoever honor there be in doing that work, and just precisely so Jesus shares the honor with those who are working with him to bless the world. Jesus recognizes a kindred relationship as subsisting between him and his disciples, him and his church. He repeatedly and habitually called God his Father, prayed to him as a Father—claimed to be God's Son, claimed God to be his Father. He taught his disciples to say to God, when praying: "Our Father which art in heaven." Yet, that God is the Father of all human beings, the Savior says is not true. Wicked people, as we learn from John 8: 44, claimed God as their Father, but the Savior told them he was not their Father. He is the Creator, the universal Benefactor; he is the Father of his own children who bow in submission to his will and have been adopted into his family, and who live in conformity to his law. He has made Jesus the Savior of the obedient children of the living God, and Christ recognizes the relationship, when teaching his disciples to say, "Our Father," as subsisting between him and them, since they are all children of the same loving God. This allegory of the vine and the branches brings out the same thought, showing that the relationship is intimate and close, as only blood relationship can be. The vine furnishes the sustaining power, the life-giving principle, the sap that runs through every branch, and through every twig and leaf of that branch; and thus the vine and the branches are made practically one. No blood relationship ever was closer than the Savior recognizes this divine relationship to be.

Indeed, I am not sure but that it is safe to say—and I

am sure it is safe, if it be true—that Heaven has practically exhausted the list of appropriate illustrations, the vocabu-
lary of proper terms, with, by, and through which to illustrate and express and impress the thought of the nearness,
dearness, and heavenly blessedness of the relationship subsisting between all the members of the spirit body of Christ
—a relationship binding Christ to that body, the same relationship binding every member to Christ and Christ to
God, making them practically one, as husband and wife
are one. Now, if this proposition be true, it is certainly a
blessed thing, that all should appreciate, to belong to the
spirit body of Christ, to be a branch of the only true and
living Vine.

All of us have some idea—have heard, it may be, or
learned—of the tie that binds together the shepherd and
the sheep of his pasture, the lambs of his fold. Many
touching little stories in history, reaching far back to ages
of the long ago, express this thought. The church is the
fold; Jesus is the Shepherd; all Christians are sheep of his
pasture, lambs of his flock. The apostle Peter says: "For
ye were as sheep going astray; but are now returned unto
the Shepherd and Bishop of your souls." (1 Pet. 2: 25.)
We should all rejoice that we can look to Jesus as such a
Shepherd. David, in the long, long ago, rejoiced that God
was his Shepherd, and cried from the depths of his grateful
soul: "The Lord is my shepherd; I shall not want. He
maketh me to lie down in green pastures: he leadeth me
beside the still waters. He restoreth my soul: he leadeth
me in the paths of righteousness for his name's sake. Yea,
though I walk through the valley of the shadow of death,
I will fear no evil: for thou art with me; thy rod and thy

staff they comfort me.   Thou preparest a table before me
in the presence of mine enemies: thou anointest my head
with oil; my cup runneth over.   Surely goodness and
mercy shall follow me all the days of my life: and I will
dwell in the house of the Lord forever." (Ps. 23.)   And
this is the sublime sentiment that every soul in the love of
Jesus may cherish every day and every hour.   Storms may
rage and tempests howl, friends may forsake and foes beset,
but even then we can look aloft to the Sun that has neve:
set, cling to the cross of Christ, and say: "The Lord is my
shepherd; I shall not want."

The blessed tie of friendship is one we all have felt, a
tie that is greatly appreciated.   Some appreciate it more;
others, less; all appreciate it some.   We all have our
friends; we may all have foes.   Jesus had foes, the apostle
Paul had foes, Elijah of old had foes.   As "man is born
unto trouble, as the sparks fly upward," it may be that he
is born to have foes, at least enough to make his friends
dear to him; is born to have clouds enough to make the
sunshine all the brighter, and to have sorrow enough to
make joy all the sweeter.   But whether we have or do not
have foes, we all have friends; and if we are worthy, we
have true friends—friends that are loving, dear, and kind,
willing, if need be, to die for us.   We all know something
of the tenderness of the blessed tie of friendship.   There
are many touching stories in history along this line.   There
is the story, brought from the shadows and sunshine of
mythological ages, of Damon and Pythias—each anxious
to die that the other might live, each anxious to be in
prison that the other might be free.   This relationship exists among all God's children and binds all God's childrer

to Jesus, the tender Shepherd and Bishop of our souls.
" This is my commandment, That ye love one another, as
I have loved you.   Greater love hath no man than this,
that a man lay down his life for his friends.   Ye are my
friends, if ye do whatsoever I command you.   Henceforth
I call you not servants; for the servant knoweth not what
his lord doeth: but I have called you friends; for all things
that I have heard of my Father I have made known unto
you."   (John 15: 12-15.)   We may know every day we
live whether we are the friends of Jesus.   If we daily do
whatsoever he demands of us, we are his friends; otherwise,
otherwise, his own language being true.

We should appreciate our worthy friends, and treat them
as they deserve to be treated, and show our appreciation of
their love and friendship.   We should sigh at the thought
of losing friends and friendship, and try to live so that we
may never know the pain of the shadow that must fall upon
the soul when sighing in the loneliness of lost affection.
But especially should we rejoice in the privilege of being
friends to Christ and of claiming him as our Friend, and
we should act so that heaven, earth, and the underworld
may see that we are not wavering, that no power in the
underworld can make us waver, so far as our fidelity to
Christ is concerned.

All of us know something of the tie that binds together
teacher and pupils in a school.   Some of us have had much
experience, all of us have had some, along these lines.
There is a tie that is tender, a tie that is strong, binding
together teacher and pupils in every good school in all the
earth.   I have seen brave men, sweet women, and precious
boys and girls sob and weep as if their heads were waters

and their eyes fountains, as if their hearts were broken, when the time came for the last song to be sung, for the last talk to be made, for the last prayer to be offered, for the last benediction to be said, for the word "farewell" to be spoken, for the tender good-byes to be uttered, and teachers and pupils to leave the spot where for many months they had labored together, to go to some place far away, it may be, from that (to them) sacred spot, with the assurance that they might never meet again on earth. The church of the living God is a school. The term "disciple" suggests this thought, meaning "pupil" or "scholar." The disciples of Plato—the pupils of Plato; the disciples of Socrates—the pupils of Socrates; the disciples of Christ—the pupils of Christ, members of the school of the Lord Jesus Christ. Each and every disciple of Christ is a member of Christ's school, and Christ's will is that there be perfect union and harmony in this school, that every member thereof may be blessed. But the separation days must come; farewells must be spoken, good-byes must be uttered. But the day is coming when, if we live aright, we shall be promoted to a higher grade. We have gone along, climbing step by step, growing in grace and knowledge of the truth, and the time is coming when we shall be promoted to a higher grade in school. We shall have angels and archangels, prophets, patriarchs, and apostles for our associates; Jesus for our Teacher; and the blessed Book, that has been our text-book here, our text-book still. This blessed book, Isaiah and Peter tell us, shall last forever. God is the Head of this divine institution, and we have the assurance that there shall never be a separation, that the term will be an eternal term. No more farewells, no more good-byes, no more tears! We should rejoice that it is our privilege to belong to this school here, and live so as to be in that school up there, dwelling in glory with God for evermore.

Of course we all have some conception, though we have not all been literal soldiers, of the tie that binds together the soldiers in any army. There is something not super-human, and yet really mysterious, about the strength and tenderness of that wonderful tie that binds together the soldier boys and binds the soldier boys to their leaders, a tie that lasts as long as they live. Many things in history illustrate this, showing the affection of the leader for his soldiers, the soldier for his leader, of common soldier for common soldier, of officer for officer, and sometimes the tie is so strong that they prefer to die together on the bloody field rather than to be disbanded. History tells us that Napoleon, far from France, the country of his adoption, and far from Corsica, the isle of his birth, on the burning sands of Egypt, himself and his soldiers almost perish-ing of thirst, was given a cup of water. Instead of drink-ing it himself, though almost dead of thirst—not will-ing, as he could not give it to all, to show himself a re-specter of persons—he lifted it up and poured its contents on the burning sands, saying to his men: "If you die of thirst, your leader dies with you." The same spirit was illustrated in the same campaign, when an unexploded shell buried itself in the sand almost at the feet of that beloved leader. It could not be extinguished, nor could it be re-moved in time to save his life. His soldiers threw them-selves around him, forming a living wall, so that no frag-ment of the shell in its death-dealing work could possibly reach the body of him they loved. The same tender tie is illustrated in the case of the French soldier who kept his solitary watch at the tomb of his loved leader on the bare, bleak, rain-drenched, wind-swept shores of St. Helena; then, when the body was removed to Paris to the splendid mausoleum prepared for it, turned away weeping when told that he could no longer guard the sacred dust, but must leave it to the care of the nation. It is part of the history of the "lost cause," for which so many brave men gave their lives, that when the battle-scarred (but not *scared*) wreck of the once bright host that had astonished the world, gave up, surrendered at Appomattox, even generals wept like children, and private soldiers sobbed and cried aloud, and many begged the leader they loved as they loved no other to gather them once again around him and hurl them in one last, hopeless charge against the victorious hosts, that they might die in the cause they loved, rather than give up and go back to the worn, wrecked, and ruined homes, many of them to weep unavailing tears over the graves of loved ones who had died of sorrow and hardship, privation and trouble, while they, the soldier boys, had been doing what they believed duty demanded for the four bloody years that tried men's souls.

The church of the living God is an army. Jesus is the Commander in chief, the Captain of that army, and every Christian is a soldier of Christ. Hence the apostle Paul says: "Fight the good fight of faith, lay hold on eternal life, whereunto thou art also called, and hast professed a good profession before many witnesses." (1 Tim. 6: 12.) "Thou therefore endure hardness, as a good soldier of Jesus Christ. No man that warreth entangleth himself

with the affairs of this life; that he may please him who
hath chosen him to be a soldier. And if a man also strive
for masteries, yet is he not crowned, except he strive lawfully." (2 Tim. 2: 3-5.) "But we see Jesus, who was
made a little lower than the angels for the suffering of
death, crowned with glory and honor; that he by the grace
of God should taste death for every man. For it became
him, for whom are all things, and by whom are all things,
in bringing many sons unto glory, to make the captain of
their salvation perfect through sufferings." (Heb. 2: 9,
10.) Jesus is referred to as the captain of their salvation,
the word being used just as in 2 Kings 5: 1: "Now Naa-
man, captain of the host of the king of Syria, was a great
man." It means that he was the commander in chief,
which history shows him to have been. This is a thought
that should rejoice every Christian—to be a soldier of
Christ, clad in the panoply of heaven, marching beneath
the fluttering folds of the banner of the Prince Imperial,
battling for the glory of God and the honor of Christ and
the salvation of souls, to fall at last, all covered with glory
divine, at the post of honor, where God demands you shall
stand until his warfare be over.

We have reunions in this life of a military character.
War over, soldiers gather at stated periods at what we call
"reunions;" and joyous times they are. But when they
meet, there is always sorrow mingled with the joy, over
the thought that some have passed away, some who once
met with them can meet no more. The years go by, and
as they meet from time to time they know that some have
passed away. There are reunions of the Blue and reunions
of the Gray, their numbers growing less and less at each

meeting, and now they are beginning to have reunions of
the Blue and the Gray, and the time is coming when these
reunions will cease, because the last representative of that
heroic time shall have passed from the stage forever.   At
these reunions there is sadness in the thought that they can
be together but a little while; but a day is coming to the
glorious army of the Lord, and that is the day I look forward to with joy unspeakable.   Though I was a young
soldier, no more than a boy when I wore the gray, for
thirty-three years I have been so busy in the work before
me that I have never had time to attend one of these reunions, though I was once within three miles of where one
was being held; but I was preaching three times a day and
baptizing in a creek near by, and had no time to go and
spend a moment there.   I suppose I shall never get time
to attend one of these reunions.   Whatsoever may be my
inclination or disinclination, I suppose I shall never have
time to do so; for as long as I am able to go three miles to
attend a reunion, I expect to be able to tell the old story of
salvation to men and women and children on the way to
everlasting perdition or everlasting glory, and I shall never
have time to spend in any other way than to work for God
and Christ and the salvation of souls.   But by the grace of
God, the encouragement of my brethren and sisters and
friends, and the leadership and sympathy of my blessed
Savior, I pray to live so that when I am done with the warfare of this life, and the time comes for the reunion of the
battle-scarred veterans of the cross, I may be accounted
worthy to be there, and may take by the hands those I have
known and loved and labored with here, brethren and sisters that have stood by me in sieges against sin and Satan

in this world. When that blessed time comes, that glorious reunion, we can press each other close and think of these times, and rejoice that we are in glory, with no thought of parting, no thought of saying good-by, no sighing and no tears; for we shall be in a land where congregations ne'er break up; where sickness, sorrow, pain, and death are neither felt nor feared; where life is eternal and a treasure sublime. The thought of that joyous reunion to me is enough to repay me ten thousand times over for all the sacrifices I may ever make until God shall call me home. I never feel that I have to bear heavy burdens; that my labors are very abundant; that I have any reason to murmur, complain, repine, or boast, or have one little feeling of pride in my soul; but I feel always that the very thought of having the privilege of being a child of God is enough to make me perfectly satisfied to go right on, and on, and on, in the labors of love God permits us to perform here, until life's fitful dream shall be over, without ever having a boastful feeling or a spirit of pride while we breathe the breath of life.

The church of the living God is a family—God our Father, Jesus our elder Brother, and we, if we are Christians, brothers and sisters, born into God's family by virtue of the divine spirit birth; members of God's family, God himself being the Father and Head. Of course we all know something of the tie binding together the members of a family, and we know something of how stubbornness or anything of a bad character in the spirit or life of any member of the family may shadow the household, shroud it in gloom, and rob every heart there of the happiness that is justly due. Apply this to the church of the living God, and let each one say: "I will be a ray of sunshine; I will scatter joy around me; I will make others happy, and will be grateful, pure, and good; I will do all in my power to make my spirit home, the church of the living God, a blooming paradise of smiles, where sorrow can never come." We rejoice in this life in the thought of belonging to respectable families. If we are Christians, we belong to the most honorable, the sublimest family in the universe, God being the Father and Jesus the elder Brother—the royal family, of which God is the Head and Jesus is the Prince Imperial, our Captain and our King.

The families here separate, the old home is abandoned. There are reunions, but they bring sadness in the thought that we can stay together but one week, or one day, or one hour; and when the time to separate again comes, it seems better not to have had the reunion, when we have to bear the sorrow that follows such reunions. But the time is coming when there will be a reunion of God's family, a grand and sublime reunion, where no such shadow shall fall upon the heart; for when the children of God gather around the great white throne, the pearly portals closed, and the doomed gone from his presence forever, we shall realize that we are to stay there while eternity shall last.

There is a relationship binding together the various parts of the human body that no anatomist, no physician, no man beneath the stars, be he Solomon or sage, has ever been able to understand—a tie of such character binding together the members of the body, and all the body to the head, that nothing can be done to any member, producing a sensation either pleasant or painful, but that it is known at headquarters just the moment the sensation is felt.

Whether hand or foot is injured, it is known instantly at the head, the head controlling and directing the body. Thus we see that whatever is done to any member of the body is done to the head. The church of the living God is the body; Jesus is its Head. " For as we have many members in one body, and all members have not the same office: so we, being many, are one body in Christ, and every one members one of another." (Rom. 12: 4, 5.) In the corresponding chapter of the next book (1 Cor. 12: 12) is this language: " For as the body is one, and hath many members, and all the members of that one body, being many, are one body: so also is Christ." The Spirit is careful to express this thought so that we may not lose sight of it— that the church is the spirit body, Jesus the Head of it, and all Christians members of it, just as all members go to make up the body, and the head is the head of that body. Then, if the analogy holds good that whatever is done to any member of the body is done to the head, then whatever is done to any member of the spirit body is done to Christ. Hence, in that description of the judgment in Matt. 25: 32-46, it is said that all nations shall be gathered before the Lord; that he shall divide them, placing the sheep on the right hand, the goats on the left; and that he shall say to those on his right hand: " Come, ye blessed of my Father, inherit the kingdom prepared for you from the foundation of the world: for I was ahungered, and ye gave me meat: I was thirsty, and ye gave me drink: I was a stranger, and ye took me in: naked, and ye clothed me: I was sick, and ye visited me: I was in prison, and ye came unto me." Then the righteous shall answer him, and say: " Lord, when saw we thee ahungered, and fed thee? or thirsty, and gave thee drink? When saw we thee a stranger, and took thee in? or naked, and clothed thee? Or when saw we thee sick, or in prison, and came unto thee?" And then the King will say unto them: "Inasmuch as ye have done it unto one of the least of these my brethren, ye have done it unto me." Then he shall say to those on his left hand: "Depart from me, ye cursed, into everlasting fire, prepared for the devil and his angels." I never touch this passage without stopping to defend my God against the slander perpetrated against him every time man intimates that God prepared hell for man. Man may go to perdition if he will, but not because God prepared it for him. It was prepared for the devil and his angels. You and I can reject God, reject Christ, reject high Heaven, but God has made no provision for us in hell; and if we go, we go to be intruders on the dark domain of Satan and his angels—not because God wills that we should go there, for he gave his Son to keep us from going there, but because we will not accept his Son. The Lord says to those on his left hand in that dread hour: "Depart from me, ye cursed, into everlasting fire, prepared for the devil and his angels: for I was ahungered, and ye gave me no meat: I was thirsty, and ye gave me no drink: I was a stranger, and ye took me not in: naked, and ye clothed me not: sick, and in prison, and ye visited me not. Then shall they also answer him, saying, Lord, when saw we thee ahungered, or athirst, or a stranger, or naked, or sick, or in prison, and did not minister unto thee? Then shall he answer them, saying, Verily I say unto you, Inasmuch as ye did it not to one of the least of these, ye did it not to me. And these shall go away into everlasting punishment: but the righteous into life eternal."

We learn, by reference to Acts 9 and Acts 22, something that confirms all that has yet been said on this point. In the former, Jesus is represented as meeting Saul of Tarsus on his way to Damascus. Saul cried out, " Who art thou, Lord?" and Jesus replied, " I am Jesus whom thou persecutest." In Acts 22: 8, the language is: " I am Jesus of Nazareth, whom thou persecutest." " I am Jesus—I am Jesus of Nazareth, whom thou persecutest." I shall not ask you if Saul of Tarsus was actually persecuting Jesus of Nazareth, for that would be asking if you believed that Jesus was telling the truth. Saul was persecuting Jesus of Nazareth. How? Was he one of the howling mob that crucified him on the cross, that went by night to the garden of Gethsemane and dragged him to his persecution? We have no evidence of that. We have all the substantial evidence we need that Saul of Tarsus had never seen Jesus; but when he met Jesus on the way to Damascus and was made literally blind, and asked, " Who art thou, Lord?" Jesus said: " I am Jesus of Nazareth, whom thou persecutest." How could Jesus say that, if Saul had never seen him in person? Just as you could certify that your neighbor had injured you if he had chopped off your hand or your foot. You could certainly testify that he had injured you, if he had injured any member of your body. Saul of Tarsus was persecuting the members of the spirit body of Christ; was on his way then to Damascus, with a band of soldiers, to arrest and drag to Jerusalem for persecution and death men and women guilty of no crime, save the crime of spotless purity and sublime devotion to the cause of Christ. He himself says: " I verily thought with myself, that I ought to do many things contrary to the name

of Jesus of Nazareth.   Which thing I also did in Jerusalem: and many of the saints did I shut up in prison, having
received authority from the chief priests; and when they
were put to death, I gave my voice against them.   And I
punished them oft in every synagogue, and compelled them
to blaspheme; and being exceedingly mad against them,
I persecuted them even unto strange cities." (Acts 26:
9-11.)   He was persecuting Christians, and as Christians
constitute the spirit body of Christ, just as your head takes
notice of anything done to any part of your body, Jesus
could and did say: " I am Jesus of Nazareth, whom thou
persecutest."   This being so, you cannot insult a child of
God to-day without offering the same insult to Christ, and
it has the same effect as if you had offered that insult to the
Lord in person.   In 1 Cor. 8, we have three verses which
we can never understand so well without this thought in
our mind.   The apostle Paul says to a real or imaginary
intelligent, strong-minded brother that the thing under discussion is neither wrong nor right in itself, provided it does
not influence another.   That brother seemed to be determined to have his own way, even if it led to the destruction
of some weaker-minded brother.   Verse 11 says: "And
through thy knowledge shall the weak brother perish, for
whom Christ died?"   And verse 12 says: " But when ye
sin so against the brethren, and wound their weak conscience, ye sin against Christ."   Christ will say in that
great day: " Inasmuch as ye did it, or did it not, unto one
of the least of these my brethren, ye did it, or did it not,
unto me."   And Paul says: " But when ye sin so against
the brethren, and wound their weak conscience, ye sin
against Christ.   Wherefore, if meat make my brother to

offend, I will eat no flesh while the world standeth, lest I make my brother to offend."

One more quotation, and I shall close. Just in the light of the train of thought before us, I want to quote from 1 Pet. 4: 14: " If ye be reproached for the name of Christ [there is no danger, unless you wear his name; but if so, there is danger of being reproached for it], happy are ye; for the spirit of glory and of God resteth upon you: on their part [upon the part of those who reproach you for the name of Christ] he [Christ] is evil spoken of, but on your part he is glorified. But let none of you suffer as a murderer, or as a thief, or as an evil doer, or as a busybody in other men's matters. Yet if any man suffer as a Christian, let him not be ashamed; but let him glorify God on this behalf "—or, as in the Revised Version, " Let him glorify God in this name." I want to quote this now through without comment: " If ye be reproached for the name of Christ, happy are ye; for the spirit of glory and of God resteth upon you: on their part he is evil spoken of, but on your part he is glorified. But let none of you suffer as a murderer, or as a thief, or as an evil doer, or as a busybody in other men's matters. Yet if any man suffer as a Christian, let him not be ashamed; but let him glorify God in this name."

Now, certainly it is not meet that I talk to you longer to impress this thought upon your mind; certainly not meet that I quote more scripture, though there is an abundance of it in reservation, to impress this on your heart. These things being true, every child of God is as near to God as self to self; these things being true, as you treat Christians, so you treat Christ, and, so far as it bears on your destiny, it has the same effect as if done to Christ personally. If you hate a child of God, the Savior takes it as hating him; if you reproach a child of God, the Savior takes it as if you reproached him; if you do good to a child of God, it is as if you did the same thing to Jesus. All these things being true, I want to ask you this question: If we love the children of the living God; if we cultivate that love, cherish the tenderest and truest and purest love for the sons and daughters of the Lord Almighty, are we not thus loving Christ? And is that not a solution of the difficulty presented in the thought that "I don't know how to love one I have never seen?" This brushes aside all difficulty; if we love one another, we love the Lord; if we do not love one another, we do not love the Lord. Hence, let us not forget that we are as near to Christ as self to self, as wife to husband. We are beneath the shelter of his protecting arm, and whatsoever insults are offered to us are offered to him. Remember that God is our Shield, our exceeding great Reward; that Jesus is our Captain, our Leader, our elder Brother, and, if we are faithful, he will crown us with glory and honor and immortality, and fill our souls with bliss unspeakable through the eternal ages of God. Certainly you need only the assurance that Jesus is willing to receive you to induce you to rush to his outstretched arms, render obedience to the gospel, and follow him, if need be, through floods and flames. He says: "Come unto me, all ye that labor and are heavy laden, and I will give you rest. Take my yoke upon you, and learn of me; for I am meek and lowly in heart: and ye shall find rest unto your souls. For my yoke is easy, and my burden is light." We pray from the deepest depths of our souls that you may have the moral courage to come to Jesus, dear, dying sinner, without one plea, except that he died to redeem you, and through the grace of God now gives you a glorious, golden opportunity to come.

CHAPTER XI.

T HE admonition of Paul to Christians is: " Bear ye one another's burdens, and so fulfill the law of Christ." (Gal. 6: 2.) To bear the burdens of others, then, is both the doctrine of Paul and the law of Christ. This does not mean that any Christian should lay his burdens upon others, to be borne for him, for Paul says: " Every man shall bear his own burden." (Gal. 6: 5.) The full measure of every Christian's duty, then, is to bear his own burdens and at the same time help others to bear their burdens. It was a proverb among the ancients that " the gods help those who help themselves." This is Christianity, if it is not so construed as to justify selfishness. The man who helps himself to relieve others from the burden of helping him is within the limits of Christianity; there is no selfishness in that. But the man who helps himself, to the neglect of others, is not a Christian; he is selfish. The proverb of the ancients, " The gods help those who help themselves," may be Christianized by so amending as to read: " God helps those who help themselves and help others." It does me good—makes me a better man— to see any one, or to read about any one, helping others. I suppose it does other people good—makes them better— to see or to read such things. As the object of this book is to do good, it is legitimate to quote letters on the subject of helping others.

On the margin of a letter from a poor widow whom he had never seen nor heard of before, expressing great anxiety to educate her son, an only child, he wrote:

"I want this boy to go to school till he graduates. My heart is set on that, and I think I will do it, but I don't see how I can manage it yet. If I had the money—but how can I ever have any money, when so many people, like this poor woman and her boy, need it?"

Some years ago he wrote me one of his friends—a business man—was financially embarrassed, and asked me if I would help him while he helped his friend. I knew nothing of his friend, but, of course, I promised to help him to the extent of my ability—which was very limited—in anything he wanted to do. Referring to this arrangement, he wrote:

"I am impressing the thought on —— that you are carrying me and it will afford me great pleasure to carry him. I assure him you will settle all bills against him in Nashville, and I will settle with you. Of course he is greatly troubled, but I assure him we will hold the fort, if he is never able to pay a dollar, and he shall owe no one a dollar, either, till he gets able and ready to pay. He is a Christian, and he will come out all right, I think; but I would carry him as long as you will carry me, if I knew he could never pay another dollar. Do all you can for him at that end of the line, pay all bills promptly, charge to me, and I will come to time every time to the tune of one hundred cents to the dollar. It is joy to me to do it. To make him feel easy and to help you carry the load, I am anxious to settle up with you, in full, to date, he and I being one.

and you not in it. Now, let us square up, and settle up,
and straighten up, in full, to date, all along the line, including all demands on him for the first half of this year.
I am not keeping accounts. What will square us up with
you to date? You say and I'll send. While this may help
you just a little, you may need more help. If so, please
say so. If I can help you, I want to do it. I want you
never to need a dollar and not get it promptly. You tell
me what you need; if I cannot help you, then I cannot—
that's all. You know not how much money I might command to help you. Try me. Well, anyhow, count ——
and me one, charge all to me, take all you can get from me,
and keep the books straight—that's all."

Answering an inquiry about his financial condition during his long and serious sickness in 1898, he wrote:

" Of course my sickness is throwing me behind, financially and otherwise, but don't you send me any money—
not one cent; if you do, I will send it back. It is a crime
in morals and against the law to receive deposits in a bottomless bank."

Inclosing a check for fifty dollars for a woman who
needed it, he wrote:

" Having just received the inclosed check, I send it to
you for Sister ——. I propose to live the rest of my days
for the good that I can do."

Referring to statement of account and vouchers sent to
him at his request, with an explanation that he was specially
requested not to pay it till it was entirely convenient, he
wrote:

"As it is a small matter, and as it is going instead of coming, I believe I'll just let the thing stand till about December 32."

The first money he received, however, he paid it, " of course."

One quotation will explain how he settles business matters and never has any arguments, disagreements, lawsuits, or unkind feelings about it:

" I have long patronized ——, of Nashville, Tenn. Some months ago they sent me a statement calling for a few dollars, when I thought I owed them nothing. I offered no protest, but requested an explanation. I have never received it. About ten weeks ago I inclosed to them twenty dollars in currency in a letter, which was some dollars and cents more than all their demands to that date. Thrice have I written them for a ' yes ' or ' no ' as to whether they received the twenty dollars. Never a word in reply. They have always treated me so nicely and honorably that I do not understand it. My impression is that they have a —— for a bookkeeper, and that no man there has any idea how I have been treated recently. Now, please go yourself in person and see Mr. —— in person. Place with him the inclosed order, settle up all—past, present, and future—and then tell me exactly how many dollars and cents to send to square me with you to the time you write, and just as much further along in the direction of the millennium as you please, and then keep me level and square, if you can. I am not willing to quit them under circumstances that might offend them. I believe that they are gentlemen in the fullest sense of the word, but I cannot understand this hitch. No apology from them is demanded or considered due. I just simply want to— want you to set me straight with them—that's all."

I called to see Mr. ——, found him a gentleman, settled the business, and forwarded statement and vouchers. In a few weeks the firm failed, and the books proved to be in a tangle; but T. B. Larimore had the confidence, respect, and friendship of everybody, and no trouble with anybody about it.

Several years ago a Christian gentleman wrote him as follows:

" I confess that I was a little hurt when I received your letter long since; but, after studying about it, I concluded that it was because you were worried so much about your school matters, and that it was written in haste, so I forgave and forgot all about it; and I have always regarded you as one of my real good friends, and have never seen the time when I would not willingly do what I thought was right and I could do for your interest. I have never had the least unkind feeling for you, I can assure you: and whenever you come through this city, be sure to call on me; and if I can ever serve you in any way, do not hesitate to command me."

On the margin of this letter he wrote:

" I thought he treated me unkindly and unjustly once— long ago—and wrote him a letter such as I would not write now. I wrote him recently, begging pardon and acknowledging that he was right and I was wrong—which was the truth."

DORMITORIES AND SOUTH YARD, MARS' HILL.

It is easy for men to settle disagreements and promote brotherly love when they have the spirit of Christ and each is anxious to bear both his own burdens and the burdens of others.

Inclosing a letter from a poor boy who expressed great anxiety to complete his education and be a preacher, he wrote:

"I send you this letter hoping you may see some way to bless this boy. Well, I'll send you this one, and then let you rest awhile. Be all other things as they may, never let me hamper, harass, or burden you, financially or otherwise. If at any time or in any way I can help you, please grant me that privilege. I am glad that I do know I will never intentionally cause even the slightest shade of a shadow of a sigh to flit across the path of anything that breathes. How much sorrow I may have caused I do not know, but I believe I have never caused any intentionally, and I know I have no desire to do so. Yes, I know I shall be more careful to always bless and never curse in the future than I have been, even till God shall call me home."

The following stanzas by Mrs. M. A. Boling, of Nashville, Tenn., were inclosed in one of his letters, in original manuscript which had never been published:

"BEAR YE ONE ANOTHER'S BURDENS."

In your pathway 'long life's highway
    You may see the steps of age
Moving slowly toward life's sunset,
    Tottering feebly off life's stage.

Hasten, then, to give them succor;
    Smooth the stones and thorns away;
Banish clouds and scatter sunshine;
    Make their last their happiest day.

In your pathway 'long life's highway
   You may see a brother, friend,
Leaving paths of truth and honor,
   While his steps toward ruin trend.

Speak a word of admonition;
   Do not be too swift to blame;
Make him see his soul's condition;
   Call him back in Jesus' name.

You may see an erring sister
   Straying far from virtue's fold,
Wandering lonely, friendless, homeless,
   In a world unkind and cold.

O, speak to her of hope and heaven!
   Tell her the words that Jesus said,
" Go thy way, and sin no more,"
   Have hungry souls of millions fed.

And she may have suffered sorrow,
   Struggled long with grief and pain,
Until by it her courage perished,
   Until wild frenzy fired her brain.

O, do not pass her by in scorning!
   Help your fallen sister rise.
Thinking not of man's approval,
   Your reward with Jesus lies.

Then do not brush aside your garments;
   Fear lest they receive a stain.
Jesus, in his loving-kindness,
   Made the vilest whole again.

Be a staff for age and weakness;
   For the fallen speak a prayer;
With the widow and the orphan
   Shed the sympathizing tear.

If your heart would sing with gladness,
   And be free from care and pain,
And would never know the sadness
   Of ever having lived in vain,

> Help to bear each other's burdens,
>   For each one must a burden bear;
> And this was God's own commandment:
>   That we each other's burdens share.

Some years ago he sent me a letter from which it appeared that people he did not know and had never seen were mistreating him and trying to injure him. He wrote as follows:

" When I am gone, may it be said—truthfully said—of me: ' He never tried by tongue or pen—never tried in any way—to injure any person, place, or thing; but studied, tried, and prayed to do all the good he could.' Why these people treat me thus, I do not know. ' Lord, lay not this sin to their charge.' ' Father, forgive them; for they know not what they do.' "

I regret that I do not feel authorized to publish the name of the illustrious man he refers to in the following letter:

" Of course you knew by reputation, if not personally, the illustrious ——, author, preacher, lecturer, scholar, and educator. His son has told me much which the world does not know, and probably never will know, about his illustrious father. He says the lack of one hundred dollars forced his father to face death, and that then, having faced it, he accepted it to save less than one dollar, because he believed it necessary, the world not knowing his needs; but that when it was forever too late to bless the fallen hero, his coffin and grave were deluged with floral offerings, any one of many of which cost more than one hundred dollars; and he believes there were tens of thousands of men and women, each of whom, that very day, would have gladly given one hundred dollars to restore him to life and health. This may not be worth relating, but I think it is. It is a case that illustrates a principle. So far as I know, history nowhere intimates that the poet Burns ever tried to save any souls; but he was Scotland's greatest poet, and history is responsible, not for the following language, but facts: He lived in poverty and died in want, having actually begged bread. Many who refused to give him bread, gladly gave gold liberally to build a costly monument to perpetuate his memory—or, to tell the truth, to gratify Scottish vanity. When his aged mother saw the monument, she said, as she brushed blinding tears away: 'Ah, Robbie, ye asked them for br'ad, an' they gie ye a stun.' Some of the strange facts in the case of the illustrious —— are: He was in Florida in January. One hundred additional dollars would have kept him there till spring opened. He knew he ought to stay there—that life might depend on it—but the hundred dollars were wanting. He was not willing to humiliate himself by making his needs known. He plunged from Florida into Northern winter. When he reached home, the frozen snow was five or six inches deep. One dollar would have taken him home in a closed carriage. He could not afford to spend the dollar. He stood in the cold wind ten minutes on the snow, waiting for a street car. Ten cents took him near home. From there he walked home over the snow. One week from that cold night he was ready for the grave. He may not have had a dollar when he reached home; if so, he deemed it his duty to save the ninety cents. If I ever write for publication for permanent preservation, I must write some on the influence of little things.

> " 'A pebble in the streamlet scant
>   Hath changed the course of many a river;
>   A dewdrop on the baby plant
>   Hath warped the giant oak forever.' "

His idea of help for the living and mourning for the dead is expressed in the following article, which he clipped from a paper and inclosed in one of his letters:

" WHEN I DIE.

" When I am dead and my life work is done; when I am about to be laid away to await the trumpet of the archangel, and my loved ones are gathered about my coffin to bid a last farewell to my remains, then I want no flowers from those who did not give me such and wish me good cheer while I lived; I want no hypocritical encomiums or fair speeches of praise from those who cursed, or blamed, or falsely accused me in life; I want no preacher display of funeral oratory from those who could not or would not fellowship me in the service of my Master.

" I despise the hypocritical cant which praises when I am dead, but cursed me as a heretic in life. I want no crocodile tears or sprig of evergreen from such. My life is ended; let me go. Turn to the living, the suffering, and give to them the sympathy and praise which may do them good. I have always despised the hypocrisy which railed at a Roman Catholic purgatory and the priestcraft which pretended to pray men through it, and then did the same thing under the name of ' a funeral.'

" If any have cheered or blessed me while living, or if there be any whose lives I have made brighter, any upon whose countenance I have provoked an innocent smile, or

FRONT VIEW, WEST VERANDA, LARIMORE'S HOME, MARS' HILL.

whose burdens I may have helped to bear—if these should attend my funeral and shed an honest tear or lay one flower upon my grave from sincere love, so be it; and may God bless them.

"I am sure that life is the time to do good to our fellow-men, and that when they are dead our opportunities toward them have forever ceased. No amount of praise can undo the evil we may have done them, nor can it atone for the good we could have done. Life's road is a hard one at best, and those who have found a spiteful sort of pleasure in throwing stones at me and across my pathway during life should not add insult to injury by professing a sorrow they do not feel, or by expressing a hypocritical praise for one they damned through life. Still, nothing men may do or say can change the destiny of the dead. His own life, now done, has worked out for him an eternal weight of glory, or sunk him down amidst the wreck of a world, through sin, to unutterable woe. No prayers or tears or words of praise can change the fact that men must reap what they sow.   JOHN T. POE."

On the margin of this clipping he wrote:

"There are volumes in that. A religious paper said, when announcing the death of a faithful old soldier of the cross whom that same paper had relentlessly persecuted while living: 'The old guard will soon be gone.'"

The following story on burden bearing in the home circle, clipped from a newspaper and inclosed in one of his letters, is especially commended as a message from him to boys and girls:

"'Can you help me for a few minutes, Marion?'

" ' I would like to, but I don't see how I can.' The tone was not impatient, but hurried. ' I have this essay to finish for the society this evening; I must go to our French history class in an hour, then to a guild meeting, and get back to my German lesson at five o'clock.'

" ' No, you can't help me, dear. You look worn out yourself. Never mind. If I tie up my head, perhaps I can finish this.'

" ' Through at last,' said Marion, wearily giving a finishing touch to the ' Development of Religious Ideas Among the Greeks,' at the same time glancing quickly at the clock.

" Her attention was arrested by a strange sight. Her tired mother had fallen asleep over her sewing. That was not surprising, but the startled girl saw bending over her mother's pale face two angels, each looking earnestly at the sleeper.

" ' What made that weary look on this woman's face? ' asked the stern, strange-looking angel of the weaker, sadder one. ' Has God given her no daughters? '

" ' Yes,' replied the other, ' but they have no time to take care of their mother.'

" ' No time! ' cried the other. ' What do they do with all the time I am letting them have? '

" ' Well,' replied the Angel of Life, ' I keep their hands and hearts full. They are affectionate daughters, much admired for their good works, but they do not know they are letting the one they love most slip from my arms into yours. Those gray hairs come from overwork and anxiety to save extra money for the music and French lessons; those pale cheeks faded while the girls were painting roses or pansies on velvet or satin.'

" The dark angel frowned.

" ' The girls must be accomplished now! ' exclaimed the other. ' Those eyes grew dim sewing for the girls to give them time to study ancient history and modern languages; those wrinkles came because the girls had not time to share the cares and worries of everyday life; that sigh comes because the mother feels neglected and lonely, while the girls are working for the women in India; that tired look comes from getting up so early, while the poor, exhausted girls are trying to sleep back the late hours they gave to study or spent at the concert; those feet are so weary because of their ceaseless walk around the house all day.'

" ' Surely the girls help, too.'

" ' What they can; but their feet get weary enough going around begging for the charity hospital and the church, and hunting up the poor and sick.'

" ' No wonder,' said the Angel of Death, ' so many mothers call me. This is indeed sad—loving, industrious girls giving their mothers to my care as soon as selfish, wicked ones! '

" 'Ah, the hours are so crowded! ' said Life, wearily. ' Girls who are cultured, or take an active part in life, have no time to take care of the mother who spent so much time in bringing them up.'

" ' Then I must place my seal on her brow,' said the Angel of Death, bending over the sleeping woman.

" ' No, no! ' cried Marion, springing from her seat. ' I will take care of her, if you will only stay.'

" ' Daughter, you must have had a nightmare. Wake up, dear. I fear you have missed your history class.'

" ' Never mind, mamma; I'm not going to-day. I am

rested now, and I will make these buttonholes, while you curl up on the sofa and take a nap. I'll send word to the guild professor that I must be excused to-day, for I am going to see to supper myself, and make some of those muffins you like. Now, go to sleep, mamma, dear, as I did, and don't worry about me. You are of more consequence than all the languages or classes in the world.'

" So, after being snugly tucked in a warm afghan, with a tender kiss from her daughter, usually too busy for such demonstrations, Mrs. Henson fell into a sweet, restful sleep.

" ' I see we might have lost the best of mothers in our mad rush to be educated and useful in this hurrying, restless day and generation,' Marion soliloquized, as she occasionally stole a glance at the sleeping mother. 'After this, what time she does not need I shall devote to outside work and study. Until she gets well restored, I shall take charge of the house and give up all societies.'

"And Marion kept her word.

"A few months later one remarked to her: ' We miss your bright essays so much, Miss Marion. You seem to have lost your ambition to be highly educated. You are letting your sisters get ahead of you, I fear. How young your mother looks to have grown daughters! I never saw her looking so well.'

" Then Marion felt rewarded."

The financial crisis of 1893 is an historic epoch in the United States. All over the country fortunes were squandered; old and conservative business firms were wrecked; homes were ruined, hopes were blighted, hearts were broken; and many men who had long stood high in the estimation of the people for integrity were imprisoned for technical violations of the law, if not for moral turpitude, in efforts to dodge disaster. When the panic was at its highest, every bank in Nashville, save one, was closed, and depositors in that one made a rush to draw their money which probably has no parallel in the history of the city. Confident of the strength and solvency of their bank, the president, cashier, and directors decided to waive the custom of banking hours, and, instead of closing at 2 o'clock P.M., keep the bank open and pay all demands as long as anybody wanted money. There were several sensational failures during the day, all business was practically suspended, and the streets were blocked by hundreds of excited spectators around the bank on which depositors were making a run. I received a few remittances by mail in the usual course of business that day, and about noon went to the bank to make a deposit. The line of men, with here and there a woman, crowding toward the bank to draw their deposits extended from the paying teller's window out through the front door, near the middle of the block on College street, up College to Union, and down Union to within a few feet of Market—nearly a block and a half in length. It had held its own at about that length since the bank was opened at 9 A.M., and all day long the clink of gold and silver and rattle of paper money never ceased at the paying teller's window till late in the evening, when the crowd dispersed, with the assurance that the bank would be open as usual and ready to pay all demands at nine o'clock next morning. When I reached the bank a full force of policemen were on duty, holding back the crowds and keeping the bank runners in line. At the door I was stopped by a policeman, who, assuming that I wanted to draw money, politely requested me to go back to Union street, near Market, and take a position at the tail of the line. When I told him I wanted to make a deposit, he stepped aside and asked me to walk in. On the inside everything was quiet and orderly. The cashier and directors were in consultation around a long table in a private office, the president was standing at the paying teller's elbow closely inspecting every transaction, and the paying teller was counting money and handing it out like a machine. This sketch of the local panic and general crisis is necessary to properly introduce his next letter. When the morning papers came out next day, they contained a list of those who made deposits in the bank during the run, and by the next mail after he saw the paper, he wrote:

" I was rejoiced to see your name among depositors during the run on the bank. Many men and business institutions are ruined when perfectly solvent by a rush of reckless people in a panic. Josh. Billings says, ' When a man starts downhill everything seems to be greased for the occasion;' but it is the part of a man and a Christian to sand the track and put on the brakes for the fellow on a downhill run, even if it must be done at great risk and heavy loss. When my lifelong friend, Mr. ——, was at the mercy of his creditors, I had in his bank to my credit —— dollars. It was intrusted to me by two poor sisters to keep for them; it was all they had, and the savings of a lifetime. When the crash came, I could have made a rush with the rest and drawn it out, but I did not do it. I have never explained the situation to the two sisters who intrusted it to me. I have simply said to them: ' Give no anxious thought to your interests there. You intrusted all you had to me; I put it in the bank; I am managing that.' They said: 'You did right; you could not have pleased us better. As to the money being perfectly safe, we never had one single doubt.' Well, if I get it, I'll use it; if not, I'll lose it; and in either event, I expect to pay them every dollar of it. Suppose I never see one cent of that money now covered up in the débris of that bottomless bank. Well, if it must so be, then so must it be; but that is only that—that's all. I can work, and I can pay; but I can't crush nor see others crush a fallen, struggling man and lifelong friend, if I can help it."

I once sent him an itemized statement of transactions through me which showed extravagant benevolence. I insisted that he was going beyond his ability and duty, to his own financial ruin, and begged him to be more careful in his benefactions and try to keep out of debt and never get entirely out of money. He wrote:

"This lengthy statement required no little time and labor; but, then, it cost me nothing. That's your way. You never do anything 'in a corner.' It's all right, of course. I shall not figure on it. You keep everything straight, square, and level. Send me whatsoever you want to send me whensoever you will, and you may always rely on my sending the needful to meet all demands. If you keep me from getting out of money, you'll have a government contract. It's more than heaven and earth have done yet. A father said of his wayward boy: 'I whip him often enough and hard enough, but he will not stay whipped.' I save some money every now and then, but so many people need it, it will not stay saved. I have just read in the

paper about the misfortune of our dear Brother ———.
Please send him for me all you are willing to risk me to
pay, and charge to me."

Of course this meant all I could raise, for I never saw the
lay I would not risk him to pay any amount he wanted and
I could command; but where I had any discretionary power
at all, even by the most liberal construction, it was the better for him and the worse for the beneficiary of his bounty.
Speaking of risking him to pay suggests the story of Albert
Marr and his mule, which he greatly enjoys. Marr moved
from Alabama to Arkansas, and a merchant demanded a
mortgage on his mule to secure a store account. Marr said:
"A man has come to a pretty pass when his credit is not
as good as the credit of a mule. I don't owe that merchant
a cent. He would not credit me; he preferred to credit
the mule. That is not my debt; it is the mule's debt; and
if the mule dies, I'll never pay a dollar of it."

There is another reason than the one given at the beginning of this chapter for publishing these letters. It is gen-
erally understood that he has received what many people,
and especially preachers, consider very liberal support at
many places in his work. Under pressure of financial embarrassment, he has in some cases made his needs known
in a way which caused good people who really loved him
to think he uses too much money and expects too much by
way of support in his work. There is some justice in the
criticism; but he has laid up no money, and has not even
had enough at all times to meet the legitimate expenses of
an economical home and an industrious wife and children.
His letters will give those who are disposed to be just the

data they need to form a correct estimate of him " as concerning giving and receiving." If he would use money
with more caution and discretion, he would have more for
himself and family, and would perhaps do more good in
his efforts to help others, without being financially embarrassed and oppressed, even if he should receive less than he
does receive by way of support in his work. I have told
him this many times, and he has frankly admitted it frequently; but his sympathies and impulses so completely
overbalance his appreciation of money that he seems to be
constitutionally incapable of systematic and successful
financiering. His friends and advisers can no more control him in such matters than they can stop the rain from
falling or the sun from shining. I once went over all this
with him, told him frankly that he was doing himself and
his family an injustice, and encouraging and aiding in their
meanness designing people who take advantage of sympathy to impose upon generosity, when they ought to be put
upon the practice of the doctrine of Paul: " For even when
we were with you, this we commanded you, that if any
would not work, neither should he eat. For we hear that
there are some which walk among you disorderly, working
not at all, but are busybodies. Now them that are such
we command and exhort by our Lord Jesus Christ, that
with quietness they work, and eat their own bread." (2
Thess. 3: 10-12.) A well-balanced Christian character
has enough sympathy to respond to all legitimate appeals
for help; it also has enough of sterner stuff to enforce the
wholesome scripture doctrine of industry and self-reliance.
However, by the next mail after I called his attention to

MISS ETTIE LARIMORE ON WEST VERANDA, MARS' HILL.

the weakness of his nature and advised him to profit by the legitimate criticisms of good people who loved him, I received the following letter from him:

" In January of the present year a stranger, whose voice and face and story touched my heart and completely controlled me, called upon me for help to reach her distant home, where a sick mother was longing and sighing to see her, assuring me that I should hear from her immediately after she reached home and mother. I gladly gave her all she asked, which was one dollar less than all I had, and almost immediately regretted that I did not give her the other dollar, and reproached myself for not doing so. She had vanished from my view, however, or my last dollar should have been hers. March is now silently stealing away, yet no tidings have come from that beautiful girl. I have not the remotest idea who or where she is, but I still regret I was selfish enough to withhold from her hand the dollar I kept. I am glad I gave her all she asked, and would gladly do the same to-day, should opportunity offer —if I had the dollars. I'm sure I'd give all I have. Of course I shall never see that beautiful child of sorrow again, and she may smile when she thinks of my weakness; but I'd rather be ' taken in ' a thousand times, and be as poor as Lazarus, than to have a heart hard enough to resist such appeals for sympathy and succor. ' When my final farewell to the world I have said,' and I am free from all sorrow and censure, may no one have reason to say: ' He withheld from me the succor and sympathy for which he knew I sighed, when he could have given me either.' This little story is a sample of many never to be told that illustrates a weakness that has always been mine—a weakness which I would not exchange for a hard, selfish heart and the wealth of all this world. When my tongue is silent, and my heart is still, and my hand can no longer help the needy, men may say, ' He lived and died in poverty; ' but I pray that God may know and truth may say, ' His soul was always sympathetic, and he never withheld the helping hand from any suffering, sorrowing soul that appealed to him for help.' "

After all, his weakness is at a point where most people, and even Christians, have too much strength. Perhaps such weakness will do more good in softening hearts that are too hard than it will do harm in encouraging and aiding unworthy and designing people who are mean enough to take advantage of sympathy to impose upon generosity.

CHAPTER XII.

SERMON—THE IRON, THE SILVER, AND THE
GOLDEN RULE.

JUDGE not, that ye be not judged. For with what judgment ye judge, ye shall be judged: and with what measure ye mete, it shall be measured to you again. [Surely no man can claim or desire more than this—to buy and sell by the same yardstick.]   And why beholdest thou the mote that is in thy brother's eye [little blemishes in your brother's conduct or life], but considerest not the beam that is in thine own eye [the greater sin of which you are guilty]?   Or how wilt thou say to thy brother, Let me pull out the mote out of thine eye; and, behold, a beam is in thine own eye?   Thou hypocrite, first cast out the beam out of thine own eye [get right yourself]; and then shalt thou see clearly to cast out the mote out of thy brother's eye [you can consistently criticise him when you get right yourself].

" Give not that which is holy unto the dogs, neither cast ye your pearls before swine, lest they trample them under their feet, and turn again and rend you.

"Ask, and it shall be given you; seek, and ye shall find; knock, and it shall be opened unto you: for every one that asketh receiveth; and he that seeketh findeth; and to him that knocketh it shall be opened.   Or what man is there of you, whom if his son ask bread, will he give him a stone? Or if he ask a fish, will he give him a serpent?   If ye then, being evil, know how to give good gifts unto your children, how much more shall your Father which is in heaven give good things to them that ask him? Therefore all things whatsoever ye would that men should do to you, do ye even so to them: for this is the law and the prophets." (Matt. 7: 1-12.)

"Therefore all things whatsoever ye would that men should do to you, do ye even so to them: for this is the law and the prophets."

Surrounded by a great throng of people in the plain, and weary of his surroundings for the present, Jesus withdrew from the crowd and ascended to the summit of a little hill nestling with becoming modesty among the mountains of the Land of Promise; and when he had seated himself, his disciples came unto him, and he opened his mouth and taught them the things that constitute the fifth, the sixth, and the seventh chapters of Matthew—a crown of radiant gems and jewels rare that have come down through the ages, sparkling and glittering and flooding the world with light divine for eighteen hundred years, and that will continue to brighten our pathway with wondrous light until we wing our flight among the stars, provided we become children of the living God, reduce these principles to practice in our lives, and prove faithful unto death.

Among these jewels we find the language: "Therefore all things whatsoever ye would that men should do to you, do ye even so to them: for this is the law and the prophets." (Matt. 7: 12.)

Man is so constituted that rules and regulations, discipline and government, are necessary in all the relationships of life. Every school must have its rules, its regulations, its government, its discipline.   It is true that there are some arbitrary rules, as there are some arbitrary teachers; but the existence of arbitrary rules no more argues against the importance of rules than the existence of arbitrary teachers argues against the importance of teachers. Every school must have its rules and regulations, its discipline and government, and these must be properly administered and properly respected, in order that the school may be a blessing to the community and a blessing to mankind.

The church of the living God is a school, all Christians being pupils, scholars, or disciples in that school; the sixty-six volumes of the Bible being the text-books for these pupils to study, that they may grow in grace and in the knowledge of the truth.   Jesus is the great head Teacher— the Teacher of teachers.   God is the supreme Head over this divine, spiritual institution, and he has sent the Holy Spirit to his children here to comfort and help them in the study and practice of these wonderful lessons.

But people are never pupils in a school until they have entered the school.   There is never a chance for them to be promoted to another grade until they have entered some grade, no chance to enter until they have matriculated, and no chance to have any honor in the school until they have entered it.   Just so with this divine institution called " the church."   We must, as responsible souls, matriculate in this school, enter it in God's appointed way, and come under the law governing its pupils, in order to be benefited, in order to be entitled to the emoluments and honors connected with this wonderful institution over which God himself presides.

Every army must have its rules, its regulations, its government, its discipline, its tactics, without which a comparatively numberless host may be routed, wrecked, and ruined by a few well-officered, well-equipped, and well-governed soldiers, submissive to the rules, regulations, and tactics of the army, as was demonstrated by the memorable crusades of the tearful, bloody long ago.

The church of God is an army. Jesus is the Leader of that army; God is at the head of the government, directing this army; and every Christian is a soldier of the cross. Hence Paul says: " Fight the good fight of faith, lay hold on eternal life, whereunto thou art also called, and hast professed a good profession before many witnesses." (1 Tim. 6 : 12.) " Thou therefore endure hardness, as a good soldier of Jesus Christ. No man that warreth entangleth himself with the affairs of this life; that he may please him who hath chosen him to be a soldier. And if a man also strive for masteries, yet is he not crowned, except he strive lawfully." (2 Tim. 2: 3-5.) In Eph. 6 we have the soldier's armor spoken of as applied to Christians: the helmet of salvation, the breastplate of righteousness, the shield of faith, the sword of the Spirit—everything connected with the armor of the ancient soldier mentioned as belonging to the soldier of the cross. In Heb. 2: 9, 10, the Savior is spoken of as the Captain of our salvation: " But we see Jesus, who was made a little lower than the angels for the suffering of death, crowned with glory and honor; that he by the grace of God should taste death for every man. For it became him, for whom are all things, and by whom are all things, in bringing many sons unto glory, to make the captain of their salvation perfect through sufferings "—

the word " captain " being used in the sense of commander in chief, the leader of the Christian hosts, battling for the salvation of souls.

Every family must have its rules and regulations, its discipline and government, in order to be a blessing to the world, as God would have all families to be. We speak of a well-regulated family—that is simply a family submissive to good regulations, to good rules, properly adminis tered, respected, and obeyed. Families must have rules and regulations to be governed by.

The church of God is a family—God the Father, Christ the elder Brother, and all Christians brothers and sisters. " The Spirit itself beareth witness with our spirit, that we are the children of God." (Rom. 8: 16.) The Bible authorizes Christians to call God their Father. This shows that they are children of God, with Jesus as their elder Brother; and as all the Christians on this earth are members of God's family, that family must have its rules of government.

Every kingdom must have its government. The church of Christ is spoken of as a kingdom: " Giving thanks unto the Father, which hath made us meet to be partakers of the inheritance of the saints in light: who hath delivered us from the power of darkness, and hath translated us into the kingdom of his dear Son: in whom we have redemption through his blood, even the forgiveness of sins." (Col. 1: 12-14.) This divine government, of course, must have its laws by which it is governed.

Every natural human body must have rules and regulations governing it—we call them rules of health—and to the extent that these rules are observed, men have greater

prospect of health, happiness, and longevity than those
who do not comply with these laws of the human body.
The church of Christ is compared to the human body: " So
we, being many, are one body in Christ, and every one
members one of another." (Rom. 12: 5.) The same
thought appears in 1 Cor. 12.

Now, then, since each of these—since the school, since
the army, since the family, since the kingdom or government, since the natural human body—must be governed by
rules and regulations, these being properly observed in
order that proper results may come; and since the church
is like all these, and God himself compares it to all these,
the conclusion comes with full force, in the light of these
illustrations, that the church must have government, must
have discipline, must have rules and regulations, to be observed by its members. The church can no more prosper
and be the institution God would have it be, without its
rules and regulations of government, than a school, an
army, or a kingdom can be prosperous without its rules and
regulations, its government and discipline. No church can
prosper without government.

We should not wonder, then, that Christ submitted to
his disciples a rule of life to govern them in their relationship to each other, to him, and to God. Hence Jesus said
to his disciples: " Therefore all things whatsoever ye would
that men should do to you, do ye even so them "—the royal
rule of righteousness, submitted by the Savior to his disciples, to be observed by them and to be observed by his
servants until time's knell shall be sounded and the redeemed shall be gathered home.

There are three rules recognized among men that have

received metallic names. The first of these in point of antiquity—and, unfortunately, the first in point of numbers, if we consider the men who have submitted to live in accordance with its requirements—is what is known as the " Iron Rule," otherwise called the " Rule of Cain," because Cain, the firstborn human being on the earth—Adam and Eve were *made*, Cain was *born*—was the first to make himself notorious by submitting to its demands. This heartless rule is based upon the Satanic principle that might makes right. All the carnage, cruelty, and crime that have cursed the earth for six thousand years, growing out of a spirit of pride, a spirit of selfishness, of greed for gold—justifying and emphasizing Burns' poetic expression, " Man's inhumanity to man makes countless millions mourn "— may be traced with unerring certainty to the shadow of the Iron Rule, the principle that might makes right. From the time that Cain murdered Abel, his soul full of hatred and envy of his innocent brother, no such act has ever stained the earth with blood that has not been committed in obedience to the demands of the Iron Rule. In all the ages there has never been a man, ambitious of conquest, thirsting for personal grandeur and greatness and glory, power and popularity and dominion, who has unsheathed his sword and marched his legions into erstwhile peaceful communities and filled them with the wreck of homes and broken hopes and blighted prospects, that he might add to his own possessions and power and dominion—doing this work for self and prompted to it by sordid, selfish, Satanic motives—who is not worshiping in the shadow of the Iron Rule. It is not necessary for us to single out some characters along that line. It is not necessary for us to go far back over the hills and plains of the long ago to Alexander, weeping because he could reach no other worlds to bathe them in blood and drench them in tears; to Hannibal, who held Rome under the heel of his tyranny for fourteen years; to Cæsar, in his eight years of Gallic wars, laying waste to a once-fair country, slaying or reducing to bondage three millions of her people; to the illustrious Corsican, the adopted son of France, as he crushes kingdoms, overturns thrones, breaks scepters, and plays with crowns as children in the nursery play with toys—it is not necessary to go to these to find worshipers at the shrine of the Iron Rule. In all this favored land we call " our country "—a Christian country—there is not a man called " husband " by a faithful, loving, and dutiful wife, who, forgetful of promises made in twilight's semisacred hour in the long ago, or sacred vows made at the hymeneal altar—vows as sacred and as binding as any oath ever administered beneath the stars—is now a cruel tyrant, to be feared, instead of the fond, compassionate husband and father, to be revered, who is not as surely a servant of Satan, a worshiper of self at the shrine of the Iron Rule, as was ever Alexander, or Hannibal, or Cæsar, or Napoleon, or any bloody tyrant the world has ever seen—a smaller, lesser, but more contemptible, specimen of the same cruel class. It does not make any difference what position—ecclesiastical, political, or social—he may fill; it does not make any difference how pharisaical he may look, how long he may make his prayers or his sermons; if that be his character, he is serving Satan to Satan's perfect satisfaction. While he may wear the livery of Heaven, he is serving Satan, and not the spotless Lamb of God, who gave his life to redeem us, who died upon the cross that we might live. It is not necessary for man to deceive himself with the idea that he is headed for heaven because he prays long prayers or preaches long sermons; for God knoweth the heart, and out of the heart cometh the issues of life. If the heart is evil, the life is not pure in the sight of God. But we can go from the family circle, from the home, shadowed by such a cruel tyrant, or from a home that is blessed by such a husband as that cruel tyrant should be, to any congregation of Christians, and in some of these congregations, it may be, we can find specimens of this same class of persons. Whenever we find the " rule-or-ruin," " boss-or-burst," " my-way-or-no-way " man in the church of God, in any congregation of Christians in the service of God, there we find the Iron Rule character, and that man can do more damage to the cause of Christ, occupying a position nominally in the church of Christ, than any seven men of equal power can do, if standing in open opposition to the church of God. Occupying that position gives him a vantage ground that no man without that nominal relationship could ever have. Of course you know, and I know that you know, that I have no reference to the man that stands up, like brave old Elijah of old, for God's right to rule. These two characters—the one who is determined to rule or ruin, boss or burst, have his way or no way, and the man who is ready to do and bear and die for God's right, standing up for his " thus it is written," " thus saith the Lord " —are as far apart as the opposites of limitless space; as far apart as the east is from the west; as far from each other as the deepest, darkest depths of perdition from the highest heights of rapture that canopy the eternal throne of God.

The one—the rule-or-ruin man—is a curse to the community in which he lives, so far as his influence is felt; the other, a blessing to all around him, a man that angels admire and that Heaven will receive at last. We may just look around in all the relations of life, and whenever we see a man who, simply because he has the power to do it, lays hold on that which is not his own, who oppresses anybody or robs anybody, then we have an example of those who worship at the shrine of the Iron Rule. If there is a man, be he pope, priest, or preacher, who has taken advantage of some technicality of law, or the absence of some important witness whose testimony would have brought truth to light, or the loss of some important paper, to get a decree of court in his favor, and, having got it, has taken property which may be the home and rightful possession of some unfortunate widow and her helpless children, when he knows that according to the eternal principles of everlasting justice he has no right to these things, but holds them simply by the decree of court and under the protection of the strong arm of the law, he is a servant of Satan, worshiping in the shadow of the shrine of the Iron Rule. No decree of court has ever made wrong right. The decree may come from the lowest court in the land, it may be appealed until it reaches the Supreme Court of the United States, and the decision of the lower courts may be upheld to the last; but still, if the first decision is wrong, the last one is wrong, and all the others are wrong. These decisions and decrees cannot make the wrong right. It is presumable, of course, and the general inference is, that the decrees of court are right, or should be, but the decree of court does not make it so; and it is reasonable to believe that there

are thousands of people to-day holding property who know that according to the eternal principles of right and justice the property belongs to others. It matters not what may be their ecclesiastical, financial, political, or social position, they are robbers; trying to get and enjoy the goods of others, they have worse than stolen them; they are Iron Rule people, and there is not grace enough in the bosom of God to save them unless they repent, make restitution, turn to God, and live the Christian life.

I am sure there is no man who would be advertised as an Iron Rule man, and there is no man who will question a single point I have made. You have the right to criticise my logic or my grammar, but I do not believe there is a man here who will criticise the principle I have laid down. There is not a man who would be willing to be advertised as an Iron Rule man. If I should call him out and say, " Here is an example of the Iron Rule man," this audience would consider it a shame, a burning disgrace. It is a strange thing that men of culture and refinement will be for years, willfully, willingly, knowingly, and intentionally, what they would consider it an unpardonable outrage for any man to either publicly or privately accuse them of being, and at the same time and during that time persistently refuse to be what they would like for the whole world to believe they are, when it is a voluntary matter and left for them to say, just as it is left for the sinner to come and be a child of God or not.

The second of these rules in point of antiquity, and one that occupies the halfway point between the deep, dark depths occupied by the Iron Rule and the heights whereon we find the law of Christ, has been called the " Silver

Rule "—otherwise, the " Rule of Confucius," because Confucius, a Chinese philosopher, who lived about five hundred years before the birth of the Babe of Bethlehem, embodied this rule in his teachings. The Silver Rule, the Rule of Confucius, is this: " Do nothing to others that you would not have others do to you." All can understand that this is a wonderful improvement on the Iron Rule, a rule of much higher grade than that Satanic and heartless rule; and yet the Silver Rule is very deficient indeed. It is purely negative. It does not actually demand that we do anything. It forbids much, but does not demand anything. It would not allow you to apply a torch to your neighbor's home, but does not require you to stop and spend three minutes in extinguishing the flames, if you should see them doing their dreadful work; it would not require you to stop and save your neighbor's child from the waves, if you saw him drowning, though it would forbid your pushing him into the water. So far as this rule is concerned, a man may step aside and let the suffering suffer, the perishing die, and never violate one single syllable in it. I am sure there is not a man in this audience willing to be classed so low as the worshipers at the shrine of the Silver Rule, living negative lives, living for self, and, while not taking time to injure others, never extending a helping hand to one single son of Adam's race. According to every principle of justice and right, there is no man who has the right to be a Silver Rule man. We are under obligations to help others, to be ready to sympathize with and succor the suffering and needy wherever we go; live to bless ever and curse never, thus obeying the injunction of Him who has said to Christians: " Bear ye one another's burdens, and so fulfill the law of Christ."   (Gal. 6: 2.)

The third, and last, of these rules has been called the " Golden Rule "—otherwise, the " Rule of Christ," because Christ was the author of it.   The Iron Rule, the Rule of Cain—" Might makes right; " the Silver Rule, the Rule of Confucius—" Do nothing to others that you would not have others do to you; " the Golden Rule, the Rule of Christ—" Therefore all things whatsoever ye would that men should do to you, do ye even so to them."

We should all rejoice that Jesus, the immaculate Son of God, has given us this absolutely pure rule of life; we should all rejoice that it is our privilege to enter into his service and live according to the demands of this rule; we should rejoice in the thought that to the extent we live the Christian life we are helping the world to live according to this divine principle, this Golden Rule.

I rejoice that I have never come to the conclusion that Golden Rule people are scarce in this world.   I may have too much confidence in my fellow-man, and may love my brethren and sisters too tenderly, constantly, and confidingly; it may be that I am often deceived by having too much confidence in people wherever I go; but I would rather be deceived and suffer along this line than to suffer under the influence of the thought that Golden Rule people are so scarce in this world that the safest way is to consider every man a scoundrel until he proves himself to be a gentleman.   All over this land are Golden Rule men and women, who, to the extent of their ability, are living up to the rule.   I remember a blessed, good woman who at one time took a journey to Texas, and on her return found she had ten dollars more money than she ought to have. She was worked up about it; she thought about it, dreamed about it, prayed over it, and suddenly she thought: " There is just one place for me to have made this mistake." She remembered that at one place she had to get the ticket agent to change a bill for her. She quietly wrote the ticket agent at that place in Texas, " Did your money balance, or your accounts balance, at the end of a certain time? " not intimating whether she had lost fifty dollars or was fifty cents ahead. She got a polite note from the agent saying that at the end of that month he was ten dollars short, and had never been able to make his accounts balance. She immediately remitted the ten dollars to him in a safe way, received his grateful acknowledgments, and felt easy. Do you say this is not worth relating? It would not be, if all who claim to be Christians were really what Christianity would make them if they would submit to its principles every day. A man with whom I was acquainted amassed a great fortune. Twenty years after his wife died he also died, leaving a son and two daughters. For some reason that has never been satisfactorily explained, he gave his fortune to his son, just leaving enough to his daughters to make the will stand the test. So far as I know, no one knows why he did so. It may be that he wished, like the elder Vanderbilt, to keep his property together; or that he believed his daughters would not know how to manage such fortunes; so he gave it all to the son. The son waited for about forty days after the death of the father, and then came the time for a decision as to what was to be done. We all see that he was confronted by a situation where he had to choose between the three rules. On the Iron Rule principle, he could have told them to get out. You say this would have been Satanic; the Iron Rule is always Satanic. On the Silver Rule principle, he could have said to himself: " These things are mine. If they want to stay here and risk their chances, live of the crumbs that fall from my table, they can stay; but these things are mine." We all know what he would have done if he had decided to go according to the Golden Rule. The forty days having elapsed, he called his sisters into the family room—that room where the hand of the mother had rocked the cradle where each in turn had slept and smiled and dreamed, all unconscious even of the loving mother's heart. He then produced three documents. A lawyer himself, he had called to his aid in preparing these papers all a lawyer's experience along that line. He had made a careful invoice of all the property, and had made three lists of equal value, one-third of the property on each list. He requested the sisters to listen while he read over these lists, and be able to decide what they considered most valuable, the second, and the least valuable. He turned to the older sister, when they had both told him they understood, and demanded that she take first choice. She threw her arms about his neck and begged him not to ask her to do this; but he insisted that she pledge her honor to take the one she really preferred, and she finally did so. The same scene was enacted between him and the other sister, who regretfully and reluctantly took her choice, leaving him one-third. Instead of all the property, he has but one-third; but we can all see that in reality he is infinitely richer than if he had all the property and ten times more. He has acted upon the principle of the Golden Rule. I am not sure but there are people who claim to be Christians, who preach longer sermons and offer up longer prayers than patient, polite people ought to have to listen to from such a source, who would not have done as that man did; and yet, sad to say, that man was not a Christian, is not a Christian to-day, and I think there is little probability that he will ever be a Christian. I am almost sure he was wrecked and ruined along that line long ago by the deception, hypocrisy, sin, and wickedness among those who claim to be children of God. As a lawyer, he had heard false swearing from those claiming to be Christians, and had lost faith in mankind and faith in his Maker, and is destined some day to go into eternity without God and without a hope of the blessings the Father promises to all his faithful children. Such lessons should make us realize the responsibility resting upon us as followers of Christ, and see to it that we never fall short of the requirements of this Golden Rule of life.

I want to touch upon a Bible example. I never like to close without closing on the solid Rock. In Luke 10: 25-37, in the story of the good Samaritan, we have a traveler, some robbers, a priest, a Levite, a Samaritan, a lawyer, and the Savior—these seven characters and classes of characters in that beautiful and valuable story—and we have these three rules brought out in it. The robbers were the Iron Rule men. "There are many of us, he is alone; we will rob him, take what he has, and leave him dead or dying by the wayside." We can see they were Iron Rule people. There came along a priest, a model of religious zeal; he saw the man, and passed by on the other side. After him came a Levite, a prospective priest; he heard the man sigh or groan, came and looked at him, passed on, dropped into the path, and left the man to die. What rule do these men represent? The Silver Rule. Then there came along the good Samaritan. He heard the groan or sigh, saw the situation, went to the man; bound up his wounds, pouring in oil and wine; led the beast up, put the man upon it, carried him to a house, secured good quarters for him, stayed by and watched him until morning, paid the bill up to that time, and told the host to take care of the sick man, and whatever it cost he himself would pay it when he came again. What does he represent? The Golden Rule. The Savior approved it, the lawyer approved it, and the Savior said to the lawyer: "Go, and do thou likewise." And all the sons and daughters of the Lord Almighty who have come after have approved it—this principle of the Golden Rule: "All things whatsoever ye would that men should do to you, do ye even so to them."

Now, this is simple, practical Christianity; and when we come short of it, we simply come short of the duties and demands of the religion we profess. When we practice it, it makes us happy and useful, and God will bless us here and hereafter. We ask you to accept a religion of which this is the fundamental principle. And now, if there are any in this audience who are in any sense subjects of the gospel call, any who are desirous of coming out on the Lord's side to cast their lot with his followers, God is willing, Jesus is pleading, mercy is lingering, Heaven is waiting, and all that is necessary is for you to sublimely resolve to abandon sin and Satan, and then carry out that resolution, and God promises you pardon and salvation and blessedness in this life, and everlasting bliss in the home of the soul; and if this be the desire of any or all of you who are subjects of the gospel call, we give you, at the close of this last and final service of the day, a chance to come. Our hearts are pleading with you, our hearts are pleading with the great I Am in your behalf; while the angels who rejoice over one sinner who repents are ready to rejoice with joy unspeakable, if you will only come to Jesus now.

CHAPTER XIII.

LETTERS—THE UNITY OF THE CHURCH.

ACCORDING to the plain teaching of the New Testament, the church is a spiritual body, Christ is head
over it, every Christian is a member of it, and there is no
organization in it but local congregations. All Christians
are "one body in Christ;" there are "many members, yet
but one body;" that one body is the church. In New
Testament times the Christians in each locality formed, or
constituted, a congregation for religious work and worship.
Each local congregation thus formed or constituted was
the church—the body of Christ—in that place, and every
Christian in that locality belonged to it because he was a
Christian, and worshiped in it and worked through it because there was nothing else for any Christian to be a member of or to worship in and work through. Thus they kept
"the unity of the Spirit in the bond of peace." There
were no ecclesiastical organizations, denominational institutions, or partisan brotherhoods in Christianity in New
Testament times. Christ and all Christians were one, as
the vine and its branches are one.

"I am the true vine, and my Father is the husbandman.
Every branch in me that beareth not fruit he taketh away:
and every branch that beareth fruit, he purgeth it, that it
may bring forth more fruit. Now ye are clean through
the word which I have spoken unto you. Abide in me, and
I in you. As the branch cannot bear fruit of itself, except

it abide in the vine; no more can ye, except ye abide in me. I am the vine, ye are the branches: He that abideth in me, and I in him, the same bringeth forth much fruit: for without me ye can do nothing." (John 15: 1-5.)

The same truth is taught with equal clearness at another place by a slight change in the figure. Christ and all Christians are one, as the olive tree and its branches are one.

"And if some of the branches be broken off, and thou, being a wild olive tree, wert graffed in among them, and with them partakest of the root and fatness of the olive tree; boast not against the branches. But if thou boast, thou bearest not the root, but the root thee. Thou wilt say then, The branches were broken off, that I might be graffed in. Well; because of unbelief they were broken off, and thou standest by faith. Be not high-minded, but fear: for if God spared not the natural branches, take heed lest he also spare not thee. Behold therefore the goodness and severity of God: on them which fell, severity; but toward thee, goodness, if thou continue in his goodness: otherwise thou also shalt be cut off. And they also, if they abide not still in unbelief, shall be graffed in: for God is able to graff them in again." (Rom. 11: 17-23.)

At still another place the figure is changed again, but the truth which is no less plainly taught is the same. Christ and all Christians are one, as the body and its members are one.

" For as the body is one, and hath many members, and all the members of that one body, being many, are one body: so also is Christ. For by one Spirit are we all baptized into one body, whether we be Jews or Gentiles.

whether we be bond or free; and have been all made to drink into one Spirit. For the body is not one member, but many. . . . But now are they many members, yet but one body. . . . Now ye are the body of Christ, and members in particular." (1 Cor. 12: 12-27.)

"There is one body, and one Spirit, even as ye are called in one hope of your calling." (Eph. 4: 4.)

"For as we have many members in one body, and all members have not the same office: so we, being many, are one body in Christ, and every one members one of another." (Rom. 12: 4, 5.)

"And that he might reconcile both unto God in one body by the cross, having slain the enmity thereby." (Eph. 2: 16.)

"May grow up into him in all things, which is the head, even Christ; from whom the whole body fitly joined together and compacted by that which every joint supplieth, according to the effectual working in the measure of every part, maketh increase of the body unto the edifying of itself in love." (Eph. 4: 15, 16.)

This one body is the church.

"And hath put all things under his feet, and gave him to be the head over all things to the church, which is his body, the fullness of him that filleth all in all." (Eph. 1: 22, 23.)

"For the husband is the head of the wife, even as Christ is the head of the church; and he is the savior of the body." (Eph. 5: 23.)

"And he is the head of the body, the church; who is the beginning, the firstborn from the dead; that in all things he might have the preëminence." (Col. 1: 18.)

" Who now rejoice in my sufferings for you, and fill up that which is behind of the afflictions of Christ in my flesh for his body's sake, which is the church." (Col. 1: 24.)

This one body is all the church there is in the New Testament, and it is all the church any Christian has any scriptural authority to be a member of now. This church includes and consists of all Christians; it is the body of Christ, and every one who belongs to Christ is a member of it. The church in the New Testament is always spoken of as one, except when local organizations in different places are referred to, and then the church is one in each place. To be a member of it is to be a Christian, and to be a Christian is to be a member of it. Every man becomes a member of it when he becomes a Christian, and remains a member of it as long as he continues to be a Christian, because that which makes a man a Christian constitutes him a member of it. No one can be a Christian and not be a member of the church any more than he can be a Christian and not belong to Christ, because the church is the body of Christ, and it includes and consists of all Christians by the plain meaning of the passages above quoted.

The plain duty of Christians is to abandon and abolish everything but this one body, which is the church, and keep " the unity of the Spirit in the bond of peace " in this one body. The formation, operation, and propagation of ecclesiastical organizations, denominational institutions, and partisan brotherhoods in religion produce strife, contentions, animosities, alienations, envyings, and rivalries among Christians, and inevitably cause open divisions which gender an ugly, partisan spirit in the body of Christ. The logical effect and constant tendency of the truth of God is to disintegrate and dissolve everything but the " one body in Christ," which is the church, and of which every Christian is a member, whether the preacher intends to do that or not, or whether he so much as knows of the existence of anything but the one body in the way of a religious institution.   The following quotation from one of his letters is in point here:

" They claim and charge that I preach against certain things, but never name them.   I simply ' preach the word,' ' unlearned questions avoid,' meddle not with other men's matters, and exhort all to ' walk in the light,' to simply take God at his word—that is, believe what he says, do what he commands, become and be what he requires, live as he directs, and trust him for what he promises.   That's all there is in that—absolutely all.   My preaching is Bible preaching.   I never try to prove any point in preaching, save by the Bible.   I just simply tell them what the Bible says, and then tell them that settles that.   At the conclusion of a successful series of meetings in ' Uncle Charlie's church,' as everybody calls it, in Bonham, Texas, in the spring of 1892, ' Uncle Charlie,' as he is affectionately called—President Charles Carlton—said to an audience that literally packed the house, and repeated it with all the emphasis and power that even he could throw into it: ' You have heard more scripture quoted—accurately quoted, too; book, chapter, and verse being given for every word quoted —in this series of meetings than in all the days of your lives besides, and you know it.'   He then called upon all who appreciated and fully indorsed my preaching and my course to say so by standing up.   Then, having requested any one who might dissent to stand up, he declared the in-

SUMMER VISITORS AT MARS' HILL.

dorsement to be unanimous, and urged all to never forget it. If my preaching, then, decapitates, uproots, and demolishes things, I am not to blame. I never sit in the pulpit or on the platform, if I can help it, and I usually help it. I sit down with the congregation till time to preach. I never, if I can avoid it, stand behind anything when I preach. I want not even so much as a table, a chair, or a grudge between me and my audience. I always read, and usually comment upon, a lesson, then reread the text— that's all. I never read anything when I am preaching —never. Every line of scripture in every sermon after I leave the text and begin to talk is quoted, and book, chapter, and verse are given, from memory."

The charge that he " preaches against certain things, but never names them," is no doubt true and false both. Any man who preaches exactly what is in the Bible, and nothing else, necessarily preaches against everything that antagonizes the Bible, whether he names other things or not, or even so much as knows whether there be any such things. No man can build up things that are not in the Bible without preaching something that is not in the Bible. In this sense the charge is no doubt true; but if the charge is intended to mean that he preaches against things designedly by cowardly insinuations and innuendoes, while pretending to be in favor of them, the charge is untrue and unjust. How can any man preach and practice exactly what is in the Bible, and nothing else, without disintegrating and dissolving, to the full extent of his influence in life and sermons, everything but the " one body in Christ," which is the church and of which every Christian is a member?

" Every plant, which my Heavenly Father hath not planted, shall be rooted up." (Matt. 15: 13.) The Heavenly Father hath planted no plant in the way of a religious organization or institution, save the body of Christ, which is the church. The plain duty of every one is, therefore, to be a Christian, and nothing else; be a member of the church, which is the body of Christ, and of which every Christian is a member, and nothing else; preach and practice all the New Testament teaches, and nothing else. The aim and constant effort of the life that is photographed by private letters in this volume have been to do this, as numerous letters, extending over a long period of years, abundantly show. On this point he wrote, several years ago:

" I am more and more confirmed in my irrevocable determination to never be a partisan in any sense; to look, in the light of God's eternal truth, straightforward to the New Jerusalem, ' preach the word ' with all the power granted me, and do all I can to comfort and save souls. That is where I am, and I am there to stay. I may be rather lonely, but I propose to stand there, if, Elijahlike, I feel so lonely as to be constrained to implore the Almighty to take away my life. Standing on the rock, building on the rock, my soul shall ever be secure. The storm rages now, but the time is coming when those who have stood with ' God, and the word of his grace,' will be appreciated. Let us bide our time. You may have no fears. You may always know—absolutely know—you run no risk in saying that I am in no sense a partisan; that I simply ' preach the word,' and leave results with God. I have always tried to do this, but have sometimes been drawn aside just a little;

never thus again. I propose to, as long as I live, adhere strictly to the Bible. In that way I can do a glorious work. On any other line my work could not fail to be a failure. No religious party may appreciate or demand my services, but on the Lord's side I am safe, though solitary and alone. Some will interpret this to mean I have no convictions, or, having convictions, have more policy than principle, but 'none of these things move me.' My position and determination are: 'Preach the word' wherever Providence seems to point the way and duty seems to demand; always hew to the line; have no hobbies, attack no hobbies; do always and under all circumstances exactly what duty demands. This is all I can do."

At another time, years ago, he wrote:

"All who know me know I am an extremist, so far as standing aloof from everything that causes strife and division among Christians is concerned, everything that is rending the church—the body of Christ—into factions. In this, as in many other things, I may be wrong; but I believe I am right, and I am trying to do my duty. I have never intentionally aided or encouraged divisions, but have always, both publicly and privately, urged Christian union and Christian unity with all my feeble might. So far as I know, I belong to nothing except that to which every Christian in the wide, wide world belongs. Thus publicly, privately, and practically I preach and practice unity all the time. I was born into the family of the Lord Almighty about twenty-seven years ago, and by the grace of God I hope to be faithful as a member of that blessed family till called to my reward, and to never be a member of any-

thing else.   Let others do as they may, the church of God
is good enough for me.   I have solemnly resolved to try to
keep my eye on the ' open, pearly portal,' and go straight
forward, neither turning nor looking to the right or the
left—simply ' preach the word,' and let professed Christians adjust their differences and difficulties in bitterness
and blood, if they will.   My earnest desire is to keep entirely out of all unpleasant wrangles among Christians.   I
do not censure those who are in it, but I must keep out of
it, if I can.   Now, if people want no preacher but a partisan preacher, they will please not call for me.   I propose to finish my course without ever, even for one
moment, engaging in partisan strife with anybody about
anything."

When this letter was read to him in the manuscript prepared for this book, he opened the Bible and read aloud,
without comment:

" 'And the servant of the Lord must not strive; but be
gentle unto all men, apt to teach, patient, in meekness instructing those that oppose themselves; if God peradventure will give them repentance to the acknowledging of the
truth; and that they may recover themselves out of the
snare of the devil, who are taken captive by him at his
will.' "   (2 Tim. 2: 24-26.)

Explaining why he never attends religious conventions,
he wrote:

" I never attend conventions of any kind.   I never have
the money; I never have the time.   In all the years I have
been preaching, I have baptized hundreds, if not thousands,

of people, while others—it may be, better than I—were attending conventions. I was doing what I believed to be my duty; they, of course, were doing the same. As to how I have spent the money I did not have to pay my expenses to conventions—well, you know where and how many hundreds of dollars of it have gone. I have never spoken of it, but during the time, the very days, set apart by many good people last year to attend a convention, under my labors eighty souls were added to the Lord. It is true I worked—preached three times and went into the water once, and sometimes twice, to baptize every day; but that was better for me—body, soul, and spirit—than attending a convention. Had I gone to the convention, the expenses had been at least thirty dollars. That thirty dollars went the way I thought it would do the most good. Conventions are a costly luxury—too costly for me to enjoy. As to where I preach, I go where I think I can do the most good. Probably I may never be able to convince some of this, but I always go and do where and as I deem best for the cause of Christ."

From a city where a religious convention met while he was in a meeting, he wrote:

" Doubtless they will expect me to take part in the convention which meets here while I am engaged in this meeting. Well, they wouldn't, if they knew me. Of course they believe it is their duty to work in the convention, else they would not be here; I know I believe it is my duty to work with all my might all my time in this meeting, else I would not be here. I do not expect them to neglect their duty in the convention to take part in the meeting; why should they expect me to neglect my duty in the meeting to take part in the convention? "

His proposition to "belong to nothing except that to which every Christian in the wide, wide world belongs; " "publicly, privately, and practically preach and practice union and unity all the time; " and "keep entirely out of all unpleasant wrangles among Christians," is eminently correct and scriptural, and "a consummation devoutly to be wished," but it is hard to do. Speaking of things which have most discouraged him in the "ministry of the word," he wrote:

"Discouragements: Envying, strife, and division; hatred, discord, and dissensions; evil surmisings, speakings, and doings; lack of love, liberality, gentleness, goodness, faith, meekness, temperance, zeal, energy, earnestness, enthusiasm, forbearance, forgiveness, patience, politeness, prayerfulness, promptness, purity, consecration, and sanctification among professed followers of the Lamb—these be the things that have discouraged me most, my own shortcomings and evil doings excepted, of course; still, I must not, do not, complain, and certainly have neither right nor reason to boast."

In the midst of a meeting, while trying hard to "keep entirely out of all unpleasant wrangles among Christians," when such wrangles were raging all around him, he wrote:

"The storm cloud is dark and threatening. It is a struggle between the church and all sorts of societies, suppers, festivals, and frolics 'for the benefit of the church.' If I have kept the count correctly, there are thirteen factions in the fracas. I may have failed to count some I have heard of, and there may be others yet to hear from. One trouble is, Christians here, in little squads, obey the good old song,

"'Observe your leader, follow him;'

and 'him' is always a man, if he is not a woman. Why can't Christians learn to be guided in all things by the Bible and follow Christ in everything? That is easy, and it is right."

In another meeting, while doing his very best to " belong to nothing except that to which every Christian in the wide, wide world belongs," he wrote:

" My home is at the home of a good brother whose Christian wife is ' presidentess ' of so many societies and things that it is bewildering to think of how much she has to do in the name of societies, and how little time she has to even think of doing anything simply ' in the name of the Lord,' to build up the blessed church, to establish which he shed his precious blood."

No one but a man who has tried it knows how hard it is, under such circumstances, to " belong to nothing except that to which every Christian in the wide, wide world belongs," without getting into a " wrangle " with somebody.

In a meeting at another place, when they had him more closely cornered still, he wrote:

" Sister —— says her preacher says: ' We must belong to something.' That means, in the context, the church is nothing. I doubt not that preacher believes Christians— members of the church of God—are nothing unless they belong to something."

BAPTIZING IN CREEK AT MARS' HILL, ANNUAL MEETING IN AUGUST.

When troubled by a faction of Christian Scientists, he inclosed the following newspaper clipping in a letter:

"Speaking of mind healing, John Gilmer Speed writes, in Leslie's Weekly: 'Some years ago a young friend of mine went to a mind healer for a lark. There was nothing in the world the matter with him, but he pretended to be the victim of terrible headaches. The wonderful healer asked no questions as to the cause of the ailment. He did not care about that, for he had one panacea which sufficed for every evil. Said he to the young investigator: "Go home, and whenever the headache comes on, sit down quietly and put your whole mind on it, thinking with all your might that you have not got a headache; then you will not have it, and will be cured." "That's easy," said my young friend. "What is your fee?" "Five dollars." "Well, sir, you put your whole mind on it and think with all your might that you have that five dollars; then you will have it, and will be paid."'"

In 1899 I had a discussion with Brother J. N. Hall, of the Baptist denomination, which was published simultaneously in the Gospel Advocate and the American Baptist Flag. In that discussion I affirmed and Hall denied that the church includes and consists of all Christians, and the same process which makes a man a Christian adds him to the one body—the church. Referring to this discussion, he wrote:

"Of course I shall read your discussion with Brother Hall. You ought to drop all other work and write a book on the church, after you collect all you can of what Hall and others say against your position—the Bible position—

on that subject. A book from you on the church of God is badly and sadly needed. While I live I am at your service, to the limit of my ability, whatsoever may be your general or special line of work; but I think the most important work before you now is to write a book on the church of God. Certainly that is needed, if anything is. The people seem to know as little about that as some doctors of divinity know about the gospel. Scarcely a sod has been turned on the broad bosom of that vast plain, save what your plow has turned, and you have simply plowed in spots. You may die—though I hope you may live many years after I am gone—and you ought to write that book now, lest you defer it till it is too late. If you had such a book ready now, I believe I could serve humanity to no better purpose than to aid in circulating it."

As an indication of public sentiment on this subject, the following newspaper clipping from a speech in an international convention was inclosed in his letter:

"President E. B. Andrews, of Brown University, Baptist: 'It is the great vice of denominationalism that it tends to ignore the church's unity and leads to the sin of schism. This is the characteristic guilt of the ultra-Protestant world to-day—of Baptists, Congregationalists, Methodists, and Presbyterians. We have a sharp sense of denomination, but almost no sense of church.'"

The following letter, written at the close of a meeting where Christians had long been divided into factions, indicates his idea as to the proper way to settle strife and promote unity among Christians:

" Eighty souls added to the Lord during the meeting—
nine the last discourse. Church troubles—none there.
A good way not to fix a church trouble is to try to fix it.
A good, sure way to unite forty pieces of lead into one
piece, leaving neither crack nor crevice between, is to warm
them up and give them a chance to get together; hands off
—that's all."

After I had read to him and he had approved the manuscript of this chapter down to this point, he inclosed the
first page clipped from the Gospel Advocate of March 15,
1900, and wrote:

" This is a glorious page. It digs things up by the roots
—things pestiferous and pernicious. This page is valuable. 'It's all wool and a yard wide.' I remember you
touch some of these things in the manuscript you have read
me for the book we are now working on. I hope you will
make them strong as possible in the book. Never hesitate
to give strength, in love and kindness of manner and style,
to anything in the book. I look to you for the strength
as well as the sense and symmetry of the book in the arrangement of all my sermons and letters and clippings.
Never hesitate to do what you deem best."

The clipping referred to is in two paragraphs. The first
paragraph is as follows:

" The following card states a difficulty and asks a question:

" ' Protection, Kan., February 24, 1900.—Of what religious denomination is the Gospel Advocate? I have
searched the paper for its religious views in vain. I know

it advocates immersion, which I like; but I cannot deter-mine whether it is of the Baptist or Campbellite persuasion. Please let me know.   Address Mrs. S. A. Ross.'

" Of what religious denomination is the New Testament? The Gospel Advocate tries to be exactly like the New Testa-ment in teaching and practice, without regard to religious denominations, and it always states its ' religious views ' as clearly as it can.   Has anybody ever searched the New Testament carefully to see ' of what religious denomina-tion ' it is?   Nobody understands that the New Testament is of any denomination.   There were no denominations in New Testament times, and there ought to be none now. All Christians were ' one body in Christ, and every one members one of another,' in those days, and they ought to be that way yet.   That ' one body in Christ ' was the church, and every Christian was a member of it.   Every Christian is a member of that same body now, and no one has any scriptural authority to belong to anything else. The Gospel Advocate is of that ' one body in Christ,' which is the church, and it is not of anything else.   It belongs to no denomination; it opposes all denominations.   It is not of the Baptist persuasion, nor yet is it of the Campbellite persuasion.   It is persuaded to be a Christian, and noth-ing else; to belong to the church, which is the body of Christ, and nothing else; to preach and practice everything Christians preached and practiced in New Testament times, and nothing else.   Is that right?   If not, why not? "

The second paragraph referred to in his letter reads thus:

" The following letter is worthy of attention in these columns because of the important question it raises:

- 15 -

" ' Palestine, Ark., February 27, 1900.—Dear Brother Srygley: As you have done so much to enlighten the readers of the Gospel Advocate on the church question, will you please give us a lesson on the " invisible church " theory? I got a Methodist to read your discussion with J. N. Hall. He says that you " did up " J. N. Hall, but that it is the " invisible church." Please dig up the " invisible church " theory, and greatly oblige your brother in Christ,

" ' RYAN BENNETT.'

" I am not sure I know what the ' invisible church theory ' is. If people would ' speak as the oracles of God speak,' they would never talk about the ' visible church ' and the ' invisible church.' There are no such expressions in the Bible, and if there is any such idea in the Bible, it ought to be expressed in the exact words of the Bible. We would then be sure we have the exact Bible idea. Any idea that is in the Bible can be expressed in the exact words of the Bible; any idea that cannot be expressed in the exact words of the Bible is not a Bible idea. There is but one church in the Bible; it is the body of Christ, and all Christians are members of it. ' There is one body, and one Spirit, even as ye are called in one hope of your calling.' (Eph. 4: 4.) ' For as we have many members in one body, and all members have not the same office: so we, being many, are one body in Christ, and every one members one of another.' (Rom. 12: 4, 5.) ' For the husband is the head of the wife, even as Christ is the head of the church; and he is the Savior of the body.' (Eph. 5: 23.) 'And hath put all things under his feet, and gave him to be the head over all things to the church, which is his body, the fullness of him that filleth all in all.' (Eph. 1: 22, 23.) 'And he is the head of the body, the church: who is the beginning, the firstborn from the dead; that in all things he might have the preëminence.' (Col. 1: 18.) 'Who now rejoice in my sufferings for you, and fill up that which is behind of the afflictions of Christ in my flesh for his body's sake, which is the church.' (Col. 1: 24.) 'For as the body is one, and hath many members, and all the members of that one body, being many, are one body: so also is Christ. For by one Spirit are we all baptized into one body, whether we be Jews or Gentiles, whether we be bond or free; and have been all made to drink into one Spirit. For the body is not one member, but many. . . . But now are they many members, yet but one body. . . . Now ye are the body of Christ, and members in particular.' (1 Cor. 12: 12-27.) The church is as visible as Christians, for Christians are the church. There was no organization in New Testament times for religious work or worship but local congregations. The Christians in any locality and in every locality were the church—the body of Christ—in that place. The thing that is 'invisible' in the New Testament is ecclesiastical or denominational organization of every kind. There is absolutely no organization but local congregations in the New Testament, and there is no scriptural authority for any other organization now. The one and only church in the New Testament is the body of Christ; every Christian is a member of it; and there is no organization but local congregations in it. That which makes a man a Christian constitutes him a member of the church, and every Christian belongs to and works and worships in and through the local congregation wherever he is.

Everything else ought to be dug up; and if I cannot dig it up, God can, and he will. 'Every plant, which my Heavenly Father hath not planted, shall be rooted up.' (Matt. 15: 13.)"

CHAPTER XIV.

SERMON——THE PRAYER ON THE CROSS.

PILATE therefore, willing to release Jesus, spake again to them. But they cried, saying, Crucify him, crucify him. And he said unto them the third time, Why, what evil hath he done? I have found no cause of death in him: I will therefore chastise him, and let him go. And they were instant with loud voices [listening to no reason, regarding no right], requiring that he might be crucified. And the voices of them and of the chief priests prevailed [that Jesus should be crucified]. And Pilate gave sentence that it should be as they required. And he released unto them him that for sedition and murder was cast into prison, whom they had desired; but he delivered Jesus to their will. And as they led him away, they laid hold upon one Simon, a Cyrenian, coming out of the country, and on him they laid the cross, that he might bear it after Jesus.

"And there followed him a great company of people, and of women, which also bewailed and lamented him. But Jesus turning unto them said, Daughters of Jerusalem, weep not for me, but weep for yourselves, and for your children. For, behold, the days are coming, in the which they shall say, Blessed are the barren, and the wombs that never bare, and the paps which never gave suck. Then shall they begin to say to the mountains, Fall on us; and to the hills, Cover us. For if they do these things in a green tree, what shall be done in the dry? And there were

also two other, malefactors, led with him to be put to death.
And when they were come to the place, which is called Calvary, there they crucified him, and the malefactors, one
on the right hand, and the other on the left.

"Then said Jesus, Father, forgive them; for they know
not what they do. And they parted his raiment, and cast
lots. And the people stood beholding. And the rulers
also with them derided him, saying, He saved others; let
him save himself, if he be Christ, the chosen of God. And
the soldiers also mocked him, coming to him, and offering
him vinegar, and saying, If thou be the king of the Jews,
save thyself. And a superscription also was written over
him in letters of Greek, and Latin, and Hebrew, THIS IS
THE KING OF THE JEWS." (Luke 23: 20-38.)

"Then said Jesus, Father, forgive them; for they know
not what they do. And they parted his raiment, and cast
lots." (Verse 34.)

Language of the loving Lord under most trying circumstances; a prayer to the Father for those who nailed him
to the cross and cursed him as he died: "Father, forgive
them; for they know not what they do." The human race
is accustomed to striking contrasts. The hovel stands in
the shadow of the palace; the pauper and the millionaire
pass each other on the street; the bridal veil and the shroud
touch each other. The life of Jesus presents some striking
contrasts. The Babe of Bethlehem, the Child of poverty
in Mary's arms, had been the darling object of God's delight, his constant companion and bosom friend, from all
eternity, and had stood at the foot of the throne of God,
with admiring angels around, rejoicing to cast their crowns
before him, while the stars that glitter were but dust be-

neath his feet. The Man of sorrows, poorer than the foxes of the fields and the birds of the air, so poor that he had not where to lay his head, and the One that created all things—all things are created by him and for him; that sighing, suffering Son of the living God, kneeling down thrice upon the bosom of gloomy Gethsemane, while the mantle of dark night was thrown around him, pouring out his soul in prayer to the Lord Almighty to remove from him the bitter cup he was about to drink, is the one who had a few weeks before that stood transfigured upon Hermon's holy height, with Peter, James, and John, Moses and Elias, around him, while he is enveloped in a bright cloud, from the bosom of which came the voice of Jehovah, saying: " This is my beloved Son: hear him." But all the contrasts that are presented to us do not show the Savior in a more glorious point of view, so far as the attractiveness of his divine spirit is concerned, than when on the cross he prayed for his murderers: " Father, forgive them; for they know not what they do."

When the Savior offered that prayer, the circumstances were such as to make us surrender body, soul, and spirit to his service. He was no intruder on earth. He had been sent by the Father in mercy to save a lost and ruined, wrecked and recreant, race. While God had sent him, he had gladly come, being glad to do the Father's will, and glad especially to do anything that might stay the tide of sin and lift the sons and daughters of men from their wrecked and ruined state and bring them home to God. He had lived one-third of a century in this world, the average length of life to-day. That life had been a life of purity and love divine. He had been unselfish, sympa-

thetic, merciful, long-suffering, forbearing, and kind; but
the spirit of partisan prejudice, the blindest and bitterest
spirit that has ever cursed the human race, had planned
for his destruction in a way that would give him most in-
tense misery, and the most of it possible, ending with his
death. He had been tried before Pilate, who found no
evil in him. Pilate had thrice asked the throng clamoring
for his crucifixion, "What evil hath he done?" and had
received no response, but they clamored louder for his crucifixion. He had been dragged up Calvary and nailed to
the cross. The great, surging mob was reviling him and
sneering at his claims to be divine. Losing all sight of his
sympathy, and his real mission, and his unselfishness, they
demanded that he demonstrate his divinity now by saving
himself and refusing to die, if he be what he claimed to be,
not understanding that that would be to thwart the purposes of God and his own purposes and leave the human
race unsaved. He called for a drink of water, but they
refused to grant him even that. The material universe
was sympathizing with him. The moment was at hand
when the rocks around Jerusalem should crumble, and the
veil of the temple should be rent from bottom to top; when
the graves should open and many of the saints be seen;
when the solar system should be darkened; when the whole
vast universe was to be convulsed, and this old earth was
to roll and rock like a bubble upon the bosom of the sea.
Notwithstanding all this, that howling mob had no sympathy; and yet he was dying for the people in that mob,
for those they loved and for those that loved them. But
instead of considering the sympathizing material universe;
instead of for that moment thinking of the mother who

bore him, and of the friends who loved him, and of the blessed women—last before the cross, first at the tomb, and first to go and tell the glad tidings of the resurrection—he spends in behalf of his murderous enemies breath that might have been spent in pleading for himself or his friends: "Father, forgive them; for they know not what they do."

There is a wonderful lesson here for us all. We should appreciate this lesson and learn from it to love the Savior all the more because of the spirit manifested in this prayer, and then walk in his footsteps and try to be like him. The Savior teaches all these things, not only by example, but by precept, admonition, exhortation, and advice. "Ye have heard that it hath been said, Thou shalt love thy neighbor, and hate thine enemy. But I say unto you, Love your enemies, bless them that curse you, do good to them that hate you, and pray for them which despitefully use you, and persecute you; that ye may be the children of your Father which is in heaven: for he maketh his sun to rise on the evil and on the good, and sendeth rain on the just and on the unjust." (Matt. 5: 43-45.) Is not that the way he did? Did he not, under most trying circumstances, pray for his enemies: "Father, forgive them; for they know not what they do?" If there are any in this audience who are not children of the living God who think they could not do that, they should at least come to God and try to do it; if there are any who are Christians who cannot do that, they should not be discouraged or give up the struggle, but study more and more the things the Savior has taught in language and in life, and learn to love him better and admire his example more, and grow

more and more like him. When Peter drew his sword in
Gethsemane, on the night of the betrayal, and commenced
using it in defense of his Lord and Master, Jesus immediately rebuked him gently; told him to put up his sword,
that they who took the sword should perish with the sword;
and said unto him: " Thinkest thou that I cannot now pray
to my Father, and he shall presently give me more than
twelve legions of angels? But how then shall the scriptures be fulfilled, that thus it must be?"   (Matt. 26: 53,
54.) And then he healed the injured man, submitted himself to the mob, was dragged to Jerusalem, and then to Calvary, and nailed to the cross whereon he died. It had
been written, and the Scriptures must be fulfilled. The
salvation of a lost and ruined race depended upon the fulfillment of that scripture. Had he then summoned more
than sixty thousand, or twelve legions, of angels, and destroyed all his enemies, and escaped out of the hands of
the mob that had come to destroy him, then the purposes
of God had been destroyed, the Scriptures had not been
fulfilled, and man had not been saved. So we can see in
that a good reason—yea, many wonderful reasons—why
the Savior did not rescue himself from the mob, or destroy
the mob, as he could easily have done by praying to the
Father for a legion of angels to execute his will, had that
been his will. But when he offered the prayer on the
cross, " Father, forgive them; for they know not what they
do," he had already been arrested in Gethsemane, he had
submitted to the injustice heaped upon him in reference
to his trial, he had already been dragged up Calvary and
nailed to the cross, and was already in a dying condition,
and it only remained for him to cry aloud and give up the

ghost, and all had been ended. So he might have wreaked vengeance on that mob then. He might have called down swift and sudden and certain destruction upon every enemy he had in all that mob, and still not have interfered with the fulfillment of the prophecy that thus it must be, but he did not do it. We cannot say that, instead of destroying that mob, he prayed for those who murdered him because if he had destroyed them man had not been redeemed; but we must look to another source for the reason for his doing as he did. There is but one reason: he was filled with love divine and with sympathy for a lost and ruined race that was perfectly sublime. So, while he had the power to summon more than twelve legions of angels from the presence of God to destroy every foe he had in the twinkling of an eye, instead of that, he lifted up his voice and prayed: " Father, forgive them; for they know not what they do." Nothing but the purest love, the sublimest, sincerest sympathy, ever induced the Savior to offer that wonderful prayer. We ought to love him all the more and appreciate him all the more because of the spirit that was manifested in that prayer, and we should show our love and demonstrate our appreciation by trying to be as much like him as we can. It was nothing unusual for the Savior to pray. On the night before he chose his apostles he prayed all night upon the lonely summit of a towering mountain. (Luke 16: 12, 13.) He withdrew himself from the presence of mortals, climbed the summit of a mountain, and there, beneath the silent, listening stars, he prayed to God from dark to dawn. He then came down from the mountain to the plain and chose his twelve disciples, to go forth, filled with the divine Spirit, to labor in love according to his will for the salvation of poor, lost, and ruined souls. This teaches us that, if we have anything important before us, we should pray, not only in public, but especially in private. On another occasion, at the close of the day he ascended to the summit of the mountain to pray to God, remained in prayer until late at night, and as it drew on toward the fourth watch of the night, realizing that a tempest had swept down upon the deep, he descended the mountain, walked upon the waves, stilled the tempest, calmed the trouble and relieved the fears of his disciples, who were tossed upon the bosom of the deep and who expected to die in the terrible storm sweeping around them. (Matt. 14: 23-33.) In Gethsemane, on the night of the betrayal, Jesus prayed. (Matt. 26: 37-45.) He withdrew himself from his disciples, and, kneeling down upon the bosom of gloomy Gethsemane, while in agony he sweat great drops of blood, he prayed to God for relief, if man might be saved without his drinking of the bitter cup so near his lips, but always saying: "Nevertheless not my will, but thine, be done." Jesus prayed for Peter, that he might not fall into the hands of Satan, told Peter so, and said to him: "When thou art converted, strengthen thy brethren." (Luke 22: 31, 32.) The whole of John 17 is a prayer, except a few words in the beginning. Jesus finished his labors here upon the earth, just before being translated to heaven, with a fervent prayer. He led his disciples as far out as Bethany, lifted up his hands and blessed them, and while he was blessing them a cloud received him out of their sight, carrying him home to glory. (Luke 24: 50, 51.)

But the sublimest of all his prayers was the prayer, when

he was on the cross, for the wicked men who murdered him:
" Father, forgive them; for they know not what they do."
Would the Lord Almighty hear and answer this prayer?
Whose prayers will he hear? Solomon says: " The sacrifice of the wicked is an abomination to the Lord: but the
prayer of the upright is his delight." (Prov. 15: 8.) " He
that turneth away his ear from hearing the law, even his
prayer shall be abomination." (Prov. 28: 9.) " Now we
know that God heareth not sinners: but if any man be a
worshiper of God, and doeth his will, him he heareth."
(John 9: 31.) " Finally, be ye all of one mind, having
compassion one of another, love as brethren, be pitiful, be
courteous: not rendering evil for evil, or railing far railing:
but contrariwise blessing; knowing that ye are thereunto
called, that ye should inherit a blessing. For he that will
love life, and see good days, let him refrain his tongue from
evil, and his lips that they speak no guile: let him eschew
evil, and do good; let him seek peace, and ensue it. For
the eyes of the Lord are over the righteous, and his ears are
open unto their prayers: but the face of the Lord is against
them that do evil." (1 Pet. 3: 8-12.) " Confess your
faults one to another, and pray one for another, that ye may
be healed. The effectual fervent prayer of a righteous
man availeth much." (James 5: 16.) Now, in the light
of these passages of scripture, we can all see and understand
whom God will hear in prayer and whom he will not hear
in prayer. We may not agree with the Lord Almighty,
we may not be willing to accept the truth, but we can see
and understand, in the light of these scriptures, what God
says about it. Our not being on the Lord's side, but on the
other side, will not prevent us from seeing what God says

about it.   Was Jesus a character that Jehovah would hear, when we look at him in the light of the life he lived and in the light of these passages of scripture showing whom God will hear in prayer?   Certainly we cannot question that. What was the character of the one who offered this prayer? He was simply immaculate; always as sinless as an inno- cent child, as harmless as a lamb, as innocent as a dove, as divine as Jehovah, as pure as the Holy Spirit himself; no guile upon his lips, no deception in his heart; sympathetic, loving, true, and pure; long-suffering, self-denying, self- sacrificing, and kind; dominated always by his desire to do the Father's will, and filled with love and sympathy all the days of his painful pilgrimage upon the earth; doing good ever, doing harm never; blessing his friends and blessing his foes; demonstrating the sublimity of that spirit in the very prayer under consideration, crying, under the most trying circumstances: " Father, forgive them; for they know not what they do."   What was the character of the people for whom he prayed?   All of us understand, of course, that it was very bad.   We are told that Pilate knew " that for envy they had delivered him up " unto death. They composed the howling mob to which Pilate thrice propounded the question, " Why, what evil hath he done?" the response being instantaneous, coming from them as if they had but one voice: " Crucify him, crucify him!   It is not meet that such a fellow should live on the earth! " This mob was composed of the men who condemned the Savior before he was bought, and bought him before he was betrayed; who wrested judgment from him when it was in his favor; who crowned him with thorns, spit upon him, buffeted him with their hands, struck him with reeds, dragged him to Calvary, nailed him to the cross, and mocked him as he died. It surely required the sublimest spirit to offer a prayer of any kind for good for such a mob as that. And what was the prayer? It was the only prayer that could do good to those people: " Father, forgive them; for they know not what they do." Of course that prayer was used in its broadest sense. When the petition was " Forgive them," the Savior willed that all their sins be blotted out, but especially he had reference to what they were doing, for he mentioned that: " Father, forgive them; *for they know not what they do* "—showing unquestionably that he had under consideration that very sin.

Was that prayer ever answered? There is no father or mother on earth—a civilized one—I am sure, with intelligence enough to be responsible in the sight of God and amenable to the laws of any civilized land, who would not gladly grant any reasonable, loving, unselfish request coming from a son or daughter in the hour of death. Well, this was the loving Son of Jehovah, in his dying hour, making this request of the Lord Almighty himself. Shall we say the Lord would not hear such a prayer as that, coming from such a source, under such circumstances, at such a time? Surely God would not refuse to answer that prayer, and not only answer it, but answer it in the way that his beloved Son willed him to answer it when he prayed: " Father, forgive them; for they know not what they do." Surely we poor worms of the dust, even though redeemed by the blood of the Lamb, justified by faith, and saved by the grace of God, may never hope that any of our prayers are to be answered, if we cannot believe that Jehovah answered that prayer of his obedient Son in the solemn hour of his tragic death. Surely God answered that prayer—answered the prayer just as it was intended in the heart of his dying Son. Hence, just what Jesus prayed for, just what the prayer was in the soul of Christ, whatever that was that found expression upon his quivering lips, God certainly heard and answered.

And now I want to ask another question, an intensely practical question; one that no pen, save the pen of inspiration, has ever touched, so far as I know; but a question, nevertheless, that all of us ought to ponder well—a question that ought to be propounded in the pulpit, from the rivers to the ends of the earth, and answered according to the word of the living God. When was that prayer answered? It was not answered instantaneously, then and there; it was not answered previous to the death of Christ, which occurred a few moments after he offered that prayer. That did not keep him from offering it, however, and that did not keep it from being answered. And this ought to suggest a thought to us: if we have been praying for the reformation and salvation of loved ones for forty years, and they seem to be as far away from reformation and salvation as when we commenced praying for them, we ought not to give up the struggle; and if we realize that the death moment is at hand and we are going to leave this world before our prayers are answered, and leave the loved ones behind us, in the midst of all the temptations of earth, we not to be here to pray for them any more, we ought not to doubt that God will bless them, and we should not hesitate to offer up the same earnest prayer; but even after our lips have ceased to talk to earthly friends, our souls can breathe this prayer to God.

That prayer was not answered before the resurrection of the Lord Jesus Christ. When he burst the bars of death and rose the triumphant Conqueror over death, hell, and the grave, bringing life and immortality to light, he did not hear that that prayer had been answered and his murderers forgiven, for they had not been forgiven. He then spent forty days upon the earth, doing the work that God had appointed him to do in that period of time between his resurrection and ascension; and when he entered God's eternal home, and was crowned with glory, coronated King of kings and Lord of lords, that prayer had not been answered. As certainly as God is God, and Christ is Christ, and the Bible is the Book of God's truth, that prayer had not been answered when Jesus was coronated King of kings in glory.

When, one week after that time, the Holy Spirit, by the will of God and the direction of the Savior, descended from the courts of glory and took up his abode in the one hundred and twenty disciples, and the apostle Peter stood up with the eleven and called that vast assembly of men and women to hear, that prayer had not been answered.

How do we know these things? It is important that we know them, and that we know how we know them. We know them by knowing what the Bible teaches on the subject. The Bible teaches that when God forgives sins he forgives them. We, in a half-hearted way, halfway forgive sins; but they are not forgiven at all, and three days after we have said that we forgive them we are thinking of them just as we did before we said we forgave them— some of us, sometimes. Not so with Jehovah; with him forgiveness is forgiveness, and we are told that when he

forgives he remembers the sins against those he has forgiven, or pardoned, " no more." " This is the covenant
that I will make with them after those days, saith the Lord,
I will put my laws into their hearts, and in their minds will
I write them; and their sins and iniquities will I remember
no more. Now where remission of these is, there is no
more offering for sin." (Heb. 10: 16-18.) That applies
to all cases, of course, but it was written in reference to the
new institution, guaranteeing forgiveness of sins in connection with that. So, then, if we can find out that God remembers and holds a sin against a man, we may know, just
as certainly as God is God, that that sin has never been forgiven by Jehovah. Here is an honest merchant doing a
small business, so he attends to it himself. He is a straightforward, conscientious, godly man. Now, there being an
account standing on his books against you, not marked can-
celed or satisfied in any way, is an evidence that you owe
him, and his reminding you of it himself, or sending his
son to remind you of it, is additional evidence that you owe
it, that it has not been paid. After it has been paid, he
does not hold it against you any longer. But he might
make a mistake, might forget that it has been satisfied; but
God does not make any mistakes, and God declares that
when he forgives sins he remembers them no more. So,
then, if we find that he remembers certain sins against certain characters, then we know, as surely as God is God, that
he has not forgiven those sins. The apostle Peter on this
occasion was surrounded by an immense multitude of people—the very same people that constituted the howling
mob around the cross on which Jesus died, and for whom
Jesus prayed that prayer. It was in the city of Jerusalem,

where Jesus was tried and where he was crucified. And now the apostle Peter, the representative of Jehovah, under the guidance of the Holy Spirit—it being God talking by the tongue of Peter—said to these people: " Ye . . . by wicked hands have crucified and slain." He had before him the very people for whom Jesus prayed, and he remembered their sin and reminded them of it. Peter brought these things to bear upon them to such an extent that it overwhelmed them. He brought down a bright flash of flaming thunderbolts from the arsenal of God on high upon their guilty souls, dark with the blood of the Lamb whom they had slain, until they were terrified and overwhelmed, when Peter reminded them that they were still guilty of the murder of God's Son. If that does not show that God had not answered that prayer, we have no use for the Bible; nor language, nor logic, nor wisdom, nor knowledge, nor all combined, can ever show anything, if that does not show that that prayer had not been answered. What does that show? It shows that the time had not come for the guilty to be pardoned; that the conditions had not been complied with; that they had not placed themselves in such relations to God that God could answer that prayer without creating spiritual anarchy. When they heard these things, they were overwhelmed, filled with consternation, but not quite despairing; for in the midst of this storm of darkness, when they realized that God would be just to hurl them down to the depths of perdition, there came a light, but it came from the cross on the wings of memory, and that gleam of light burst from the bosom of the most wonderful prayer that has ever fallen from lips divine: " Father, forgive them; for they know not what they do."

Still they lived, still they remembered that prayer, still they know that it has not been answered, for Peter tells them, by the power of God, that they are guilty. God remembers their sin; Christ is praying for forgiveness for them, and God says when he forgives sins he remembers them no more. So, welling up from the stricken souls in that assembly, comes the cry: "Men and brethren, what shall we do?" Christ has been preached to them, and they believe him to be the Son of God. They realize that they have murdered God's Son and are guilty of a crime that may send them to the regions of endless despair; but Jesus was merciful and prayed for their forgiveness as he died upon the cross, and it might be, as God had spared them for fifty days, that they could obtain forgiveness yet, and they cry out, "Men and brethren, what shall we do?" in order to be rid of that terrible sin, in order that the prayer of the Savior be answered. The apostle Peter answers: "Repent, and be baptized every one of you in the name of Jesus Christ for the remission of sins, and ye shall receive the gift of the Holy Ghost. For the promise is unto you, and to your children, and to all that are afar off, even as many as the Lord our God shall call. And with many other words did he testify and exhort, saying, Save yourselves from this untoward generation. Then they that gladly received his word were baptized: and the same day there were added unto them about three thousand souls." (Acts 2: 38-41.) Then and there God answered the prayer of the Savior by forgiving three thousand of the murderers of Christ. Every time one was added to the church the prayer of the Savior on the cross was answered. When did God answer that prayer? When they heard the gospel, believed the gospel, and obeyed the gospel, thus taking upon themselves the yoke of Him whom they had murdered but fifty days previous to that time.

Shall we, in the light of this wonderful lesson, imagine that God will pardon poor, lost, ruined sinners, just because we pray for them, while they do nothing more than simply allow us to pray for them? Shall we presume to be so much more influential with God than is his own Son that God will answer such prayers offered by us without requiring of the sinner obedience, when he would not answer thus the prayer of his dying Son? Can we hope that God will pardon sinners before they obey the gospel, when he would not do such a thing in answer to the sublimest prayer ever uttered, and that prayer the prayer of his dying Son upon the cross? We ought to rejoice that Jesus offered this wonderful prayer. It ought to make us love him better and serve him more faithfully, and make us rejoice that we have denied ourselves and taken up his cross; it ought to make us determine that we will dare and do and die to make this work an eternal success; it ought to fill our souls with sympathy and love and unquenchable zeal, and make of us an invincible, unconquerable host in the service of Him who prayed on Calvary's rugged brow, " Father, forgive them; for they know not what they do; " it ought to induce every wanderer in this audience to come back to Christ, to induce every sinner who is a proper subject of the gospel call to arise in the strength of Israel's God and come to Jesus, who prayed for his enemies, who prayed for his friends, who begs you to come and take his yoke upon you and find rest and be eternally blessed. Now, if there are any in this audience who realize their lost condition, we are going to give you an opportunity to come. God is willing, Jesus pleads, mercy lingers, truth instructs, and Heaven waits. You are dying, your souls are drifting toward the desolate shores of eternal darkness, without God and without hope; but it is the privilege granted you by high Heaven to cease your drifting, to rise and come to Jesus now, without one plea, save that he died to save you. He begs you to come and bow in meek submission to his will, take his cross upon you, be buried into his name, wear it, enter into his army and fight the battles he would have you fight for the glory of God, the honor of Christ, and the salvation of souls, until God shall call you home to enjoy the bliss of heaven forever and ever. He guarantees that the Lord Almighty will accompany you through the dark valley of the shadow of death, and then upon the bright, golden shore will crown you with glory and honor and immortality, and thrill and fill your souls with bliss unspeakable amid the fadeless flowers of his eternal home—that land where friends never part, where good-byes are never uttered; where sickness, sorrow, pain, and death are unknown; where hearts never bleed nor break, where life is a treasure sublime. If it be the will of any of you through pure motives to come, we wait to lovingly welcome you, and pray that you may come.

CHAPTER XV.

LETTERS—SYMPATHY.

THE true Christian is touched by sympathy in the joys and sorrows of others. "Rejoice with them that do rejoice, and weep with them that weep." (Rom. 12: 15.) "Now ye are the body of Christ, and members in particular." (1 Cor. 12: 27.) "But now are they many members, yet but one body." (1 Cor. 12: 20.) "That there should be no schism in the body; but that the members should have the same care one for another. And whether one member suffer, all the members suffer with it; or one member be honored, all the members rejoice with it." (1 Cor. 12: 25, 26.) The Fatherhood of God and brotherhood of man is a foundation idea in Christianity. The man who does not feel the joys and sorrows of others is not a Christian. There is scripture truth as well as pathetic sentiment in the old song:

> "Blest be the tie that binds
>   Our hearts in Christian love;
>   The fellowship of kindred minds
>   Is like to that above.
>
> "We share our mutual woes,
>   Our mutual burdens bear;
>   And often for each other flows
>   The sympathizing tear."

Heaven and earth are not very far apart when Christians sing "with the spirit and with the understanding also."

" How sweet, how heavenly, is the sight
   When those that love the Lord
In one another's peace delight,
   And so fulfill the word;

" When each can feel his brother's sigh,
   And with him bear a part;
When sorrow flows from eye to eye,
   And joy from heart to heart;

" When, free from envy, scorn, and pride,
   Our wishes all above,
Each can his brother's failings hide,
   And show a brother's love;

" When love in one delightful stream
   Through every bosom flows;
When union sweet, with dear esteem,
   In every action glows! "

Inclosing a letter from an afflicted sister, he wrote:

" Years ago I baptized Mrs. —— and her daughter. Learning very recently that she had lost her health, I wrote her. Letter inclosed tells the rest of the sad story, so far as the letter goes. Long ago she told me much of her life story—one of the saddest of the sad. I must go to see her some time, if I can. If I could write as you can write, I could sit by her bedside a few hours and write a true story that would thrill the world. Storms have swept over her, chilling blasts have blighted her, and hope in her bosom sees nothing this side of the river of death. As I read her letter I could not but realize my own unworthiness. How far I fall below the standard for those who love the Lord! "

The following letter indicates the extent to which he sympathizes with all who are in trouble or distress:

"In a letter just received, one of my dearest friends says:

" 'You always look so sad. Why should you ever look sad? I believe I have never seen you look real happy, except in your best efforts in the pulpit. Tell me: Why should you ever look sad, when you have so much to make you happy?'

"I had never thought of that; but, really, I believe I am always sad, except when I am preaching or helping somebody in some way. How can I be otherwise than sad, except when I am preaching or helping some one bear a burden, when so many souls are blighted by sin and burdened with sorrow?"

Inclosing a sensational story of sin clipped from a newspaper, he wrote:

"One of our boys the first session of school at Mars' Hill. I baptized his wife when she was a little girl, beautiful and innocent. I hope the story is not true; but if it is, sin has struck me a hard blow in a tender place once more. It grieves me when any of my Mars' Hill boys or girls sin or suffer. I wish I knew some way to help them. Mrs. Larimore—at work, of course—is singing as I write:

"'Jesus, I my cross have taken,
    All to leave and follow thee.'

Trying to be everywhere and do everything, she is sometimes near me and sometimes far away; sometimes her singing seems strong and sometimes weak, but still she sings. She and Ettie have been getting little Christmas presents ready for ' the children ' far away, and now Ettie has gone to mail them. This is a perfect May day; but the sunshine, birds, and squirrels cannot keep me from thinking of loved ones far away. Where are the boys who have preached and the girls who have sung here in the sweet long ago? I wish we could call together all the children of the Mars' Hill family yet alive, and live and love in one happy band a few brief days, as we lived and loved in the years of sunshine and shadow that are now gone forever."

A poor woman who was in feeble health, and was bitterly persecuted by religious partisans because she had abandoned all denominations to be a Christian and nothing else, and to be a member of the church, which is the body of Christ, and nothing else, wrote him a very pathetic letter about her sickness, poverty, and trouble. Inclosing her letter, he wrote:

"I do wish you would go to —— and interview Mrs. ——. I believe it would do you good, and that you could write a true story of her life that would be as interesting as a novel and as thrilling as the 'Arabian Nights.' She is a pure, intelligent Christian, relentlessly persecuted— suffering martyrdom—for her fidelity to Christ."

The wide range of his sympathy with sorrow and trouble will be strikingly manifest when a scene of distress in a far different station in life is placed in juxtaposition with this case of sympathy for an unfortunate woman "in sickness, poverty, and trouble." There is no respect of persons or of stations in life with sorrow and affliction, and there should be no social castes in sympathy and helpfulness.

From religious convictions he is opposed to war and all other acts of cruelty, but he appreciates courage and heroic

MARS' HILL, ALABAMA—1876.

endurance of hardships in those who go to war from convictions of duty, and he keenly sympathizes with bereaved hearts in blighted homes whose loved ones fall in the army. When telegraphic dispatches erroneously announced the death of General Wheeler, he wrote the children at home as follows:

" The sad message announcing the death of your illustrious father and my friend has just now reached me. I am overwhelmed with sadness and sorrow as I think of the long ago, of my old-time commander, of my friend whom I can never meet again. Brave, true, and faithful man! Only a few weeks ago I received from him a characteristic letter, which I shall preserve with special care. Had your fearless, faithful father lived, no man could ever have supplanted him in the district he represented in Congress so long, so faithfully, so wisely, and so well, as mortal man can never supplant him in the heart of his country—for which he died. Others have left the field of death and danger to occupy a safe place in Congress; he left Congress to battle for his country where the fight was fiercest, the danger greatest. Others have left the front and retired to the rear on mere pretense of being sick; he, sick unto death, left the rear and rushed to the front, against the earnest protest of surgeons and friends. Honest man, sublime soldier, faithful friend! To say that you, his bereaved children, have my sincerest sympathy, is but to truthfully say what tens of thousands of others could just as sincerely say. May the loving Lord sustain you in this the second sore trial of your young lives."

In this letter there is no word of bitterness, no spirit

of animosity, no approval of war. He saw in General Wheeler an "honest man," a "sublime soldier," a "faithful friend," an "illustrious father;" in the sorrow-shrouded home he saw "bereaved children." It is such a letter as he could have written, and no doubt would have written, and General Wheeler and the rest of mankind would have approved, under similar circumstances, to the "bereaved children" of any soldier of the same qualities who fell in the other army. The following letter will be appropriate in this connection:

" HEADQUARTERS UNITED STATES FORCES,
" CAMP WYCKOFF, MONTAUK POINT, LONG ISLAND,
"September 20, 1898.
"T. B. Larimore.

" My Dear Friend: I thank you very much for your kind letter. No one can possibly appreciate the crushing severity of the blow. Although my son was only seventeen and a half years of age, he was a strong, well-grown man. He was good in all that word can imply, and had so twined himself around our hearts that we all loved him with the tenderest devotion. Four of us—my daughter, my two sons, and myself—were in the campaign, and although I had often thanked God for letting us all come back, I fear I did not feel as much gratitude as I should for such a blessing, and I also fear I did not feel the sympathy I should for others who lost their dear ones; but in the grief I now suffer I realize it all.

" With high regards,
" Truly your friend,
"J. WHEELER."

This correspondence, of course, was on the occasion of the death of General Wheeler's son. With all this, he preaches constantly against war and all other forms of violence, takes no part in politics, and, to the extent of his influence, keeps everybody out of personal strife of every kind. One of his old pupils, and a lifelong friend, was thinking about becoming a candidate for Congress, with very flattering prospects of election if he would make the race. When asked how Larimore felt about it, he said:

"Larimore is squarely against it and would keep me out of the race if he could, even if he knew I would be elected."

After several days' search for the body of a man who was drowned in the Tennessee River at Florence, Ala., he wrote:

"Body of —— still in the river. Telegrams have been sent to points below to keep a lookout. Really, I think it better never to find it now, it has been so long lifeless. I think if he were my own child, I would greatly prefer that the body should never be seen again. I wish I could think of something comforting to write to the bereaved family; but what can man do to comfort hearts under such circumstances? Language is a feeble thing, eloquence is dumb, under such circumstances."

Expressing a desire to encourage and assist a young author with his first book, he wrote:

"—— thinks his book will be out by October. I may never read it, may never have time; but I know he is a good man, and I hope his book is good. I have just ordered three copies of 'Biographies and Sermons' sent to three sisters who want to read it, but are not able to pay for it."

Distressed by the financial losses and business complications of a Christian woman in the midst of one of his meetings, he wrote:

" I urge this dear, sorrowing sister to put all of her business into the hands of our mutual friend and brother, Attorney —— —, of Nashville. Please see him for me, and ask him as a favor to me to do all he can for her. She is all right. Her heart is crushed. I assure her that with all of her business in his hands, she may feel perfectly safe—easy. Of course, if some one has to go to Chicago to look after her interests, he can do that, and I believe he will do it better than anybody else. She has been in serious trouble for several days. I know not the details, but I know she needs help. She cannot talk to me at all with dry eyes. I am to call immediately to see her. I am nervous. I wanted to write many things, but will close and go to see our sorrowing friend and sister."

Illustrating the idea that every Christian ought to be anxious to help others without receiving any help himself, he inclosed in a letter the following clipping from a newspaper:

"A little girl wrote the following letter to Santa Claus:

" ' Dear Santa Claus: My father works very hard, but can't make a living for us all. I wish you would get him a better job, so he could make a living and not have to work so hard. You need not bring me anything.' "

He is even careful not to be a burden to others in his efforts to help them.   On this point he wrote:

" Much matter such as I send you may be burdensome to you.   If so, please say so.   I am trying to help you, and I don't want to hinder you by my efforts to help.   As ever and always, all I send you is yours ever after it leaves me, to be used as you may wish.   I have some envelopes addressed to you—left over from last year—but I have had one hundred more addressed to you, giving me, say, one hundred and twenty-five with which to begin the new year."

The extent to which people trust him and rely upon him for assistance frequently places him in an embarrassing position.   For instance, two of his friends were trying to negotiate a trade.   Each asked him to manage the matter and close the trade under confidential instructions, without knowing what the other had done.   One authorized him to pay twelve hundred dollars as a maximum; the other authorized him to take one thousand dollars as a minimum. He closed the trade at eleven hundred dollars, and, of course, both parties were grateful to him and gratified with the bargain.   One would have taken a hundred dollars less than he received; the other would have paid a hundred dollars more than he gave for the bargain.   He wrote about it as follows:

" Still, my conscience is not quite easy.   I know I have earnestly endeavored to do my whole duty; but, then, whether I look toward the one or the other, I am just a little troubled.   You see, they both trusted me fully; indeed, the whole thing was in my hands.   Now, have I betrayed any confidence?   I could have added one hun dred dollars to the wealth of either at the expense of the other. Well, I know I have earnestly endeavored to do my whole duty. I hope I have missed both Scylla and Charybdis, but my vessel is shaky—seriously so."

His most intimate friends, and even his own wife and children, have often remonstrated with him for buying things he did not need, when he did not have money to pay for things he really needed. The following letter, written in the midst of one of his greatest meetings, will probably shed some light upon this mysterious freak of his character:

"A sweet, modest girl came to me to sell me a costly book that I did not need and could not well afford to buy. When I told her I neither needed it nor could afford to buy it, she said:

" 'Well, then, please write me a commendation of the book, that others may buy it. I have myself and an invalid mother to support, and have just taken an agency for this book, hoping to make something that way, and I am to-day having my first experience as a book agent.'

" I said: ' I am sorry, but I have never read the book.'

" She said: ' Dr. Solon, Dr. Solomon, Dr. Socrates, and Dr. Sampson—all the pastors in town—gave me good certificates this morning, and I am sure they will be helpful to me.'

" I said: ' Well, the Doctors have read the book, of course, or they could not testify to its merit.'

" She said: ' No, sir; they all told me they had never seen the book, but that they were glad to help me all they could.'

"I said: 'Did they all subscribe for the seven-dollar book, or for the cheaper binding?'

"She said: 'They didn't subscribe at all. I haven't sold a book yet. Maybe I don't know how. It's hard to get a start.'

"Just then I saw her beautiful, big, brown eyes were filled with tears that silently stole down and kissed the roses on her cheeks. I knew I was to be far away from there, probably forever, before the time she hoped to begin delivering books; but, being neither iron nor steel, I could not resist all that, of course. I subscribed for the book—best binding—paid for it in advance, told her I might be gone long before the book was to be delivered, tried to encourage her; bade her good-by, probably forever; have never seen the book, of course; have never heard of the sweet child since, and have no thought of ever seeing her again."

When I thought I saw the dawning of brighter days for him after a long pull in hard places, I wrote him as follows:

You have every reason to be cheerful over the situation and outlook. I know something of how things have stood and of how they now stand with you. I know you have had a heavy load to carry, and I have sat up with you many a night for the last two years; but I see the way clearer for you now than I have seen it in a long time. As for myself, I am going under the clouds as you are coming out. I feel now like you used to write—blue. I will do the best I can."

The last part of this letter was unguarded expression of transient depression from overwork and petty cares. I ought not to have written it, and, in fact, I did not know I had let it slip till he returned my letter and wrote as follows:

"I really wish to know what is meant by my emerging from the clouds as you go under. I understand neither my coming out nor your going under. If my coming out causes your going under, then I want to not come out; if my going under will keep you out, I want to go under. If I can help you, tell me how."

Of course he could not help me, because I had nothing much to do and needed no help. The incident is of no consequence, except as an illustration of his readiness to help to the extent of his ability in any emergency, regardless of consequences to himself.

Several years ago two or three very desirable positions were offered to him through me, to all of which he replied at once in the following words:

"I must forego the pleasure and profit of accepting any position—editorial, educational, financial—any position whatever. Please pardon me and give all the good things reserved for me to others."

Inclosing two telegrams received the same day, asking him to preach funerals of different persons—one in Alabama and the other in Tennessee—when he was in a meeting in Missouri, he wrote:

"'O why should the spirit of mortal be proud?' I baptized Miss —— long ago. She was 'salt of the earth.' The other sister, Miss ——, was one of the sweetest saints and most charming young ladies I have ever known. She voluntarily promised me in 1894 that she would sit at the feet of Jesus till God should call her home."

Inclosing a letter filled with delicate expressions of appreciation, gratitude, and esteem from a judge who had and still has a wide reputation as a lawyer and a potent factor in politics, he wrote:

" I stood by the judge and helped to save him once—long ago, when he was a young man—when a powerful combination of big men tried (unjustly, as I then believed and still believe) to crush him and ruin him. If I am any judge of true manhood when I see it tested, he is every inch a man. He does not need any help now, but I want you to call to see him and tell him you come at my request, because I want ' all my friends to know all my friends.' He will know you when you tell him that."

CHAPTER XVI.

BELOVED, when I gave all diligence to write unto you of the common salvation, it was needful for me to write unto you, and exhort you that ye should earnestly contend for the faith which was once delivered unto the saints." (Jude 3.)

There was nothing like affectation in the use of the word "beloved" among the disciples in the long, long ago, and there should be nothing like affectation in the use of it among God's children to-day. There was no impropriety in it then, and there is no impropriety in it now. Had it not been proper, it had not become and been a part of God's revelation to his church. Christians were taught in apostolic days to love one another with a pure heart fervently. "Seeing ye have purified your souls in obeying the truth through the Spirit unto unfeigned love of the brethren, see that ye love one another with a pure heart fervently." (1 Pet. 1: 22.)

The Savior said to his disciples: "This is my commandment, That ye love one another, as I have loved you." (John 15: 12.) And if we loved one another as we ought, sympathized with one another as we should, and were ready, willing, and anxious to bear one another's burdens, and so fulfill the law of Christ (Gal. 6: 2), instead of its being embarrassing for us to express our affection for one another in a proper way, it would be stimulating and en-

couraging.   Then the world might say, " Behold how they
love one another! " as was said when Jesus came to the
grave of Lazarus and wept: " Behold how he loved him! "
Just as we depart from that blessed state of pure love, and
become jealous and envious, and learn to hate one another,
and slander, misrepresent, and abuse one another, the cause
of Christ languishes, souls are bewildered in darkness where
there should be light, and Heaven might weep, if there
could be weeping there.

When Jude was about to write to Christians about the
" common salvation," he gave all diligence to the work before him.   He was writing in reference to things involving
the salvation of souls; he was writing as the representative
of the cause of Christ on earth; he was writing, not for himself, but for God, and it was eminently pertinent and
proper and right that he should give all diligence to the
work before him.   When we are about to speak or write
on any subject, we should be faithful and careful, and, as
Christians, prayerful; but especially is this true when we
are about to speak or write about spiritual things, since the
soul's eternal interests are then involved.   He was writing
as the Spirit guided him.   Now, as it was needful for him
to give all diligence to the work before him when he was
about to write to the saints of the common salvation,
though himself inspired by the Holy Spirit, how much
more needful that we should be anxious and careful when
we are about to write and speak of spiritual things, since we
are not guided by the Spirit in the sense in which he was!

Jude wrote to the brethren upon an important subject.
Of course he had not written to them by direction of God,
had he not had something of importance to say, for God's

Spirit would not direct him to write anything that was not important. He wrote to the brethren in reference to salvation. Salvation in any sense is important. Salvation of one about to perish in the flames of a burning building—salvation in the sense of snatching that body from the blazing building and life-destroying flames—is, of course, of great importance; the salvation of a loved one from impending death and the gloomy grave is, of course, something of great importance; but Jude was about to write to the saints about another kind of salvation. We use the word " common " in two common senses. We use it, for instance, in the sense of inferior. A lady goes into a dry-goods store; she calls for something, naming the article. The polite salesman has a bolt of that goods on the counter, and he says: " Madam, here is something of that kind." She says: " This will not do; it is a common article. I want the very best." He does not say a word, just pushes it aside, turns to the shelf, takes down another bolt of that line of goods, and says: " This is the very best made." He knows just what she means by the word " common." Well, we know, of course, that Jude does not refer to the salvation he wrote about as common in that sense. Then we use it in the sense of general, and, instead of the term " common " as used in that sense conveying the idea of inferiority or low grade, it frequently applies to the very highest grade—that is, the best and most important. For instance, we refer to the light of the sun, moon, and stars; the atmosphere we breathe, the water we drink, as " common " blessings, from the fact that they are blessings to all of us in common—general blessings. Such blessings are more important than gold and jewels and diamonds, because we could live without any of them; but without any of these " common " blessings, life could not last upon the earth. Still, we call them " common "—common because they are of universal application, all of us have access to them. The pauper and the prince may breathe the air; enjoy the light of the sun, moon, and stars; dip the gourd or goblet into the water of the bubbling spring and drink that which will slake the thirst and bless the man. So we speak of these as " common " blessings. Jude wrote to the brethren of the " common " salvation. We know that it was not in that sense, but this of universal application. It is the salvation that goes hand in hand with faith under the great commission that says: " Go ye therefore, and teach all nations, baptizing them in the name of the Father, and of the Son, and of the Holy Ghost: teaching them to observe all things whatsoever I have commanded you: and, lo, I am with you alway, even unto the end of the world. Amen." (Matt. 28: 19, 20.) " Go ye into all the world, and preach the gospel to every creature. He that believeth and is baptized shall be saved; but he that believeth not shall be damned." (Mark 16: 15, 16.) It was salvation belonging to all nations, and not simply to the Jews, as even the apostles believed in the days of the infancy of the church of Christ, a delusion that was dispelled from the mind of Peter when he realized, at the house of Cornelius, that God intended to admit the Gentiles into covenant relations with himself. " Of a truth I perceive that God is no respecter of persons: but in every nation he that feareth him, and worketh righteousness, is accepted with him." (Acts 10: 34, 35.) Salvation offered to the entire human race, and not a salvation offered simply to the favored,

elect, predestined, predestinated, and before-the-founda-
tion-of-the-world-ordained few, for whom alone the Savior
died, shedding no drop of blood for the already condemned, irrevocably damned-before-the-foundation-of-the-
world many.   This the Holy Spirit teaches clearly in the
language: " But we see Jesus, who was made a little lower
than the angels for the suffering of death, crowned with
glory and honor; that he by the grace of God should taste
death for every man.   For it became him, for whom are all
things, and by whom are all things, in bringing many sons
unto glory, to make the captain of their salvation perfect
through sufferings."   (Heb. 2: 9, 10.)   " Who in the days
of his flesh, when he had offered up prayers and supplications with strong crying and tears unto him that was able
to save him from death, and was heard in that he feared;
though he were a Son, yet learned he obedience by the
things which he suffered; and being made perfect, he became the author of eternal salvation unto all them that
obey him."   (Heb. 5: 7-9.)

Now this was the salvation that Jude was about to present to the brethren, and about which he was going to write
when he said he gave all diligence to write unto them of
the common salvation.   It was needful then for Jude to
write unto the brethren and exhort them that they should
earnestly contend for the faith that was once delivered to
the saints.   That was in the earliest days of Christianity.
It was when many were living who had seen the Savior
face to face.   There were eyewitnesses to his miracles still
living, and yet there was indifference, there was careless-
ness, there was prayerlessness, there was lukewarmness,
there was coldness, there was sin among the saints to a

sufficient degree to justify Jude in saying it was needful to write unto them and exhort them to a diligent discharge of duty's demands, exhort them that they should earnestly contend for the faith that was once delivered to the saints. All this being true, we should not be discouraged when we find that we need to be exhorted day by day to a discharge of duty's demands upon us, and we ought to remember that we are actually taught in God's Book to exhort one another, "so much the more, as ye see the day approaching." (Heb. 10: 25.) We ought to do that, and if we loved one another as we ought to love one another, it would never be an offense to one of us to be exhorted, publicly or privately, to be more earnest in the service of God. If we do become offended when brethren, either publicly or privately, exhort us to be more faithful in the service of God, that shows that we need to be exhorted, and need more than we get, and need other things that are not offered us at all. One thing is sure: if we display a bad spirit when in loving kindness we are exhorted to do our duty, we need to repent and to pray God in the name of Jesus Christ to forgive us the sin of allowing ourselves to drift into that state where we can become so easily incensed.

"It was needful [and he would not have written if it had not been needful] for me to . . . exhort you that ye should earnestly contend for the faith which was once delivered unto the saints." Webster defines "contend" "to strive, to struggle." Jude says he earnestly exhorts the brethren to contend for the faith that was once delivered to the saints—to strive, to struggle. Jesus says: "Strive to enter in at the strait gate: for many, I say unto you, will seek to enter in, and shall not be able." (Luke

13: 24.) Paul says: " But foolish and unlearned questions avoid, knowing that they do gender strifes. And the servant of the Lord must not strive; but be gentle unto all men, apt to teach, patient, in meekness instructing those that oppose themselves; if God peradventure will give them repentance to the acknowledging of the truth; and that they may recover themselves out of the snare of the devil, who are taken captive by him at his will." (2 Tim. 2: 23-26.) Here seems to be a palpable contradiction, and it is a fair sample of things that are considered contradictions in God's Book. Jesus commands his disciples to strive; Jude wrote to the brethren of the common salvation, and exhorted them to contend, which means to strive; and Paul declares positively that the servant of the Lord must not strive. Yet there is no clash, confusion, discrepancy, or contradiction here. There is a verse in the Bible that harmonizes all these, in the light of which we can see our way out, and see clearly what God would have us do: " Only let your conversation be as it becometh the gospel of Christ: that whether I come and see you, or else be absent, I may hear of your affairs, that ye stand fast in one spirit, with one mind striving together for the faith of the gospel." (Phil. 1: 27.) That strife that Paul says God forbids is bitter strife, contention—when one brother contends for his way and resolves to have his way, regardless of results; and another brother in the same congregation resolves to have his way; and even some of the blessed sisters become involved, and are wrangling, and disputing, and pulling different ways against each other. Then we have the strife that Heaven condemns. The servant of the Lord, as he values the salvation of his soul and the salvation of the souls that

may be influenced by him, does not dare to persist in any
such strife and contention. I want to quote Paul to Timothy again, while your mind is filled with that thought, and
you can see all this: "But foolish and unlearned questions
avoid [that is, questions that are not taught here by divine
authority], knowing that they do gender strifes. And the
servant of the lord must not strive; but be gentle unto all
men, apt to teach, patient, in meekness instructing those
that oppose themselves; if God peradventure will give them
repentance to the acknowledging of the truth; and that
they may recover themselves out of the snare of the devil,
who are taken captive by him at his will." Paul was writing to Timothy, a young preacher, and this applies especially to all God's preachers. "Only let your conversation
be as it becometh the gospel of Christ: that whether I come
and see you, or else be absent, I may hear of your affairs,
that ye stand fast in one spirit, with one mind striving *together* [not against each other, not each for his own preference, opinion, or hobby, but] for the faith of the gospel."

Jude tells us how we are to contend as well as for what
we are to contend. We are to contend earnestly; not
roughly, not harshly, not bitterly, not unkindly, not in a
haughty, overbearing demeanor, rule-or-ruin, iron-rule, Satanic spirit—no, not that; such a spirit ought never to
be allowed to enter into the household of faith—but earnestly. Men and women are no less earnest in their plead-
ings because of not being rough in them. Is that poor wife,
with aching, bleeding heart; with disheveled hair and up-
lifted face, from which tears that would not stain an angel's cheek are dropping, bowed at the feet of her husband,
begging and pleading with him tenderly and tearfully to

remember vows he made to her in twilight's semisacred hour in the long, long ago, to abandon his unkindness, abandon his dissipation, abandon his waywardness, return to his first love, be what the husband of a pure wife ought to be, what the father of boys and girls should be—is she lacking earnestness because she is not heaping vile maledictions and direful curses and mountains of abuse upon his head and heart? Is that distressed mother whose prodigal boy is killing her day by day, breaking her loving, trusting heart, lacking in earnestness when she throws her arms about him and presses him to her bosom, and sobs and sighs and weeps and prays, and begs him, with all the tenderness characteristic of a mother's purest and tenderest love, to flee from the depths of deep disgrace, agony and sorrow? Is she lacking in earnestness because she is not calling her boy bad names, telling him that he is not worthy of the mother that bore him, the father who has protected him, or the home that has sheltered him; not worthy to dwell among human beings, nor yet among clean beasts, but only to go and wallow in the mire and filth with the hogs? It is not necessary to answer this question. Everybody knows the answer.

By the language we have already quoted we are positively forbidden to be rough. We are not allowed to be rough with any one, but clearly required to be gentle to all men. A man in the service of God must be a gentle man, and especially one occupying the position of a preacher. A preacher must actually be a gentle man, his gentleness going out toward all other men.

We must contend for what? Not for Campbellism, not for Mormonism; for it was seventeen hundred years after Jude wrote this before Campbellism or Mormonism was known in the world or had an existence. Not for Judaism, for Judaism had already been abolished. Jesus took it out of the way, nailing it to the cross. " Blotting out the handwriting of ordinances that was against us, which was contrary to us, and took it out of the way, nailing it to his cross." (Col. 2: 14.) " Having abolished in his flesh the enmity, even the law of commandments contained in ordinances; for to make in himself of twain one new man, so making peace." (Eph. 2: 15.) Not for our personal preferences, our opinions, our hobbies, our whims, our systems, our fancies, or our fads, because, if that had been the case, that would necessarily have led to confusion and strife, which God condemns. Not that. What was it? Not for any creeds, discipline, confessions of faith; they had not so much as been dreamed of; but " for the faith which was once delivered unto the saints." The Revised Version throws a little light on that, " for the faith which was once for all delivered unto the saints." That for which they had to contend had, once for all, been delivered unto them; therefore nothing more modern than God's revelation to man. Man may contend for his own personal preferences, his fancies, or his fads; he may contend for Campbellism or Mormonism; he may contend for any creed or all the creeds in Christendom since God's revelation to man has been made, and spend threescore years and ten earnestly contending for these things, and never have the right to quote this language from Jude in justification of his course; and why? There is nothing in that to justify him to contend for these things. We should all earnestly contend " for the faith which was once for all delivered unto the saints." Certainly this is so simple that every soul beneath the stars

responsible in the sight of God ought to be able to understand it in a moment, and we can tell whether we are in
line with this demand of Heaven by the way we are living,
by the way we are pleading, for what we are pleading. If
we are lovingly and gently pleading, earnestly contending
for the faith that had been, once for all, delivered unto the
saints, standing fast in one spirit and with one mind, striving together for the faith of the gospel, then, leaning upon
the strong arm of Providence, we may rest our souls on this
book for authority for what we are doing; but if we get
away from that, be in any other state, contending for anything else, any system more modern than the book of Jude,
any party or system raised or established on earth subsequent to the day when Jude wrote this book, then we are
out of harmony, out of line, with these things, and there is
no authority coming from high Heaven for one word we
utter, for one syllable we write.

We are simply to take God at his word, believe what he
says, do what he commands, become and be what he requires. This has never made a Campbellite since the world
was made, because there is not a single sentence, sentiment,
or syllable in God's Book intimating that God ever required
anybody to be a Campbellite. Take him at his word, obey
what he commands, become and be what he requires, do as
he directs, and lovingly trust him until he shall call us
home, and he will crown us with glory and honor and immortality, and thrill and fill our souls with bliss unspeakable; and if we are in harmony with these things, let us rejoice and be glad and go on and on and on. If we are out
of harmony with them, let us flee from the gathering storm
to the outstretched arms of the loving Savior, abandon the

wrong, accept the right, and reduce it to practice while we live, and God will bless and strengthen, shield and sustain, and save us.

If there are any in this audience who are in any sense subjects of the gospel call, we invite you to come.   God is willing, Jesus is pleading, mercy lingers, and Heaven waits.

CHAPTER XVII.

LETTERS——KINDNESS.

KINDNESS is a prominent trait of Christian character. One of the cardinal graces which Peter admonished all Christians to add to their faith is " brotherly kindness." (2 Pet. 1: 7.) An eminent man wrote a book on charity, entitled " The Greatest Thing in the World." Of faith, hope, and charity, Paul says, " The greatest of these is charity; " because, among other things which it does and does not, " charity never faileth." One thing which makes charity " the greatest of these " and " the greatest thing in the world " is, " charity suffereth long, and is kind." (1 Cor. 13: 4, 8, 13.) A really kind man will manifest the spirit of kindness toward every class of human beings, including even criminals, and will be kind to the very beasts of the field and the birds of the air. "A righteous man regardeth the life of his beast: but the tender mercies of the wicked are cruel." (Prov. 12: 10.) On kindness in general, to birds and beasts in particular, he wrote:

" You know kindness has always been a prominent characteristic of Mars' Hill life and teaching, howsoever unkind I may have been myself. When the Hill was covered with teachers, pupils, patrons, parents, and children, birds built their nests and brought up their young in the yard, and sometimes in the houses, and were perfectly safe and at home there. You remember, of course, one wren hatched and cared for a brood annually in a gatepost in front of the north entrance to the Mars' Hill home; another, in our church house—Bible Hall—where the little birdies and their patient mother may have slept soundly and dreamed sweetly while 'The Old Ship of Zion,' 'Am I a Soldier of the Cross?' and 'How Firm a Foundation!' made the building tremble. Many birds of many kinds, and pretty, playful squirrels are still safe, and seem to know it, there, though in many respects the place has greatly changed. Kindness has an influence over man, beast, and bird that is not always fully understood and properly appreciated. Many a team has been balked and ruined by cruelty, that could have been easily controlled by kindness; many a child has been crushed and worse than killed by cruelty, that would have developed into noble, useful, happy manhood or womanhood under the fostering care of Christian kindness. The cruel scolding and fault-finding habit is a sin and a shame and an unmitigated curse to the human race, if not, indeed, to other races. Cruelty is a curse to all animate creation. It touches my heart to think of bird or beast coming to me for shelter, sympathy, or succor. Some strangers, armed with a shotgun, passing through our little orchard, 'flushed' a covey of partridges, and sent a load of shot after them. Those that were wounded flew toward the house. One of the little things fell dead at the doorstep; two others fell on the veranda. When wounded they flew to the house, but were dead when they reached it.

> "'O thou that dryest the mourner's tear,
>   How dark this world would be,
>   If, when deceived and wounded here,
>   We could not fly to thee!'

But there is life for the faithful there."

A PAIR OF HERSCHEL'S FRIENDS.

Touched by the death of a little dog, he wrote as follows:

"Tony was as pretty a little black-and-tan terrier, I think, as I have ever seen. He belonged to Virginia Stucky, a sweet little girl who 'was bred in Old Kentucky,' and who has always lived in Louisville. Virginia gave Tony to me because her mother considered it not convenient for her to keep him. Virginia brought him to me a few hours before I left Louisville for a brief visit home. Telling me good-by, she started home; but, returning, she stood in solemn silence a few moments, looking tenderly upon the little pet she should never see again, and then, softly and sweetly saying, 'Good-by, Tony,' hurried away from Tony forever. We—Tony and I—reached Mars' Hill next day about noon, having left Louisville about midnight. Tony was an affectionate little fellow, devotedly attached to his 'old Kentucky home' and to 'the girl he left behind him;' hence I did not wonder that he cried nearly all the way. Like some other lovers, however, Tony was somewhat fickle, and he, in a very few days, succeeded in transferring his affections completely to Mrs. Larimore, who, sympathizing with the little stranger, captivated him by kindness. His devotion to her was simply marvelous. He seemed to consider it his whole duty to keep constant watch and ward over her, and to allow no other living thing to touch her. When Mrs. Larimore, Toppie, and Ettie left home to spend a few weeks with me in Louisville, Dedie said: 'Mamma, Tony will grieve himself to death about you while you are gone.' She was correct about it. He refused to eat, could not be comforted, wandered about the home premises evidently looking for the absent loved one, and died a few days before she returned home. Poor

BILL.

Tony! I've always been sorry he did not live to meet the one he loved, whose return ten days earlier, I believe, would have prolonged the life of the affectionate little lover indefinitely. Even dogs have hearts, and we should never abuse them. Their affection is unfeigned; their friendship is sincere and as lasting as life."

At the close of a long and successful meeting he inclosed a photograph of an unusually large, fine-looking rooster, and wrote as follows:

"It has occurred to me that a biographical sketch and photograph of Bill might interest you. About two weeks after our meeting began, Bill broke the shell and fluttered out into a blinding, blue blizzard that froze all the chicks in the nest, except him. Bill survived on the principle of 'the survival of the fittest.' He, however, like millions of important factors in the human race, had not survived, but for the timely aid of a sympathetic, self-sacrificing woman. Having been carefully 'thawed out,' Bill was admitted to all the privilegs of my home—places, too: kitchen, dining room, pantry, and parlor. He 'fared sumptuously every day,' and grew marvelously. He became the talk of the town, and was the point in many a joke. About the time the meeting closed, probably two or three days before, he was taken to a first-class photographer; a good negative of him was taken, from which the photograph I send you was made; the photographer offered a dollar for him, the offer was accepted, and Bill became the property of the admiring photographer. You can form an idea from the photograph of Bill as to the length of the meeting. The meeting was about two weeks longer than Bill. I preached twice every day and three times every Sunday—three hundred and thirty-three sermons—and never missed a sermon. I feel as well this morning as Bill looks. I leave here for my next meeting by the next train."

A few historical incidents and newspaper clippings will illustrate his sympathy for criminals. While on a preaching tour in Arkansas several years ago, he visited the convict coal mines at Coal Hill. The mining camp was in a bad sanitary condition, the convicts had been cruelly treated, and some of them had been killed by brutal guards. An appeal was made to the prison officials to remedy the situation. The Prison Commission and the Board of Commissioners directed that a thorough investigation be made, and that the case be brought before them on its merits. His sympathies were touched by the gloom, wretchedness, and hopelessness which hung over the camp, and he frequently referred to the matter and sent many newspaper clippings on the subject afterwards. Some of the guards at Coal Hill were discharged and indicted by the grand jury for cruelty to the convicts, the question of leasing the convicts to private corporations became a political issue in the next State election, the Coal Hill lease to a mining corporation was abrogated, the convict camp was broken up, and the matter was a sensational topic in newspapers throughout the country—all this within a few weeks after he was there. In so far as the question was a political issue, he neither expressed nor possessed any partisan bias, but he watched the developments and progress of the case very closely from a humanitarian point of view. On the margin of a newspaper clipping inclosed in one of his letters, giving an account of the trial, conviction, and sentence of a man to be hung in Alabama for murder, he wrote:

" One of the guards who cruelly treated, and probably murdered, convicts at Coal Hill, Ark."

A few years later the question of leasing convicts to private corporations attracted attention in politics in Tennessee, and he inclosed in a letter, without a word of comment, the following editorial from a daily paper:

" Under existing conditions, the whole contract system is abominable; but, for the matter of that, so is our whole prison system. We need to reform it altogether.

" It is urged that convicts must not be kept idle, that they must earn their living, that the people should not be taxed to feed and clothe an army of criminals, and so forth, and so forth. Let us see how this works. The State arrests a young fellow who, let us say, in a drunken quarrel has stabbed a companion. He is hurried away to prison; he is brought into court, tried, and convicted; he is sent to the penitentiary for five years, or for ten years, or for life. All the while a young wife and half a dozen little children are left without their natural protector and their support. They huddle in a corner of the courtroom; they hear the lawyers yaup; they listen to the verdict. The case is closed. The young father is bundled off in one direction in chains; the young family is turned off in another direction in tears. The State takes the time, the earnings, the life of the one to itself, leaving the other to starve. The mother dies of despair; the boys grow up thieves; the girls grow up harlots. The law is vindicated; the taxpayer is protected; the criminal classes are replenished.

" Is it not damnable? Does not the society which tolerates such monstrosities deserve all the evils it entails upon itself? The State has no right to take that man's labor from his wife and children and give them no equivalent. It should punish the guilty, not the innocent. Every dollar that is diverted in this way from the natural needs of the helpless to the uses of the public is base blood money that should and does carry with it the curse of God.

" There will never be peace in this land until the voice of justice, speaking for the lowly, is heard above the demands of rapacity, which holds its festival annually in all our legislative chambers.

" Tennessee has sown the wind; now she is reaping the whirlwind. Not a soldier, not a gun, should be sent to Coal Creek. If one drop of blood is shed there, it will cry to Heaven for vengeance. Take the convicts away, Governor Buchanan; call an extra session and disperse the contractors, and you will hit it about right. It may be that you will not have much law on your side, but you will have plenty of equity. Down with contract convict labor! "

On the same subject, with no word of comment, he inclosed in a letter the following editorial from the Courier-Journal:

" If we are to have repeated in Tennessee the iliad of human wrong and woe which has made Pennsylvania rich, then Tennessee were better blotted out of the memory of men.

" That fruitful and famous State has no blot upon its escutcheon. Its history is one long prose poem of heroic effort and splendid achievement. Through the veins of its people flows an unbroken stream of Scotch-Irish blood. Valor and integrity, good sense and good will, spring, like a tropic flora, in spontaneous growth, from that pure source of so much that is great and noble and good in our national life.

"Tennessee is twin sister to Kentucky. The two, like the ladies Rosalind and Celia, have gone hand in hand, one and inseparable, through a century of sunshine and shadow, of glory and daring, until from the blockhouse in the wilderness has been blazed a home for men unequaled in the world, and blessed by every abundance out of the very hands of God. If the lust for money is to make a craze among the people; if it is to put a poison in their blood; if it is to divert the currents of healthy life and thought away from their natural channels into a dark and turbid river of unfathomable depth, bearing upon its surface the Babylonian splendors of a shameful prosperity, while carrying beneath the degradation and suffering of thousands of men, women, and children, condemned, like galley slaves, to hopeless penury; if, in a word, the outcome of the camp fires of Robertson, Sevier, and Jackson, and their contemporaries, and the end of the civilization of the pioneer church, whose simple music must still echo in strains of Heaven-sent melody and piety, and love and pity, through hearts that have not forgotten the teaching of the fathers— if all this is to come to naught but greed and gain, ghastly wealth and grimy squalor, and the dread contrasts that make life at the centers one horrible pageant of debauchery, rapine, and want, then, indeed, were it better that Tennessee had never been; for, as surely as time lasts, shall it be written of her, as of an older sinner:

" ' She has scourged the weak and the lowly
  And the just with an iron rod;
She is drunk with the blood of the holy,
  She shall drink of the wrath of God.'

" The people of Tennessee, of Kentucky, of the United
States, may as well understand now, as later, that, no less
than the less favored peoples of the Old World, we have to
meet the social question in most of its forms. In Europe,
girt round by feudal bonds and tenures, pressing men and
women closer to the wall by the ever-increasing swell and
force of numbers, the conditions are sharper and more
urgent than in a young country, with its great area of terri-
tory not yet occupied and its vast resources ill accessible
to the humblest toiler. But in republican America the
same agencies are at work which originally prevailed in
the ancient monarchies, and to which may be traced many
of the evils that shadow these closing years of the nine-
teenth century.

" In dealing with them, and in order that we may em-
ploy a wisdom that is at once practical and humane, we
must take them, seriatim, as they come before us.

" This whole Coal Creek business is the offspring of an
abomination to which the law has given its sanction. In
the olden time, when might had a mind to lord it over right,
it took its good claymore in hand and went out in search
of adventures. It slew its weaker adversary, appropriated
to itself his lands and cattle and kine, and came home in
triumph, bringing stores of spoil and attended by knights
in armor and slaves in chains. Then it gave itself a title
and founded a dynasty, and got poets to sing its praises and
fools to make it merry, and historians to write down genius

and prowess for mere brute force and cunning, thieving craft and cruel pillage. Modern rapacity is more ingenious and less manly. The older ruffian at least took its life in its hand and gave its enemy a chance. Its degenerate scion finds safer and surer means of achieving its desires. It organizes a corporation; it gets a charter; it hires a lobby; it leases an organ; it buys a Legislature—and there you are! Millions to a few, misery to all others; with the law to sustain the proceeding, and, if need be—just as in the days of yore—troops to enforce it!

"The case of the Coal Creek miners is an intensification of the old, old story, for it is made stronger by the convict-contract feature. Here we have the State using its power as a State to extract blood money from its own citizens, and, by the act of doing so, denying to honest men the opportunity to earn an honest living. Among disinterested and considerate people there cannot be two opinions upon this point. All of us know how these contracts are attained, though it may be doubted whether any of us are fully conscious of how they operate. We know enough, however, to be assured that the system is infamous and brutal, and that the foot of an enlightened and humane public opinion should be put upon it to stamp it out forever.

"Governor Buchanan is essentially a man of the people. His nomination and election were effected by purely popular agencies. He is a Tennessean to the core, a veritable product of the soil. His fathers fought to reclaim that earthly paradise from the savagery of nature, and prayed to the Lord of hosts for his blessing upon the work of their hands. The men who slung their rifles over their hunting shirts and followed ' Old Hickory ' to New Orleans to drive

CONGREGATION AND MEETING HOUSE, MARS' HILL—ANNUAL MEETING IN AUGUST.

back the legions of monarchy and keep America free could not have divined that they were laying the foundations for a possibility such as that which faces the Tennessee authorities at this moment. The men who knelt in prayer under the ministrations of Lindsley and Doak, and sent from God's temples to the skies the swelling anthem of the ' Old Ship of Zion,' could no more be induced to force their fellow-citizens to submit to the wrong that these miners have rebelled against than they could have been made to acquiesce in sin and pay the devil homage. There is but one true course for Governor Buchanan to pursue. He should turn a deaf ear to those who talk about ' the majesty of the law; ' he should give a cold shoulder to the attorneys who yaup about the sanctity of contracts; he should go back to Nashville, carry the troops and the convicts with him, call an extra session of the Legislature to convene at once, and recommend the abrogation of the lease system. By thus taking the bit in his mouth, he will avoid useless turmoil, and, it may be, the shedding of innocent blood; will escape responsibility for a line of consequences that can work only hurt to the common weal, and, perhaps, ruin to this immediate region; will discharge his duty as a wise magistrate and fulfill the best traditions of his State and people. In such a policy there is nothing whatever of pusillanimity. When His Majesty, the Law, is in the wrong, it becomes the first of obligations in the executive head to see that the wrong is limited until constituted authority can be invoked to apply the remedy.

" These miners are right; their demands are reasonable. Woe to the men who order a military advance against them! "

Larimore loves the people, and his love for his auditors is probably one secret of his success in winning souls to Christ. In the midst of a meeting he wrote:

" My heart already begins to feel the pressure of the blessed influences around me, and I am beginning to realize that it will be hard to leave many whom I already tenderly love here. Many of the sweetest faces and finest specimens of noble manhood I have ever seen meet me in the house of the Lord here. Already I am in love with the congregation, and my work has scarcely begun."

He recommended and located a worthy young man to teach school. Some weeks later he wrote, inclosing a letter from the young man:

" He sent me the money referred to in his letter to pay me for getting him a position as teacher. Of course I sent the money back to him by the next mail and wrote him the best—most encouraging—letter I could."

Referring to his sensitiveness, he wrote:

" They have little ' chatterboxes ' here which, they say, accurately record every word I speak. They call them— well, I'm not sure what they call them. The first time I met Miss ——, she begged the privilege of taking down what I preached, provided the ' machine ' did not disturb me. She explained what kind of noise the little thing would make, and said: ' Now, if it disturbs you just the least bit, please tell me so or give me some signal, and it shall disturb you no more.' I assured her it would not disturb me in the least, and that it would afford me great pleasure to know my preaching was either pleasure or profit to her. She has become a fixture in our meeting. She has a neat table just to my left, where she sits facing my left side—a little back of me—screened from the audience, except a faithful few, by a curtain that adds grace and beauty to the scene, and there she rapidly and accurately records what I say. The first night she worked her machine on me the weather was perfect; the night was bright, balmy, and beauteous. Not one fleecy cloud flitted between us and the stars. I stepped to the front of the platform and began to talk. My mind was completely absorbed in my work. The little 'chatterbox' began to click. To me, the sound was exactly that of sleet driven by a brisk, biting, chilling blast against the great stained-glass windows at my back and on either side—windows occupying probably two-thirds of the space across the rear end of the building. Immediately I felt a strong, freezing current of air pouring upon me. I instinctively shivered; then, wondering why the windows had been lowered at my back, I—still talking, but mechanically—turned to glance at the storm through the open windows and ask some one to close them, when, to my astonishment, I saw the windows behind me were closed. At that moment I thought of the busy little machine, instantly comprehended the situation—understood the cause of all my trouble—was perfectly comfortable, and felt the current of cold air no more. After dismissing the audience, I examined the windows thoroughly, and was clearly convinced that imagination alone had caused all that trouble. To say I am—body, soul, and spirit—as sensitive as a barometer, is certainly no exaggeration."

CHAPTER XVIII.

SERMON——COMMUNION.

WHEN ye come together therefore into one place, this is not to eat the Lord's Supper. For in eating every one taketh before other his own supper: and one is hungry, and another is drunken. What? have ye not houses to eat and to drink in? or despise ye the church of God, and shame them that have not? What shall I say to you? shall I praise you in this? I praise you not. For I have received of the Lord that which also I delivered unto you, That the Lord Jesus the same night in which he was betrayed took bread: and when he had given thanks, he brake it, and said, Take, eat: this is my body, which is broken for you: this do in remembrance of me. After the same manner also he took the cup, when he had supped, saying, This cup is the new testament in my blood: this do ye, as oft as ye drink it, in remembrance of me. For as often as ye eat this bread, and drink this cup, ye do show the Lord's death till he come. Wherefore whosoever shall eat this bread, and drink this cup of the Lord, unworthily, shall be guilty of the body and blood of the Lord. But let a man examine himself, and so let him eat of that bread, and drink of that cup. For he that eateth and drinketh unworthily, eateth and drinketh damnation to himself, not discerning the Lord's body. For this cause many are weak and sickly among you, and many sleep." (1 Cor. 11: 20-30.)

- 19 -

We hear some very strange questions propounded in reference to the communion spoken of in the paragraph I have just read. We are asked sometimes: " In what kind of communion do you people believe? " Well, if the term " you people " means the people who accept the Bible as their creed, discipline, and confession of faith, the lamp to their feet and the light to their pathway; the people who are satisfied with the way, the will, and the word of the Lord; people who are just trying to be Christians, and nothing else, then the answer is: We believe in communion with the Lord; believe that every child of the living God should enjoy the sacred communion that he allows to the divine institution the Bible calls " the church of Christ," " the church of God "—the church to which the Savior referred when he said: " Upon this rock I will build my church; and the gates of hell shall not prevail against it." (Matt. 16: 18.)

We are asked if we believe in *free* communion. We have no faith on that subject. It is utterly impossible for that to be any part of our faith, provided our faith is the faith God would have us have, for that faith " cometh by hearing, and hearing by the word of God." (Rom. 10: 17.) And the word of God says nothing about free communion; so, of course, if our faith is Bible faith, and if we respect the elements thereof as drawn up by the Lord Almighty himself, that question can have nothing to do with our faith, and cannot be an article or element therein. So, if you ask me that question, it will be necessary for me, in order to give you an intelligible and intelligent answer, to ask you what you mean by it. If you mean by " free communion " a communion in which all the communicants are to be, to the extent of their ability, free from envy, free from jealousy, free from prejudice, free from bigotry, free from selfishness, free from the pharisaic I-am-more-holy-than-thou spirit, free from anything and everything contrary to the will of God and contrary to the spirit of Him who became the Babe of Bethlehem, the Man of sorrows, and who died on Calvary's cross for the sins of a lost and ruined and recreant race, I think, then, the communion must be free—as free as the communicants can make it. Of course, with human weakness we may never be able to make it free, but we must try, remembering that one of the very A-B-C lessons, given by the Holy Spirit to his children while they are babes in Christ, is this: " Wherefore laying aside all malice, and all guile, and hypocrisies, and envies, and all evil speakings, as newborn babes, desire the sincere milk of the word, that ye may grow thereby: if so be ye have tasted that the Lord is gracious." (1 Pet. 2: 1-3.) Yet we are not to become discouraged and refuse to commune, imagining that it will be an abomination in the sight of the Lord to do so. If we find ourselves unable to make the communion absolutely and perfectly free, we must remember that we may not, in human weakness, ever reach that point, but we must do the best we can; and unless the communion is free to a great extent, it cannot be acceptable to Him in whose heart was no deception, whose lips never uttered guile.

We are sometimes asked if we believe in *open* communion. If you propound that question to me, you bewilder and perplex me, just as when you ask the other question. There is not a cloud that floats over the earth, there is not a bud on any twig of any tree in any forest, that does not have as much printed upon its bosom, or locked up in its folds, upon the subject of open communion as is found in the whole realm of God's revelation to man. Of course, then, this untaught question cannot become an article of faith with us, cannot enter into our faith, since "faith cometh by hearing, and hearing by the word of God." To the Christian, a necessary element of faith is to know just what God says about it; and since the Bible says nothing on that subject, it cannot be an element of our faith. I will just have to ask you what you mean by it. If you mean by "open communion" a communion in which every soul communing is to be open, frank, and free with God, every soul rejoicing to know, "Thou God seeth me," "The Lord knoweth me;" a communion in which every communicant is to be in such a condition as not to dread the consequences of God's turning Heaven's search light upon our souls, and calling the angels and archangels to see the condition of the communicants, every soul rejoicing to know that the day is not far distant when, our life work having been completed, our life is to be henceforth and forever an open book before God—now, if that is what you mean by open communion, then I think it should be open, and that unless it is open to a very grea. extent it is not acceptable in the sight of God.

But we are sometimes asked if we believe in *close* communion. We can just look up to the heavens that bend in blue beauty above us, and, look wherever we will, we can see just as much written by the finger of God in flaming, living light—every letter bedecked with radiant gems and jewels rare, flashing in the sight of God forever—on the subject of close communion, as we see anywhere in God's

Book. So I will just have to ask you what you mean by that untaught question. If you mean by "close communion" a communion in which every soul communing is in close, sympathetic union with every other soul communing, and where all who are communing love each other with pure hearts fervently, and long to get closer to each other, the sentiment of each soul being, "Nearer to God every moment"—not only during the communion, but at all other times—"Nearer, my God, to thee;" every soul saying within itself, "More like Jesus, more like Jesus would I be, every day and every hour until God calls me home;" "Closer to thee, my Savior, draw me by the tenderest cords of love, and still I realize that I am ever too far from thee;" each soul determined, by the grace of God, to eliminate from its thought and practice, as near as possible, everything that may come between that soul and God—now, if that is the sentiment to which you refer when you ask if we believe in close communion, then I can safely say that the communion should be close; and the closer, the better for all concerned.

But, remember, I have made no effort in the world to answer any of these questions from a Bible point of view. The Bible says nothing about it. From the beginning of Genesis to the end of Revelation there is absolutely not one syllable about *close* communion, *free* communion, or *open* communion. Then you ask: "Why do preachers preach about it so much?" It may be that we can never be able to understand why the world has drifted so far away from God that the pulpit proclaims more that is unknown in the Bible than that which is written there. While we have made no effort to give a Bible answer to these questions, and while our faith does not touch them, since our "faith cometh by hearing, and hearing by the word of God," and the word of God mentions none of them, still we think, if the hypothetical meanings suggested be the meanings in your mind in reference to these things, that the communion must be free, open, and close, or it is not acceptable in the sight of God.

Well, do you ask why the religious world is divided on this question? Why not ask why the religious world is divided at all? These are the questions that divide the religious world. The taught questions are not dividing. We bring in the untaught questions, and then wrangle and dispute and debase ourselves, and, unless we are careful, may condemn our souls over these questions, whereas, if we would go by what is given, work in the light of God's truth, we would glorify God, honor Christ, and be eternally saved.

Well, does some one ask: "Who is to decide the question as to who shall be invited to come to the table of the Lord and who shall be forbidden?" When you raise that question the gospel preacher feels a little more at ease, because he need not go outside of the Bible when he comes to consider this question. I read a few moments ago what ought to be satisfactory. Paul wrote to the church of God at Corinth: "Let a man examine himself, and so let him eat." Now, whenever God says to all his children, "Let a man examine himself, and so let him eat," this is saying to each one of his children: "You must examine nobody but yourself; you must not examine your neighbor." So, if we are Christians, we are positively forbidden to settle that question for anybody but ourselves, and I would not presume to invite the most saintly soul—not the faithful old mother in Israel who has been serving God for fifty years, or the elder who has borne the burden of Christian work for three-score years and ten—would not think of inviting either of these souls to come to this table, nor would I think of just waving my hand to any one in the house and saying to him: "Stand back!" Why? That is a prerogative that belongs to the Lord Almighty alone. I cannot, dare not, assume to supplant God. God says to all his children in reference to this institution: "Let a man examine himself, and so let him eat." If I am God's child, then God tells me positively not to invite any soul and not to deter any soul from this privilege. He says to you: "Let a man examine himself, and so let him eat." Certainly I can never hope to reach a higher position in this life than a humble, faithful servant in the house of God. Whether I am a humble, faithful servant of the Lord is not for me to say, of course, unless I say it to myself when solitary and alone; but certainly I can never hope to reach a higher position on earth than that of a humble, faithful servant in the house of God. Would it not be strange conduct for a servant to presume to stand at the door of the dining room and say to one of his master's guests, "Come in! I think you and I agree in our hobbies and fancies;" and say to another, "Stand back! You and I differ in our opinions." That would be fearful. No servant would do that. God forbid that his servants shall do anything remotely resembling that! So he says: "Let a man examine himself, and so let him eat." But some one says: "There is a very serious difficulty there. Some one might be mistaken; some earnest, honest man might believe himself to be entitled to the communion, not being entitled to it—might believe himself a child of God, and not be a child of God—and not being entitled to the communion, but believing himself to be, might commune, and thus eat and drink damnation to himself." Well, what made you think that? "In such a case would not a man be eating and drinking damnation to himself?" Well, no, not that I know of. If the Bible teaches that, I have not studied it as carefully as I ought to have studied it, and I ought to have studied it more before I tried to teach; and certainly, when I have been preaching for one-third of a century, I ought to have known it if the Bible teaches it. "But didn't you read a little while ago about 'He that eateth and drinketh unworthily, eateth and drinketh damnation to himself?'" Yes, sir, I read that; but you would not be willing, I am sure, for any one to occupy the position of teacher for your children after they have left the nursery and passed through the kindergarten—and I rather think you would not be willing for any one to be a teacher in the nursery or kindergarten—who did not know that "unworthily" is an adverb, and modifies, restricts, and qualifies the manner of doing a thing instead of the condition of the one who does it. It is not an adjective, but an adverb. "He that eateth and drinketh unworthily, eateth and drinketh damnation to himself, not discerning the Lord's body." A gentleman and a lady walk into this house and take a seat next to the door. Contrary to their wishes, they get in a little late. They are not entitled to the communion, but think they are. I do not mean they are not entitled because they come in a little late, but they are not entitled to communion. They think they are, however, and partake of it with as good intentions and pure motives as any man or

woman in this audience. When the cup is passed, they
put it to their lips and taste the wine that symbolizes the
blood that was shed on Calvary, but they are not really
God's children. They have been misled and confused;
they have not been taught it was their duty to do those
things without the doing of which they never can be his
children, but they are not aware of that. Now they are
not eating and drinking damnation to themselves; they
are not cursing themselves or anybody else, and not acting
badly in doing that. But two other people come in here.
Reckless, weak, and wicked, they have no respect for themselves, their friends, or their God. They take a seat in the
back of the house, and after a while the bread is passed
around. He looks around, breaks off a piece, nibbles at it,
and looks around at her as if to say: " I have done something wonderful." And then she takes a piece, and he
giggles and she giggles, and he giggles and she giggles.
The cup is passed around and the same thing is enacted.
People who could do that could laugh and dance and frolic
over their own mother's grave. The latter spirit would be
no worse than the former. Now, they would be eating and
drinking damnation to their souls. It is the manner in
which you eat and drink. " He that eateth and drinketh
unworthily." But that question suggests no necessity for
setting aside God's law. Now, suppose we make an honest
mistake, do we eat and drink damnation to our souls? No,
it is not true. But where is the man who can know our
motives, our thoughts, better than we can know them?
God knew that he and we alone could know, so he leaves it
as a matter between each disciple and the Lord.

The loaf represents the body broken for the sins of a lost

and ruined and wrecked race; the fruit of the vine—if the Bible calls it "wine" in that connection, I am not aware of it; it does call it "the fruit of the vine"—the fruit of the vine represents the blood of Jesus that was shed on Calvary that we that love him might live with him in glory forever. This institution is the institution that represents his death, just as baptism represents his burial and resurrection. In the Lord's Supper and in baptism we have the death, burial, and resurrection of the Lord Jesus Christ clearly represented and memorialized, and we are led to remember all these things.

As to when we are to partake of this institution, all the Bible tells us is to lead us to the conclusion that it is on the first day of the week. "And upon the first day of the week, when the disciples came together to break bread, Paul preached unto them, ready to depart on the morrow; and continued his speech until midnight." (Acts 20: 7.) So the first day of the week was the day to partake of the Lord's Supper; and if you ask me which first day of the week, I say there is but one; no week has more than one first day in it. But does the Bible say they met on the first day of every week? It says that just as often as it says the Jews were commanded to keep every Sabbath, or seventh day, as a rest day. The commandment to the Jews was: "Remember the Sabbath day, to keep it holy." God knew there never would be and never could be a week that had more than one Sabbath day in it; he knew there never would be and never could be a week that had more than one first day in it. So the children of the living God are to meet on the first day of the week to break the loaf, representing the broken body, and to partake of the fruit of the vine, representing the blood shed for the remission of sins, thus participating in the joys and blessings of free, open, and close communion with the Lord. We should all rejoice, when the first day of the week dawns, in the thought that it is the birthday of the Savior from the tomb. God has hidden in the great chambers of his own mind, unrevealed, the birthday of the Babe of Bethlehem, so that no mortal on earth knows the month of the year in which the Savior was born. Of course we know something of what man has guessed about it—that it was on the night of what we call " December 25 " that the Babe of Bethlehem was born—and hence it is that every year now closes with a period of drunkenness, gluttony, and rowdyism and sin such as the world knows at no other period of the year, all this drunkenness, gluttony, and revelry and sin being in memorialization of the birth of the Babe of Bethlehem, the Prince of Peace, over whose humble cradle the angels shouted: " Glory to God in the highest, and on earth peace, good will toward men! " There is not a sentence in God's Book—there is not one word we could give as evidence that would be reliable as to what time of the year it was, except we know that in the tentless fields the shepherds were keeping watch, in a latitude about the same as Virginia; and hence it is probable that the monk who guessed it was about December 25 missed it as far as he could miss it and hit the year at all. But we do know the birthday of the Savior from the tomb, and God has given us the glorious privilege of memorializing his birth from the tomb, and we ought to rejoice that we are God's children and have the privilege of coming to the Lord's table and memorializing the death of Him who died that we might live.

Above these untaught questions we ought to think of the death of Christ—that the world was in a lost condition; that generations were being born and buried without a hope of escape from the dreadful weight of sin; that Heaven saw our helpless, hopeless condition, and Jesus fled to our relief. He became the Babe of Bethlehem, the Man of sorrows, died on Calvary's cross, and was buried in a borrowed tomb, and arose bringing life and immortality to light, flooding the world with light divine, and lifting our souls to God. We know we can become God's children, followers of the Lamb, and upon the birthday of the Savior from the tomb can come to the house of prayer and be partakers of the loaf that represents his broken body, and the fruit of the vine that represents his blood. We ought to remember, when the emblems are passed, that no one in this house can sit in judgment on another, or shall say who may take and who may not take, but remember that God says: " Let a man examine himself, and so let him eat." While those who are God's children are rejoicing in this privilege, those who are not can rejoice in the thought that it is their privilege to obey the gospel, and become sons and daughters of the Lord Almighty, and enjoy the privileges granted to his children while we live, and at last, in the promise of God, enter the blissful home above when the soul leaves the crumbling clay and soars away to dwell beyond the stars forever.

If any who are subjects of the gospel call will now accept in the strength of manhood or the gospel invitation, arise womanhood and come to Jesus without one plea, except that he gave his life to save you. Jesus, from the holy heights of glory, begs you to come, and we wait to lovingly welcome you, and pray that you will come.

CHAPTER XIX.

SERMON——THE GREAT COMMISSION.

AND when the Sabbath was past, Mary Magdalene, and Mary the mother of James, and Salome, had bought sweet spices, that they might come and anoint him. And very early in the morning the first day of the week, they came unto the sepulcher at the rising of the sun. And they said among themselves, Who shall roll us away the stone from the door of the sepulcher? And when they looked, they saw that the stone was rolled away: for it was very great. And entering into the sepulcher, they saw a young man sitting on the right side, clothed in a long white garment; and they were affrighted. And he saith unto them, Be not affrighted: Ye seek Jesus of Nazareth, which was crucified: he is risen; he is not here: behold the place where they laid him. But go your way, tell his disciples and Peter that he goeth before you into Galilee: there shall ye see him, as he said unto you. And they went out quickly, and fled from the sepulcher; for they trembled and were amazed: neither said they anything to any man; for they were afraid.

" Now when Jesus was risen early the first day of the week, he appeared first to Mary Magdalene, out of whom he had cast seven devils. And she went and told them that had been with him, as they mourned and wept. And they, when they had heard that he was alive, and had been seen of her, believed not.

"After that he appeared in another form unto two of them, as they walked, and went into the country. And they went and told it unto the residue: neither believed they them.

"Afterward he appeared unto the eleven as they sat at meat, and upbraided them with their unbelief and hardness of heart, because they believed not them which had seen him after he was risen. And he said unto them, Go ye into all the world, and preach the gospel to every creature. He that believeth and is baptized shall be saved; but he that believeth not shall be damned." (Mark 16: 1-16.)

The language of the last two verses is what is known as the " Great Commission." It is great in contrast with all other commissions, human and divine, that have ever been given; it is great in its origin, originating from Jehovah; it is great in design, the design being the salvation of souls; it is great in its extent, reaching from the rivers to the ends of the earth, to the end of time, and, in its influence, through vast eternity. Jesus previously sent his disciples out under a commission (Matt. 10), but he restricted them in their labors to the lost sheep of the house of Israel. He forbade that they should teach the Gentiles; he forbade that they should preach to the Samaritans; and he required that they should preach simply and solely to the lost sheep of the house of Israel. Had no greater commission than this ever emanated from the lips of the Lord of glory, then no man under a commission from Jesus or Jehovah could, being true to that commission, preach to us, we being Gentiles, not Jews; had no greater commission than this ever been given by divine authority, then no mortal had ever had divine authority to preach to any one outside the family of Abraham, the father of the faithful. Of course it was proper and right for the disciples to be restricted to the lost sheep of the house of Israel under the commission the Savior gave, as recorded in Matt. 10; and the evidence by which we know it is right is that it was that way, for we know that whatsoever the Lord doeth is always right. God had had the Jewish family under special protection, care, and development for centuries. The day had almost come when the middle wall of partition between Jew and Gentile was to be obliterated, and a new institution established upon better promises than those on which Judaism was based—an institution where national lines would not be regarded, but where, as the apostle Paul teaches, "there is neither Greek nor Jew, circumcision nor uncircumcision, Barbarian, Scythian, bond nor free: but Christ is all, and in all." (Col. 3: 11.) But while that day was at hand, it had not quite arrived when the Savior gave that other commission, nor had it quite arrived when he gave the great commission, but it was so near at hand that he deemed it well that the great commission be given. The Savior had come to this world of death for the ransom of the race. He had suffered, had bled, had died, and had been raised from the tomb; he had lived among, communed and associated intimately with, the disciples forty days after his resurrection, and he was just ready to ascend to glory, and there were but a few moments left then of his pilgrimage here on earth in which to give the commission that was to bless the world, and he used just so much of that time for that purpose as was necessary. He said to his disciples: " Go ye into all the world, and preach the gospel to every creature. He that believeth and is baptized shall be saved;

but he that believeth not shall be damned." National
limitations were disregarded: Go to the Gentile as well
as the Jew. Geographical limitations were ignored: " Go
ye into all the world." Class limitations were not regarded: " Preach the gospel to every creature." Go to the con-
tinents and the isles of the sea, to the busy emporiums of
the earth, the lesser cities, the minor towns, the villages,
and the quiet rural districts, throughout the length and
breadth of the habitable globe—wherever there were suffering, sorrowing, sinful, sighing people to be blessed, and
lost and ruined souls to be saved. These disciples personally and through their influence were to go, and wherever
they went they were to preach, and when they preached
they were to preach the gospel of the Son of God—the good
news, the glad tidings of salvation through Jesus. They
were to tell the story of the cross. The Savior did not leave
them in doubt and darkness as to what they should preach.
He did not commission them to preach their opinions, their
personal preferences, their hobbies, their fancies, or their
fads, but he commissioned them to preach the gospel—only
this, and nothing more. Now, all gospel preachers from
that day to this have preached under that commission.
That was the last and final commission from high Heaven
to man. Man has no authority to preach, save in harmony
with this commission. Hence, of course, all gospel preachers recognize that this is their license, their authority—not
human, but divine—to preach. Had they just simply been
licensed to preach, they might have preached Judaism, or
some modernism, or their own personal preferences or opinions, theories or speculations, and claimed this commission
as authority for doing that. But since the Savior was care-

ful to tell them what to preach, then no mortal can preach the things I have just enumerated and have any right to claim this commission as authority for that preaching; and if this be not the authority for preaching that the man who preaches has, then he has no divine authority. It follows, therefore, that if I preach my opinions, my personal preferences, my hobbies, my fancies, or my fads; if I preach Judaism, or any modernism, or any other ism, then I am preaching without divine authority. But if I simply preach the gospel, do my very best to lead the lost to the Lamb of God that taketh away the sins of the world, teaching them what God says they must do to be saved, then I can lay my hand on this blessed Book and claim that this commission is my authority for preaching.

Matthew, Mark, and Luke all give the commission in part—rather, each one gives a phase of the commission, and, putting all these records together, we get the commission in its entirety, with whatsoever the Lord Almighty recognizes as being a part thereof. Matthew says that the Savior, on this memorable occasion, just before he ascended, said to his disciples: " Go ye therefore, and teach all nations, baptizing them in the name of the Father, and of the Son, and of the Holy Ghost: teaching them to observe all things whatsoever I have commanded you; and, lo, I am with you alway, even unto the end of the world. Amen." (Matt. 28: 19, 20.) Mark says: " Go ye into all the world, and preach the gospel to every creature. He that believeth and is baptized shall be saved; but he that believeth not shall be damned." (Mark 16: 15, 16.) Luke says: " Thus it is written, and thus it behooved Christ to suffer, and to rise from the dead the third day: and that repentance and

remission of sins should be preached in his name among
all nations, beginning at Jerusalem." (Luke 24: 46, 47.)
Now, taking these three records and putting them together,
we find that the Savior commissioned his disciples to preach
the story of the cross, and teach the people faith, repentance, and baptism for the remission of sins. "Teach all
nations, baptizing them." "He that believeth and is baptized shall be saved." "Thus it is written, and thus it behooved Christ to suffer, and to rise from the dead the third
day: and that repentance and remission of sins should be
preached in his name." Taking the three, then, we have
the conditions that the disciples were to make known to a
lost and ruined world, from the rivers to the ends of the
earth—faith, repentance, and baptism. Then the Savior
commissioned, or commanded, them: "Tarry ye in the city
of Jerusalem, until ye be endued with power from on high."
(Luke 24: 49.) Having said these things, he led them out
as far as Bethany, lifted up his hands and blessed them,
and was taken up while he was praying blessings upon
them. A cloud received him out of their sight, and he was
carried home to glory, where he was crowned King of kings
and Lord of lords.

Now, how did the disciples understand this commission?
It is very important for us to know that. How can we
know it? How can we learn what they understood by the
commission? If we can follow their footsteps and find
what they preached under this commission, find what they
induced people to do who followed their instruction, then
we have demonstrated—demonstrated so clearly that we
cannot fail to understand—exactly how they understood
the commission under which they labored. There is noth-

ing simpler than this. In reference to temporal affairs, we can understand this clearly. There is a great battle being fought upon a plain diversified by little hills. We are occupying a position on some mountain peak overlooking the dreadful carnage. A man commanding ten thousand men is stationed on a little height. We see a courier start from headquarters to go through the stream of shot and shell. We are satisfied that he is bearing orders to the man commanding the ten thousand men. He goes and hands him the document, and the general commanding these soldiers reads the order, and immediately gives the command for his men to fall into line. He places himself at the head of the column, and he marches over ground already slippery with blood and almost covered with the dead and dying; he crosses the plain and mounts a hill where there is a battery that is doing dreadful execution in the ranks he is leading on. He loses three thousand men, but he captures the battery and silences it. Can we understand his commission? How did he understand it? He understood it just as he carried it out, if he is a true soldier.

Vessels sometimes sail under sealed orders—that is, the captain of the vessel receives orders to go to a distant port, and then receives sealed orders as to what he is to do when he gets there. He gets a sealed letter and sails away. We wonder what his orders are, and keep in close touch with him by means of the facilities for disseminating news at the present day. We find he has just reached the distant port to which he was sent at seven o'clock in the morning, and has cast anchor. At noon a telegram comes informing us that at nine o'clock he commenced shelling the town near by, and that the town is now in withering flames. Can we understand how that man understood his sealed orders? No trouble about that, conceding he was a true servant, as he should have been to have been in that place.

It is just as easy to see how these disciples understood their commission on the very same principle precisely, provided we can find them at work under that commission, hear what they preach, see what they do, what they induce people to do under their labors. Can we do this? Yes. Where shall we go for all the information that earth can have in reference to that? Go to Acts of Apostles. This is all the information we can get, except a few incidental allusions which we find in the Epistles written to the churches. Practically we find all in this book, and a moment's reflection will enable you to see the fitness of this title. You can see that every principle of good sense bearing upon the subject points to Acts of Apostles. In the King James Version of the Bible—and it may be in all versions—it is called " The Acts of the Apostles." Uninspired men gave that title to it. It is not " The Acts of the Apostles "—that is, not all the acts of all the apostles—but "Acts of Apostles." This title is in harmony with the book. These apostles are the ones commissioned to preach the gospel; these acts are their acts under that commission. Let us follow them and see how they understood their license to preach, the commission under which they labored.

They were to tarry in the city of Jerusalem until they were endued with power from on high. Repentance and remission of sins were to be preached to every creature among all nations, and that work was to begin at Jerusalem. Chapter 1 of Acts of Apostles tells us nothing of their preaching. It simply informs us that they returned to Jerusalem after having received the commission, and stayed there waiting for the fulfillment of the promise of the Savior that they should be endued with power from on high. In chapter 2 of Acts we find this: "And when the day of Pentecost was fully come, they were all with one accord in one place. And suddenly there came a sound from heaven as of a rushing mighty wind, and it filled all the house where they were sitting. And there appeared unto them cloven tongues like as of fire, and it sat upon each of them." Now, these people were simply brought to the city of Jerusalem, the very spot to which material had been previously brought for the building of Solomon's temple, and it was there that the spiritual building called " the church of God " was to be established. The Holy Spirit came, took up his abode in this material, and there was the church of God in its infancy. Now when that time came they were to begin to preach under this great commission, and the apostle Peter, to whom Jesus had promised to give the keys of the kingdom of heaven, standing up with the eleven, called upon the surging sea of humanity about him to listen to what he had to say, and commenced preaching. Now this is the first preaching ever done under the great commission. Those who received it were positively forbidden to preach under it until then, until the descent of the Holy Spirit then and there, and they were just as positively required to begin preaching immediately after; they could not wait longer and not be in rebellion against God. But the Savior said: " Upon this rock I will build my church; and the gates of hell shall not prevail against it. And I will give unto thee the keys of the kingdom of heaven: and whatsoever thou shalt bind on earth shall be bound in heaven: and whatsoever thou shalt loose on earth shall be loosed in heaven." (Matt. 16: 18, 19.) That language was addressed to Peter, he having just said, " Thou art the Christ, the Son of the living God; " and the Savior had replied, " Blessed art thou, Simon Barjona: for flesh and blood hath not revealed it unto thee, but my Father which is in heaven." So we have Peter—the right man—in Jerusalem—the right place   at the right time—at the time of the descent of the Holy Spirit to occupy the material, or take up his abode in the material, prepared for the church of the living God—commencing the work he was required to do, and that was to use the keys of the church that was just established. He preached the birth, the life, the death, and incidentally the burial, and directly and specially the resurrection, of the Lord Jesus Christ, his ascension to glory, his coronation as King of kings and Lord of lords, and his sending the Holy Spirit to the earth to bless and save a lost and ruined world.   Remember, it had been but fifty days since the crucifixion on the cross, and those who murdered him were there and heard what was said, and Peter told them that they with wicked hands had crucified and slain God's Son, and that God had raised him from the dead, because it was not possible that he could be holden of death.   The apostle referred to David and Joel; to the life of the Savior and to his teaching; to his claim of being divine, and proved it, so that those who heard him believed it.   When they heard that he had been raised from the dead, because it was not possible for him to be holden of death; that he had been raised to glory, and had been crowned King of kings and Lord of lords, with the privilege of exercising all power in heaven and earth; that he had exercised that power by sending the Holy Spirit, they were shocked and horrified and terrified at the thought of their helpless, hapless, hopeless condition while they remained as they then were. They realized then that their souls were stained with the innocent blood of the Son of God, whom they with wicked hands had slain, and that unless something could be done to relieve them from the pressure of that dreadful sin they must be eternally lost; and though they had ignored the tears and sighs and prayers of the Savior as they nailed him to the cross, and cursed him as he died, they remembered that he was loving, tender, merciful, and kind; that as he hung upon the cross, quivering and trembling, every muscle writhing in agony, every feature distorted with pain, he prayed from the depths of his stricken soul: " Father, forgive them; for they know not what they do." This thought would naturally bring the light of hope to their hearts, a hope that they might some time in Christ find pardon for their agonized and guilty souls, and they cry out: " Men and brethren, what shall we do? " Now remember that this is the beginning of the work under this great commission; remember that high Heaven, through and by the power of the Holy Ghost, is ruling, reigning, controlling, and directing this work; remember, Peter holds the keys of the kingdom of heaven—the church that had just been established, born, and brought into being. How did he understand his commission? What is the condition of these people? They are lost and ruined sinners, they are the murderers of the Son of God, and they believe what Peter has preached to them. They believe Christ to be the Son of God, and hence in terror that rends their souls

they ask: " Men and brethren, what shall we do? "   Peter
replied: " Repent, and be baptized every one of you in the
name of Jesus Christ for the remission of sins, and ye shall
receive the gift of the Holy Ghost.   For the promise is
unto you, and to your children, and to all that are afar off,
even as many as the Lord our God shall call.   And with
many other words did he testify and exhort, saying, Save
yourselves from this untoward generation.   Then they that
gladly received his word were baptized: and the same day
there were added unto them about three thousand souls."
(Acts 2: 37-41.)   What did Peter understand to be the
conditions of pardon that he was to proclaim to a lost and
ruined world?   Faith, repentance, and baptism, the divine
record being true.   Certainly all of us can see this.

Now, let us go on with them to chapter 8 of Acts of
Apostles.   We are told that after the death of Stephen the
Christians at Jerusalem were all scattered abroad, and went
everywhere preaching the word—all of them, the apostles
excepted—and that Philip went down to Samaria and
preached Christ unto them.   " But when they believed
Philip preaching the things concerning the kingdom of
God, and the name of Jesus Christ, they were baptized,
both men and women."   (Acts 8: 12.)   But, remember,
they were not ready for baptism until they had repented,
for repentance and remission of sins were to be preached in
his name, beginning at Jerusalem; and Peter, with the keys
of the kingdom, had said to those who believed: " Repent,
and be baptized every one of you in the name of Jesus
Christ for the remission of sins, and ye shall receive the
gift of the Holy Ghost."   (Acts 2: 38.)   So, then, in this
instance, while we have faith and baptism expressed, we

have repentance just as clearly implied, and we have faith, repentance, and baptism just as proclaimed for the remission of sins—the faith and baptism clearly expressed, repentance as clearly implied. Going farther down in this chapter, we have this: "And the angel of the Lord spake unto Philip, saying, Arise, and go toward the south unto the way that goeth down from Jerusalem unto Gaza, which is desert. And he arose and went: and, behold, a man of Ethiopia, a eunuch of great authority under Candace queen of the Ethiopians, who had the charge of all her treasure, and had come to Jerusalem for to worship, was returning, and sitting in his chariot read Esaias the prophet. Then the Spirit said unto Philip, Go near, and join thyself to this chariot. And Philip ran thither to him, and heard him read the prophet Esaias, and said, Understandest thou what thou readest? And he said, How can I, except some man should guide me? And he desired Philip that he would come up and sit with him. The place of the scripture which he read was this, He was led as a sheep to the slaughter; and like a lamb dumb before his shearer, so opened he not his mouth: in his humiliation his judgment was taken away: and who shall declare his generation? for his life is taken from the earth. And the eunuch answered Philip, and said, I pray thee, of whom speaketh the prophet this? of himself, or of some other man? Then Philip opened his mouth, and began at the same scripture, and preached unto him Jesus. And as they went on their way, they came unto a certain water: and the eunuch said, See, here is water; what doth hinder me to be baptized? And Philip said, If thou believest with all thine heart, thou mayest. And he answered and said, I believe that Jesus

Christ is the Son of God. And he commanded the chariot to stand still: and they went down both into the water, both Philip and the eunuch; and he baptized him. And when they were come up out of the water, the Spirit of the Lord caught away Philip, that the eunuch saw him no more: and he went on his way rejoicing." (Acts 8: 26-39.) We have in that case faith and baptism positively expressed, and repentance just as clearly implied, because of what I have already stated and because of this: He was, judging from the language, a descendant of Abraham, and in order to enter Christ he had to abandon Judaism or anything else he believed that was contrary to the gospel of Christ, which had just then been preached to him by Philip, to turn from the wrong, to accept the right. So we have faith and baptism clearly expressed and repentance as clearly implied, the baptism preceded by the confession: "I believe that Jesus Christ is the Son of God." (Acts 8: 37.) Remember that Philip was laboring under this great commission, and this shows us how an inspired man in the long, long ago understood that commission.

In chapter 9, verses 22-26, we have the conversion of Saul of Tarsus, subsequently the apostle Paul. Briefly stated, it is this: He is journeying to Damascus with a band of soldiers to arrest Christians to take them to Jerusalem to persecution and death. He met the Savior; a brightness above the brightness of the sun shone around him. Literally blinded, he cried out: "Who art thou, Lord?" To this the Savior replied: "I am Jesus, whom thou persecutest." And the records show that he believed Christ to be the immaculate Son of God, and he said: "Lord, what wilt thou have me to do?" He was told what to do. He went to the city of Damascus and remained there in a blind, praying, fasting condition for three days and nights, awaiting the fulfillment of the promise that he was there to be told what he must do. Heaven sent an inspired man to him, and he found him in that fasting, praying condition, for unquestionably he was penitent at that time. Now, finding him in that condition, that inspired man of God caused his sight to come back to him, and thus God proved to Saul that the man who came to him was backed by divine authority. Then the inspired man said to him: "Arise, and be baptized, and wash away thy sins, calling on the name of the Lord." (Acts 22: 16.) He did so, and then, without conferring with flesh and blood, he went forward to battle bravely for Jesus until he died.

In Acts 16 we have an account of another conversion, this same man Saul, then the apostle Paul, being a prominent figure in connection with it. "And at midnight Paul and Silas prayed, and sang praises unto God: and the prisoners heard them. And suddenly there was a great earthquake, so that the foundations of the prison were shaken: and immediately all the doors were opened, and every one's bands were loosed. And the keeper of the prison awaking out of his sleep, and seeing the prison doors open, he drew out his sword, and would have killed himself, supposing that the prisoners had been fled. But Paul cried with a loud voice, saying, Do thyself no harm: for we are all here. Then he called for a light, and sprang in, and came trembling, and fell down before Paul and Silas, and brought them out, and said, Sirs, what must I do to be saved? And they said, Believe on the Lord Jesus Christ,

and thou shalt be saved, and thy house.   And they spake
unto him the word of the Lord, and to all that were in his
house.   And he took them the same hour of the night, and
washed their stripes; and was baptized, he and all his,
straightway.   And when he had brought them into his
house, he set meat before them, and rejoiced, believing in
God with all his house."   There we have faith and baptism positively expressed, and repentance as clearly implied, for this man was a pagan.   He accepted Christ and
rejected paganism.   We have the faith and baptism clearly
expressed and the repentance as clearly implied.

"And Crispus, the chief ruler of the synagogue, believed
on the Lord with all his house; and many of the Corinthians
hearing believed, and were baptized."   Again we have
faith, or belief, and baptism positively expressed and the
repentance as clearly implied.

Now, I am not able to tell you why, in the commission,
belief is mentioned but once, and repentance and baptism
are mentioned twice.   The Bible does not tell you, and I
cannot tell you, but it is just that way.   Nor do I know
why, in so many of these conversions, belief and baptism
are so forcibly expressed, and repentance not directly mentioned.   I do not know, because the Bible does not say,
but I am glad that repentance is always implied.   "And
the times of this ignorance God winked at; but now com-
mandeth all men everywhere to repent."   (Acts 17: 30.)
That quotation, in connection with the many other clear
passages of scripture, should be satisfactory evidence that
repentance is an essential condition of salvation.   But putting all these together, we have this: The apostles were
teaching people to hear the gospel, believe the gospel, re-

pent of their sins, confess their faith in Christ, confess that
they do believe that he is the Son of God, be buried with
him by baptism into death, and raised to walk in newness
of life; and having done that, they have a positive guarantee that their past sins are blotted out, that God will hold
them against them no more forever. They were then born
again, born of water and of the Spirit; were saved in the
sense that their past sins were blotted out, to be remembered against them no more. Then they were to live the
Christian life, being raised to walk in newness of life, and
be faithful unto death, and God would take them home.

CHAPTER XX.

LETTERS——FRANKLIN COLLEGE.

FRANKLIN COLLEGE, near Nashville, Tenn., was the last school T. B. Larimore attended. It was a remarkable institution, and Tolbert Fanning, its founder and president, was a man of varied talents and decided ability. His brother, A. J. Fanning, who was associated with him in the work at Franklin College many years, was noted especially as a mathematician; but was a man of few words and plain speech, without any gifts of oratory. The author of this volume was especially anxious to recognize in it Franklin College and the philanthropic labors and eminent talents of the Fannings, and the editor was fortunate in securing a picture of the institution and a brief article descriptive of the workings of the college from H. R. Moore, of Huntland, Tenn. When T. B. Larimore left Franklin College, the Fannings gave him a letter of commendation, which he highly appreciated and carefully preserved. To show his appreciation and put the autograph in permanent form, he greatly desired to have a facsimile of the letter in this book, but had not time to find it among his files of papers the few hours he could spend at home before the book had to go to press. When he abandoned the search, for lack of time, and reluctantly consented for the book to go to press without the letter, he wrote as follows:

" My Dear Friend and Brother: Looking in vain for

"DEDIE."

the Fanning letter I am so anxious to find, I have found something that has opened a fountain in my heart.

" Three days before Dedie's marriage, when she handed me a plate of such biscuits as she alone could make, I took two, but could not *eat*. I wrote a few lines, wrapped them up, and put them away in a safe place. The same was repeated on the morning of her marriage day. She cooked breakfast, as usual, that day. The four (4) biscuits are well preserved. Copies of the pages in which they are wrapped are herewith inclosed."

The " few lines " referred to are as follows:

" Made and baked by Dedie, December 27, 1897—three days before her marriage. Blessed child ! Our firstborn, she is the first to leave us. At 3 P.M., December 30, 1897, our family circle must be broken by, not death, but marriage. There is a land where love-bound circles are never broken. The thought of that makes life worth living."

On another sheet of paper to which he refers was written: .

" Made and baked by Dedie on the morning of her marriage day—December 30, 1897. Dedie is not only a good cook and a clean cook, but she is a good, pure, sweet Christian. She has been pure and sweet and good all her life. Home can never be home as it *has* been, sweet child ; but there is another home—a brighter and better home—where ' they neither marry nor are given in marriage,' and WE shall be perfectly happy forever there."

At the close of his long meeting in Nashville, in which

the sermons in this book were preached, he drove out
to Franklin College, which is now the Fanning Orphan
School, and wrote as follows:

> " 900 South College Street,
> " NASHVILLE, TENN., April 9, 1900.

" Mr. Woodfin, Birdie, and myself have just returned
from Franklin College and Hope Institute—twin institutions about five miles toward the gates of the morning
from Nashville, and about three hundred yards apart.

"A high fence, dividing the space between them about
equally, was the dangerous, dreadful ' dead line ' over
which boys and girls threw kisses there a generation ago.

" Sister Lipscomb, at the Institute, and Sister Mary
Fanning, at the College, received me so cordially and
treated me so kindly that I almost imagined I had found
some of the same sweet spirits that loved and were loved
there in the long, long ago. May the Lord always abundantly bless these sweet sisters, those they love, and those
who love them.

" Scarcely anything I saw there to-day looked natural.
Nearly everything looked less—very decidedly less—than
when I was one of the boys there three and thirty years
ago. This cannot be justly attributed to my feeling less
important then than now, I am sure; for, marvelous as it
may seem, my mission, when I first visited those institutions, was to assist the giants who then taught there in
teaching.

" It takes time and experience—much of both—to convince some of us that man knows but little here below, nor
knows that little long; but the Fannings—Tolbert and

- 21 -

Jack—made a believer of *me* in a very few days. It was a clear case, and they argued it wisely and well. They taught me that I needed to be taught, convinced me, and I gladly became a schoolboy again. They taught me how to think, how to talk, how to teach.

" When I left them, to stem tides of trouble I knew not of, one of them handed me the little letter, approved by both, herewith inclosed. The other said: ' I have never failed to read a man correctly when I had a good chance. You may never accumulate a fortune, but you will never depart from the faith or disgrace the cause of Christ.'

" Many years have come and gone since those things were written and said, and I—have not accumulated a fortune yet.

"About one hundred feet from the main entrance to Hope Institute, directly in front of it, just outside the yard, about thirty feet from the front gate, under a square pyramid of massive stones, sleeps the silent dust of an entire family—Tolbert and Charlotte Fanning.

" Why so little has been written and published about these two marvelous characters, A. J. Fanning, and others associated with them in their wonderful work, mortal man may never know. Had I the power to tell the story of their eventful lives, the story should be told.

" I hate no one. I am sure I love all in the sense in which the Lord demands that I love all. Nor man, nor beast, nor bird would I harm. I sincerely sympathize with the whole human race, with *all* things that can suffer or be sad. I would draw no invidious comparisons ; I would speak disparagingly or disrespectfully of none. I cherish no unkind feeling toward any person, place, or thing. I know *no* preacher who cannot be helpful to *me*, if I will listen diligently to what he may say. To say Solomon was the wisest of men is not to speak disparagingly of sages of other ages, countries, or climes.

" Now, I want to say I have known but one Tolbert Fanning. From the days of my youth until now, I have considered pure, chaste, clean oratory, free from profanity, balderdash, and slang, and backed by purity, consistency, earnestness, fidelity, and brains, the sublimest of all the sublime powers of man. I have never fallen at the feet of orators or worshiped at the shrine of oratory, but I have always loved to linger there. In all my life I have heard but one orator whom I deem it reasonable or admissible to compare with Tolbert Fanning. That man was the great and gifted lawyer and statesman, Daniel Voorhees, ' the tall sycamore of the Wabash,' whose oratory thrilled the greatest nation on the globe. As I heard him plead with power and pathos for the life, liberty, reputation, and honor of a prominent prisoner in the prime of life, whose beautiful wife—beautiful enough to be the bride of the prince imperial of any realm—sat in solemn silence by his side, weighing well every word, and anxiously waiting to take her husband home—which she was permitted to do in less than an hour after that wonderful oration was ended—I could almost see Tolbert Fanning, and hear his melodious, stentorian voice, as, in faultless English and perfectly rounded periods, he preached, as no other man I have ever heard *could* preach, the gospel, ' the power of God unto salvation.' Wonderful men were they!

"Alone I went into the chapel, and stood where I had so often seen that wonderful gospel preacher stand. The

stillness and silence of death were there. I looked at the
bare walls, the clean floor, the vacant seats; thought of the
loved of long ago, and instinctively said: ' O, *why* should
the spirit of mortal be proud?'

" Then, though the day was bright and the room was
light, I could not see even the vacant seats, but with Memory's eye of love, that neither time nor tears can dim, I
saw Julia, Josie, Jessie; Mottie, Bettie, Katie; Anna,
Fanny, Pattie; Maggie, Mary, Mollie; Alice, Lena, Sallie; Ella, Emma—a great throng of angels, pure and sweet,
too numerous to mention ' one by one.' I was again living
in the sweet long ago. The tide of time receded; I was
young again. We had met to work and worship in the
name of the sympathetic ' Man of sorrows.' The day was
dark as gloomy Gethsemane. Somber clouds shrouded
the scene and seemed to practically blot out the sun; livid
lightnings startled us; distant thunders rocked the earth;
the heavens sighed and moaned and wept; rain poured
down in torrents. Our great teacher announced ' Sorrows ' as the song for us to sing. Then I heard the rustle of clean cambric, calico, and linen—' linen pure and
white '—as the throng of angels, every one of whom I
dearly loved, arose to sing. Sister Fanning closed her
eyes, folded her arms, and led that throng of purity, love,
and beauty in singing, as, it seemed to me, only she and
those sweet girls could sing. May they ALL forever sing,
with *other* angels, where sorrows are unknown.

" Many years have come and gone since those happy
girls and hopeful boys last together sang ' Sorrows.' ' Sorrows, like tempests,' have swept down upon some of the
sweetest souls there then. Some of them are inexpressi-

TOLBERT FANNING.

(325)

bly sad. Some of them are living in poverty. Fortune seems to have favored a few. The cold, cheerless grave has claimed some. As these eventful years have silently slipped away, I have wandered up and down in the earth to tell the sweet old story of Jesus and his love. From ocean to ocean, from the lakes to the gulf, have I gone; but I have never heard sweeter strains of sacred song, music more nearly divine, than when I heard Sister Fanning and those precious pupils sing ' Sorrows ' before many, if any, of them knew what sorrow was.

"I shall hear some of those sweet souls sing ' Sorrows ' no more, but I hope to hear Sister Sallie Joe Carlton sing ' One Step at a Time, Dear Savior,' again and again and again; and I hope to hear ' the saints and faithful ' sweetly sing, wherever I may go, till God shall call me home.

" May the Lord, who loves and leads us, as, ' one step at a time,' we journey to the tomb, so bless us ALL in all our efforts to do the right, that, when done with all the toils and trials and troubles and tribulations and temptations and tears and sorrows of time, we may enter into the rest that remains ' to the people of God,' to roam and rejoice among the fadeless flowers, peerless beauties, and halcyon scenes of God's eternal home forever.

" From the Institute, I walked alone to the College. A gate has supplanted the stile on which we crossed the ' dead line ' when we were boys and girls. As I closed the gate behind me, I almost imagined I saw Overton coming to meet me. Pure, precious, tender-hearted boy! When I would walk to some place in ' the woods ' to *try* to preach on Sunday, I might expect him to be ' waiting and watching ' for me, and to meet me on the lawn and kiss me, when

I reached home, about the time of the setting of the sun. In looks, language, love, purity, and manners, he was more like a sweet girl than an average boy. Tender-hearted, affectionate, and true, ' he loved, not wisely, but too well.' His love for one he worshiped was not requited. She was all the world to him, but she would not be his. He could not live without her. Friends found him dead in his room. I doubt whether a handsomer, purer, truer boy has ever died.

"May the Lord grant that, when I get home, Overton may be at the gate, ' waiting and watching,' to welcome me. I long to meet and know there the loved who have known and loved me here.

"Miss Mary Fanning, the charming daughter of two marvelous mathematicians, met me at the College, and did all in her power to make my few-minutes' stay there pleasant as possible. I could not recognize any resemblance between her and her father or mother; but she may have inherited the mathematical genius of both. If so, she is certainly a mathematical prodigy. Be that as it may, I am sure she is a good, sweet child, and I pray that she may be happy forever.

"What changes time has wrought! I could recognize and definitely locate scarcely anything there, except the old dining room and kitchen in the basement. All above the basement has disappeared. If living witnesses, facts, and figures did not forbid, antiquarians might conclude that the dining room and kitchen had not been used as such for at least one thousand years. I went into the dining room through the same old hole in the wall; went into the kitchen and climbed out *over* the wall. That part of the scene is the personification of utter desolation.

" Slowly and sadly I walked back to the Institute, where Mr. and Mrs. Woodfin were patiently waiting for me. Not a word was spoken. No mortal but myself knew how I felt, and I could not express my feelings. Just as I was taking my final, farewell look at the dear old place, and wishing we had not taken the trip I had been so anxious to take, a sweet little motherless girl—Miss Irene Newman—came to tell us good-by. Mr. Woodfin, who loves little girls, as all good men do, tenderly embraced and kissed the precious little treasure, and I think we *all* felt better.

" Our journey home was uneventful. Our conveyance was comfortable and my company was charming, but I was too sad to talk. About sunset we reached home.

" ' Some sweet day ' we shall reach our eternal home. Then shall we be not sad, but glad ; and there shall we rest and reign and rejoice forever. Till then let us live as Heaven would have us live."

HUNTLAND, TENN., April 10, 1900.

Dear Brother Srygley: Your kind favor to hand, for which I am very much obliged. I am pleased to learn that you are inclined to utilize the picture of the old Franklin College building in embellishing the " Letters and Sermons " of your friend and preceptor, the gifted T. B. Larimore.

The picture was taken from a number of The Naturalist, a most excellent and ably edited monthly, conducted in

FRANKLIN COLLEGE, NEAR NASHVILLE, TENN., T. FANNING, PRESIDENT.

the long ago by President T. Fanning, Prof. Joseph S. Fowler, Prof. I. N. Loomis, and, it may be, other members of the Franklin College Faculty.

The dim old picture has had a place in my old scrapbook for nearly forty eventful years. I turn it over to you most willingly, that it may in future occupy a more becoming and conspicuous place in the book named.

But for the fact that the old Franklin College building has long since been destroyed, the picture would be insignificant and of no importance to any one.

But a dwindling remnant of the many students who were beneficiaries of that grand old school during the forties, fifties, and early sixties, still survives the disintegrating forces of time, scattered far and wide throughout this goodly land. The shadows of those that are left are falling far to the east, but perchance the bent of their minds, by the weight of years, is such that their thoughts can be easily attracted, and their fond memories readily awakened, by the pleasing environments that the picture may suggest. The influences of Franklin College have to a marked degree been favorable to our progressive Christian civilization. Its founder and able conductor was a remarkable man and a towering benefactor in his day and generation. Men like unto President Tolbert Fanning have never gone in gangs. If in early life he had entered any secular vocation, his great ability and peculiar force of character were such as to have warranted eminent success. As a preacher, teacher, and editor, he made an indelible impress on his surroundings for good. For years after the organization of Franklin College, her students were required to devote a certain part of their time, during certain seasons, to manual labor. Approved methods in agriculture and horticulture were taught and practiced; various kinds of mechanical work were encouraged and industriously prosecuted. Under this régime the work of the college was highly satisfactory to all concerned. President Fanning's faith in the wisdom and practicability of the manual labor system, in connection with the regular work of an institution of learning, was never shaken; but the presence of various influences from time to time conspired to gradually relax the rule, and finally resulted in its abrogation.

Franklin College at all times was peculiarly fortunate in having good material for the development of a high order of physical, mental, and moral manhood and womanhood. Her requirements and observed methods were such as not to be specially attractive to the ease-loving sons and daughters of the wealthy, nor to the indolent, unaspiring poor. The great majority of her students came from frugal, industrious, practical-minded families; from the world-moving middle classes with which our Southland was then, and is still, well supplied. Like many other institutions of learning at that time, graduation at Franklin College meant something. It implied the completion of the announced curriculum without modification or variation. Comparatively few of the students completed a replete course of study. In no grade or department was shoddy, superficial work tolerated.

No inducements were offered to those who were not inclined to cheerfully comply with the rigid demands imposed alike on all. There was probably no school in the land that afforded worthy, aspiring young men, without money, better opportunities than did Franklin College.

It was evidenly the pride and pleasure of President Fanning to cheerfully help such students. His ability to see over, under, all around, and square through o boy, was such that his benefactions were rarely misplaced or lost.

As a disciplinarian, he was impartial, exacting, austere, and severe. His methods were trying on petted, spoiled boys who did not know how to toe a mark—to submit to rules. As a teacher, he was sometimes patient, at other times impatient, but at all times clear and thorough. His rebukes for not spelling and pronouncing common English correctly and for doing violence to the rules of grammar were severe and impressive. His methods were to first draw out and develop the thinking and retaining powers, and then cram and fix principles thereon. He made a specialty of the Bible, grammar, logic, rhetoric, geology, chemistry, mental and moral philosophy, and the history of philosophic and metaphysical pretensions and theories. In his department he was a signal success. As a preacher, he was critical, argumentative, and aggressive. His comprehensive knowledge of the Bible and his great familiarity with sectarian, philosophic, and metaphysical speculations and theories enabled him to draw the line clearly and prominently between the real, on the one hand, and the imaginary, on the other; between the right and the wrong in matters pertaining to Christianity. His presentations of the all-sufficiency of the Bible in matters of religion, and of the delusive and popular innovations made thereon by the tall, progressive sons of science, were persistent, clear, and powerful. Old students still remember the respectful, yet fierce and uncompromising, war he was accustomed to make on much of the prominent and popular

religious and philosophic teachings of the times. He may
have had charity for the human frailties of religious partisan leaders, but certainly had but little patience with their
misleading pretensions. He maintained that faith in the
most approved systems of moral philosophy and in the best
and most popular religious creeds ever formulated by human authority was vain and delusive. He also maintained and insisted that such authorities held by religion-
ists were only productive of acrimonious differences among
the thoughtful, and soul-blighting indifference among all
others. In matters pertaining to man's eternal welfare,
he held and taught that human creeds break down every
barrier of correct thinking, and let fancy loose to play
her wildest freaks and most meaningless dreams, and
breed delusions and impostures, and decoy honest men and
women into dangerous extremes, and that they weaken
confidence in the divine appointments of the New Testament and lead their adherents to underrate the truth and
sufficiency of God's unerring waybill from this to a happier
state of being. His faith in the Bible as God's revealed
will to man was deep and abiding. He relied on its divine
teachings as to the nature and consequences of sin in this
life and in the life to come. Not only so; he relied on its
revelations in reference to all spiritual light as to religious
duties and obligations with a tenacity that knew no wavering or compromise. It is a notorious fact that he saw and
foretold, at least forty years in advance of his time, the infidel and skeptical tendencies of speculative sectarianism
and metaphysical philosophies that are now rife in many
high places. He severely denounced orthodox tendencies,
as at times indicated on the part of some of his own

prominent contemporary brethren, to such an extent that he was regarded by such as a captious alarmist; but the divers speculations now afloat in the stylish and fashionable religious world, seen by all discerning men, show the wisdom and sagacity of his protests. With the hand of a master he drew the dividing line that separates God's written revelation, on the one hand, and the misleading and delusive philosophic *a posteriori* and *a priori* methods, on the other, as to reliable sources of spiritual light, as but few could. But I must forbear further expressions as to the well-known characteristics of this great and good man, and hastily indicate the regular routine of the work of Franklin College, under his wise and efficient supervision.

Had you been a student there from January, 1853, to July 4, 1857, you might recall the work of a week and find that it ran about thus: President Fanning (known to all students and most intimate acquaintances as " Ole Boss ") rang the college bell about daylight each morning for devotional exercises, consisting of New Testament reading and prayer. The roll was first called and absentees reported. The penalty for absence was simply " no breakfast." A chapter was read by students by paragraphs. Close attention was paid to the proper pronunciation of words, the observance of punctuation marks, and the emphasis of certain clauses to properly express the meaning. Questions were frequently propounded and explanations made. This exercise being over, students went to their rooms and awaited the breakfast bell, and thereupon promptly assembled in the long hall on the first floor and formed in line in front of a teacher, or, in the absence of a teacher, some member of the senior class, who gave orders, when all were ready, to march in double file to the dining hall. Hats were hung on pegs, and each went in order to his place at the table. Standing, thanks were given, then all sat down and went to eating. The menu was not epicurean, but, as a rule, satisfied all who had been accustomed to plenty at home and who had been blessed with a good mother's training as to manners. All left the hall at the same time in good order. The students were then at liberty to go to the spring, get wood, stroll on "the Chicken road," or study. At 8 o'clock A.M. the bell called all to business—some, to recitation rooms, all others to their rooms for study. All were busy, and their work was changed and controlled each hour by the college bell till 12 o'clock M. A few minutes after 12 M. all went to dinner in the same order as at breakfast. At 1, 2, and 3 o'clock P.M. the bell rang and all were similarly engaged as in the forenoon. At 4 o'clock P.M. all assembled in the chapel again for roll call, for two or more declamations by students, and for announcements and short lectures by the Faculty. Then the students were free for such recreations and duties as they desired till about 6 o'clock P.M., at which time they again formed in line and marched to supper. Soon after supper the bell again called all from refreshment to labor. At 10 o'clock P.M. the rule was to extinguish all lights and retire for the night. Saturdays were devoted to society work. The best students, as a rule, took great interest in this work. There were two literary societies—the Apolonean and Euphronean—each of which had a well-furnished hall and an ample library. There was no little rivalry between the respective members in getting new members and in excelling in debating and other society work. The exercises were conducted in the most orderly and dignified manner. Few deliberative bodies observe parliamentary rules as they did. Each was chartered by the State, and was an ornament to the college and a blessing to most members. About 10:30 o'clock Sunday morning, the students, the young ladies of Sister Fanning's school and of Minerva College, with the teachers, and others of that locality, assembled in the college chapel for preaching. Then and there President Fanning delivered most excellent and carefully prepared sermons. The beloved F. M. Carmack preached occasionally during his connection with the college as a teacher. The singing, in which all were encouraged to participate, was good. At 2 o'clock P.M. the members of the Franklin College congregation assembled for the Lord's Supper. Prof. William Lipscomb hung a bag on the corner of the stand, or pulpit, for contributions. At certain seasons of the year President Fanning had the students to assemble in the chapel, after the meeting of the church on Sunday evenings, for a most rigid and critical drill in from one to five chapters in the Old Testament Scriptures. These Old Testament exercises, and those in the New Testament every morning during the week, were closely studied by most students. At about 7 o'clock on Sunday evenings the young ladies and gentlemen of the schools named again assembled for singing, Scripture reading, and a lecture on some interesting subject or current topic, usually delivered by President Fanning. These lectures were very entertaining and instructive to the young people for whom they were intended. The leading thoughts in new meritorious books were at times presented and discussed; scenes and occurrences in his travels were at other times presented. He often, on these interesting and instructive occasions, discoursed on the laws of health. In insisting on the importance of rigidly conforming to Nature's laws in order to maintain health, he would sometimes say: " It is a sin to be sick. You can violate man's laws, under certain conditions, with impunity, but you cannot trifle with God's laws as contained in the Bible or in nature." On other occasions he would give, with much force and clearness, the distinctive characteristics of a gentleman and of a lady. Still at other times he would dwell with effect on the admirable characteristics of a brave man and of a true woman. He often said: "A crazy fool will strike his fellow-man or shoot him when mad; a brave man has the courage of his convictions, and amid the most trying surroundings will do right, will be a man. A true woman will not place the highest estimate in stylish gewgaws, but in purity, culture, and character."

President Fanning, his good wife, and the entire Faculty occasionally encouraged the social commingling of the young ladies and gentlemen who were under their supervision. Certain times would be named, abundant refreshments provided, and a day be most happily spent in an adjacent grove, or an evening in the spacious chapel and halls of the college. President Fanning, who on all other occasions held the students at full arm's length, would on these rare occasions be one of us. He appeared to enjoy " the pleasure of introducing " the most timid and verdant specimens of the occasion and have them mated for talks and promenades. The tendency was to eliminate timidity and develop composure and free and easy general demeanor.   Sweethearts were claimed and recognized.   In many cases courtship and happy marriages resulted.

But this hasty missive has gone beyond contemplated bounds.   There is no easy stopping place amid the environments of boyhood's happy days and scenes, days and scenes that will be held dear as long as fond memory is true to her sacred trust.   Truly and sincerely yours,

H. R. MOORE.

FRANKLIN COLLEGE ALUMNI.

Class of 1846—A. J. Fanning, Tennessee.

Class of 1847—J. H. Embry, Kentucky; A. L. Johnson, Kentucky; John King, Kentucky; S. H. Parsons, Louisiana; P. R. Runnels, Tennessee.

Class of 1848—C. N. Anderson, Kentucky; E. W. Carmack, Mississippi; S. S. Bush, Tennessee; A. G. Gooch, Tennessee; S. R. Hay, Illinois; W. A. C. Jones, Alabama; W. Lipscomb, Tennessee; Joseph Nelson, Tennessee; H. B. Rives, Alabama; J. P. Smith, Louisiana; N. B. Smith, Kentucky; J. S. Williams, Texas.

Class of 1849—J. E. Campbell, Texas; D. Lipscomb, Tennessee; A. J. Swepston, Mississippi; A. J. Wyatt, Kentucky.

Class of 1850—S. Y. Caldwell, Tennessee; J. B. Clark, Mississippi; S. V. Clark, Mississippi; J. V. Cook, Texas; S. C. Crawford, Arkansas; W. R. Cox, Tennessee; W. Y. Houston, Texas; J. P. Houston, Alabama; L. S. Lavender, Alabama; J. L. McCutcheon, California; P. G. Rives, Arkansas; J. C. Roberts, Tennessee; M. A. Smith, Georgia; D. J. Towson, Tennessee; F. D. Wright, Mississippi.

Class of 1851—Benjamin Abbott, Arkansas; Isaac Bush, South Carolina; F. M. Carmack, Mississippi; D. Galbreath, Texas; J. G. Hester, Kentucky; O. S. Laws, Ohio; T. G. B. Sanders, Alabama; F. L. Taney, Louisiana.

Class of 1852—R. R. Caldwell, Tennessee; E. W. Herndon, Missouri; L. Hodges, Mississippi; A. B. C. Jones, Missouri; S. S. Laffitte, South Carolina; W. T. Richardson, Tennessee.

Class of 1853—A. H. Appleton, Kentucky; G. W. Bailey, South Carolina; C. K. Barnes, Tennessee; A. J. Caldwell, Tennessee; R. E. Fortson, Louisiana; S. L. Freeman, Tennessee; A. P. Reid, Mississippi; E. D. Warder, Kentucky; J. P. Warder, Kentucky.

Class of 1854—H. G. Davis, Alabama; T. W. Watkins, Tennessee; K. M. Vanzandt, Texas.

Class of 1855—W. C. Hubbard, Tennessee; W. I. Lipscomb, Tennessee; T. K. Powell, Tennessee; G. B. Lipscomb, Tennessee; J. E. Scobey, Tennessee.

Class of 1856—T. T. Baudwoin, Louisiana; W. C. Bromly, Mississippi; J. J. Jolly, Alabama; M. A. Jolly, Alabama; W. L. Collins, Tennessee; J. T. Settle, Mississippi; W. M. T. Thompson, Tennessee.

Class of 1857—H. R. Moore, Mississippi; W. F. Fulgham, Tennessee; I. L. Vanzandt, Texas; A. L. Anderson.

Class of 1859—John Smith Poyner, Robert H. Powell, Wallace Powell, E. G. Sewell, G. M. Atkerson, Eleanor R. Hill, Sarah A. Harris.

Class of 1860—Thomas A. Head, James Alexander, J. S. McCorkle, L. P. Swain, Thomas W. Davis, J. J. Scott.

FOUR GENERATIONS OF LARIMORES.

CHAPTER XXI.

SERMON——EXISTENCE AND VALUE OF THE SOUL.

(Sermon delivered by T. B. Larimore at South College Street Church, Nashville, Tenn., on January 28, 1900.)

THEN said Jesus unto his disciples, If any man will come after me, let him deny himself, and take up his cross, and follow me. For whosoever will save his life shall lose it: and whosoever will lose his life for my sake shall find it. For what is a man profited, if he shall gain the whole world, and lose his own soul? or what shall a man give in exchange for his soul? For the Son of man shall come in the glory of his Father with his angels; and then he shall reward every man according to his works." (Matt. 16: 24-27.)

The mind is so constituted that it is never satisfied with its conquests. This is clearly demonstrated in life almost from the cradle to the grave. A little boy starts to school, and begins to try to learn the simplest principles of the English language. He learns the English alphabet; he learns to spell, to read, to write; he leaves the first reader, second reader, third reader, fourth reader, fifth reader behind him and goes into history; he masters one book after another, and all the time sees brighter fields before him and new wonders calling him to go forward and make other conquests. Thus he may go on forever, but still there are tempting hills and towering mountains before him that he longs to climb. He may measure the comet's path, tell the distance of the stars, and fathom the depths of space; but even then his mind will long to take a loftier flight, and from that lofty height plunge into deepest depths, that it may bring from thence knowledge that man has never gained. Thus it is that the mind is never satisfied in the sense that it is content to rest without further conquests. Now, the Savior understood all this, and knew that the preparation of the soul for eternal blessedness was in importance above all else, and he desired and designed that naught on earth should fully and completely satisfy this longing of the soul. So he submitted to the human race a sublimely simple proposition in loss and gain—a proposition simple enough to interest children, yet sublime enough to engage the attention of sages, of angels and archangels: "For what is a man profited, if he shall gain the whole world, and lose his own soul? or what shall a man give in exchange for his soul?"

Man cannot absolutely, completely, and fully gain the whole world; life is too short and man's powers are too limited for that; but we have all the reasons necessary to convince us that if he could and should gain the whole material world, with all its wondrous wealth, pomp, pageantry, and power, even then he would realize, as he had never realized before, that there is an aching void this world can never fill. Of course there are no historical characters by whom to prove that proposition, from the fact that no human being has ever completely and thoroughly gained the whole world; but history does furnish examples of men who have practically done so in the line of their sordid, selfish, and all-absorbing ambition; and history also tells us that such characters were never satisfied. Probably no man ever lived, not even Napoleon excepted, who had greater longings for conquest, for dominion, for military, political, and regal glory and splendor, than Alexander the Great. That longing seemed to be natural, to have been inherited, manifesting itself in the days of his childhood by prominent characteristics that followed him to the day of his death. When but a youth, learning from his teacher that there are worlds innumerable, the information made him miserable. His teacher asked him why. He said: "There are numberless worlds, and I have not conquered this one yet." When his illustrious father, Philip of Macedon, was conquering the divided States of Greece, one by one, and all Macedon was filled with joy, Alexander, the prince imperial, was perfectly miserable. Some one asked him why, and he replied: "My father will conquer the world before he dies, and leave me nothing to do." Now, certainly, if this world can give the bliss for which we sigh; if one possessing such longing for conquest and dominion could subdue the earth, sway the scepter over all its nations, and have access to all its wealth, he would be happy. Let us see. Just as this ambitious youth reached his majority, his father suddenly and mysteriously died, and it has come down through all the ages from then till now that it was thought and softly whispered all over that land that Alexander put poison into his cup to get him out of the way.

Combining the Macedonian hosts with the Grecian phalanx, thus forming an army invincible, Alexander began his career. Vast armies fell before him, like grain before the modern reaper; proud nations fell before him, like trees uprooted by tempests. The day was at hand when Alexander started from Macedon's capital on that eventful morning when all the armies that opposed him and all the nations that defied him were subdued. Alexander was the conqueror of the world. No nation on earth to oppose him, no man under the stars to question his right to anything he might claim. Virtually the whole wide world and its possessions belonged to him. Was he happy? If this world can make a man happy, he was certainly happy. He had reached the goal of his ambition, while he was in the very prime of young manhood, just at the age to be most gratified by his conquests, just at the time when he could enjoy them most. So, if this world can give the bliss for which we sigh, Alexander must have been happy. Let us see. An historian of that age drew a pen picture of the world's conqueror, seated upon the summit of a rock against which the billows of the sea are beating. He is watching the waves as they chase each other over the deep, deep sea, casting their whitecaps at each other like children at play, while great tears drop from his cheeks. Why does he weep? Does he weep because of the wail of weeping widows, the sigh of homeless orphans—because of the destruction, devastation, and desolation he himself hath wrought? Is he thinking of homes that had still been happy homes, had his sword not slain their defenders and his torch reduced them to ashes? Does he weep because he remembers the wreck and ruin wrought by his own ruthless hand, that the world might call him great? Not that. He wept because there was no more bloody work for him to do—no armies to vanquish; no nations to conquer; no sons, husbands, fathers, lovers, brothers, to butcher. With legions around him ready for battle, he knew there were none to meet them; with power to march his legions, drip ping with blood, he knew of no unconquered land to devastate and destroy. He has conquered the world; now what shall he do? He turns away in disgust and disappointment from the restless scene and sighing sea before him, gives himself up to dissipation, to indulgence, to revelry. He drinks until he is drunken; at midnight, when he is already intoxicated, he fills to the brim thrice the enormous cup of Hercules with the sparkling waters of temporal and eternal destruction, and pours the contents into his stomach. Delirium, in which he raves like a maniac, ensues. Disappointment, dissipation, and debauchery suddenly send him in madness and despair down to the dark depths of a drunkard's grave. Such is the sequel to the story of the man who is called Alexander the Great, the conqueror of the world.

Well might the blessed Savior, knowing human nature to perfection and understanding the vanity of all things earthly, with his disciples around him, telling them of the law of life eternal, assuring them that if they saved their temporal lives by denying him they should lose their souls, but if they died in defense of the right eternal blessedness should be their reward, ask the question: "For what is a man profited, if he shall gain the whole world, and lose his own soul? or what shall a man give in exchange for his soul?"

But I am reminded that thousands of intelligent persons deny the existence of the soul, on the ground that reason should not recognize or concede the existence of the soul, since our natural, corporeal senses fail to demonstrate or detect such existence. This is infidelity, of course; but it is the duty of Christians to meet skeptics, infidels, and

atheists—skepticism, infidelity, and atheism—respectfully,
kindly, and courteously, with reason and revelation, in the
spirit of love. Those who deny the existence of the soul
on this ground assume that it is absurd to concede the existence of the soul because the corporeal senses can neither
demonstrate nor detect its existence, and then they positively affirm there is no soul. The conclusion is illogical,
because the premise is untrue. The major premise is:
Nothing exists the existence of which cannot be demonstrated or detected by our corporeal senses just as they are.
This is the argument: There is nothing in existence the existence of which cannot be demonstrated or detected by
the use of these corporeal senses just as they are. These
corporeal senses can neither demonstrate nor detect the existence of the soul; therefore there is no soul. Is that true?
Is the major premise of that argument true? Is it true
that nothing exists the existence of which cannot be demonstrated or detected by the use of the corporeal senses with
which we are endowed, just as they are? To propound
that question to any intelligent audience is to answer it, for
every responsible soul certainly ought to know it is hard to
find a more absurd proposition. Look whithersoever we
will, we find evidence of its absurdity. Let us dip from
the bright bosom of a bubbling spring a glass of water,
pure and clear as crystal. Let the sunlight kiss it while
we look for traces of life in it. Let us bring to bear upon
it all the power of our natural senses just as they are. We
find no trace of life in it. Is it true, then, that there is no
life there? No. In that glass of water there are millions
and billions and trillions of creatures possessing all the
necessary powers of life and locomotion, there being thou-

sands in every drop, and each tiny drop, it may be, a boundless, fathomless, limitless ocean to the little creature that sports in its depths. There is, as the world now knows, life in the very dew that rests on the lip of beauty. Shall I say there are no living creatures in that limpid water, in that precious dew, because I have never seen them?

The telescope reveals millions of worlds that the unaided eye of man has never seen. Shall I say no stars ever shine in the blue depths of space, save the few blazing worlds that my eyes behold, simply because I have never seen them?

Seven acorns are taken from the same forest, the same tree, the same bough. Forty of the best scientists of this skeptical class or school on earth are permitted to take first choice, and first choice again and again, until they have chosen six of the seven acorns, leaving the seventh untouched. They take these six acorns to their laboratory to examine them in the interests of science, simply and solely to try to detect in these acorns life or anything like life. Baby forests are wrapped in the bosoms of those tiny acorns. Do they find them there? They hope to make discoveries that will cause Christians to blush because they claim there is a soul in the human body, yet have never been able to see it. They subject every part of these six acorns to every possible character and degree of scientific analysis. On these acorns, and all parts of these acorns, they bring to bear all their power, aided by all such instruments as can now be used in such scientific research, just to discover life or the life principle, or even a trace of the forests shut up in those tiny shells—anything to which they can point with pride and say, " This is it! " that they may then consistently challenge Christians to show them the soul. When their work is done their failure is complete. In the meantime the hand of a little child plants the acorn they left in a broad field where nothing can prevent the growth and development that are desired. The silent dews gather, the gentle showers fall, the bright rays of the sun come, and the acorn begins to swell, the shell breaks, the surface of the earth opens, a tiny green shoot appears, a stem supports two little leaves; the stem grows; the two little leaves multiply, are rocked by the winds and warmed by the sun; the tree grows taller and taller, until, a giant oak, it bears thousands of acorns; many of these produce oaks, and these oaks produce acorns, and many of these acorns produce oaks, until at last a vast, magnificent forest covers the once unoccupied field. As these trees bathe their boughs in the battlements of heaven bending above them, we remember that every tree, every twig, every leaf in all that forest sprang from the bosom of one little acorn that was an exact duplicate of each of the six acorns that those skeptical scientists examined in vain with all their skill, wisdom, and power, hoping to find some trace of life therein.

An eagle, proud emblem of American prowess, liberty, and power, builds her nest high up on some lofty crag above a fathomless abyss. Now there are seven eggs in that nest. Our skeptical scientists have recovered from the embarrassment of their failure to find an oak in an acorn, and are ready to try something else. They manage mind, muscle, and money so as to reach that nest. They take first choice, and first choice again and again, until they have robbed that bird of all her eggs but one. They bring them down and take them to their laboratory, where they scrutinize and analyze them as they did the acorns. When they have done all possible for them to do, they are forced to admit that failure has met them at every point. No trace of bird or life have they found. In the meantime that mother bird, directed by a power that man cannot understand, planted in her breast by Him before whom a sparrow cannot fall unnoticed, makes the best of the situation. She subjects the one egg left to a temperature that is absolutely perfect for the purpose designed. In process of time there is the sound of a gentle rapping, tapping, on the inside of that egg—that shell. What is that? Some living thing in there? No; no life there, as certainly as there is no soul in the body; for those solons, scientists, sages, skeptics, who deny the existence of the soul because they cannot demonstrate its existence, have already taken six eggs from that selfsame nest, examined them thoroughly, and utterly failed to find anything like bird or life. There is no window or door in the shell to admit anything that might make that noise, and no life within it (these scientists have failed to find life there); but still the tapping proceeds. It is not modern spirit rapping, for the lights do not have to be turned down before the rapping can begin. The sun shines, the stars glitter, but the rapping goes on. It is just as strong when the sun is poised upon the meridian as at midnight. It is, therefore, not modern spirit rapping. That settles that. Finally the shell is broken, for the workman within that shell has not been wasting time and energy by knocking around promiscuously and at random, as many men, who might otherwise be a success, do. Whatever it is inside that shell has never learned that the constant dropping of water will wear away stone, or that patient, persistent perseverance is sure to be rewarded; but still the work goes on.   The shell is broken; and then, with a precision that the wisdom of Solomon and the skill of Hiram combined could not have excelled, the little workman elevates or lowers his mallet and begins to work away in another place.   An exact semicircle is made—a regular, smooth semicircle; the shell is broken halfway round.   By this time the workman becomes impatient, wants more elbow room, spreads himself; the shell is no longer one, but two; it is empty, and an eaglet is in the nest.   Where did it come from?   From where neither sight nor science can find bird or life, as neither sight nor science can see the soul within the fleshly shell in which we journey to the tomb.   The time has now come for the mother's work to change—not to rest; mothers get very little rest in this world.   They should certainly so live as to enter into " the rest that remaineth to the people of God," and should so train their little ones that they may meet them there.

The mother's work changes.   She goes on distant journeys, over mountain high and deep abyss; across fruitful fields smiling in summer sunshine; down into deep, dark, gloomy gulfs and flowery, fruitful valleys, in quest of food for her baby bird.   Bearing a precious morsel, she homeward flies, happy because her labors have been crowned with success.   She brings it to her baby, and is glad.   The baby bird has nothing to do but lie in the nest—its eyes closed, its mouth wide open—swallow, sleep, and grow. The mother continues her labor of love till she is almost a skeleton, and the baby bird has grown to greater proportions than its mother has ever had, and weighs three times as much as its mother weighs now. Still, that bird that has grown to such ponderous proportions sympathizes not with its self-sacrificing mother—seems to regard it as a matter of course that thus it must be. There are birds without wings in this strange world that act too frequently and too long upon that same sad principle, not thinking of mother as they should—mother never complaining, of course. She wants to work for her children, and her labors seem light to her, on the principle that love's labor is always light. Some such children never realize what they are doing until some sad day, at the setting of the sun, they return from the gloomy graveyard, the silent city of the dead, to the home that mother can brighten and bless no more, and then begin to realize the meaning of " What is home without a mother? " May the God of all grace so bless you that not one of you may ever, under such sad and sorrowful circumstances, have cause for sighing and self-reproach.

It has been a bright, balmy, beautiful, glorious day, the brightness simply broken here and there by far-away, fleecy clouds, like angels hovering over earth and then speeding away into the depths of space. The mother bird is almost exhausted. Her child has rested till it is restless—tired, indeed, of resting. The sun sets; twilight's semisacred hour comes; darkness approaches; through the rent mantle of night a bright star smiles upon the bird in the nest; then another, another, and another, until the whole heaven is a sea of beauty and splendor—an ocean of stars. The mother bird, near her nest and babe, is resting now, that she may be able to work to-morrow. The young bird is restless; an unutterable feeling possesses it. The night ends; day dawns; the young bird looks far away toward the gorgeous, glittering gate of the morning, and sees towering mountain peaks kissed into gleaming, glittering glory by the rising sun, that wraps them in a mantle of light as he ushers in another bright day. A feeling akin to the sublime takes possession of the restless bird. He rises, shakes the dew from his pinions, plunges like a thunderbolt from on high down into the darkness beneath him—down, down, down, until his pinions brush the bosom of a beautiful little limpid lake asleep in the arms of the valley below; then up, up, up, like a trusting soul on the wings of prayer, until the hills cannot be seen and the mountains seem mere specks on the surface of the earth. There he rests on outstretched wings, and then we remember that that bird—a thing of beauty, power, and sublimity—came from the egg that was rejected six times by the skeptical scientists when they chose six of the seven eggs in that nest in which this one alone was left.

Thus all nature, vocal with praises of the great I Am, declares and demonstrates the absurdity of the claim that there is no soul because we cannot detect it by the use of these corporeal senses just as they are, just as God has, in his wondrous wisdom, goodness, and power, graciously given them to the sons and daughters of men.

Now, I must come down out of the clouds—no, I must arise and come up out of them, out of the mists and fogs—and give you the light of a few quotations from God's word. I never feel easy—feel that I have done my duty—if I close a discourse so as to leave my audience in the treacherous quicksands of human wisdom, speculation, or thought.

Duty demands, and I always desire, that those who patiently hear me preach be left trusting God and resting upon the solid rock of his eternal truth. Now, let us go to the bosom of God's blessed Book for an answer to that phase of whatever it may be pertinent, proper, and right to call it, that claims to believe the Bible, to accept the Bible as evidence, and still denies the existence of the soul.

In Gen. 35 we have an account of the death of Rachel, the beloved wife of Jacob. In verse 18 we have this language: "And it came to pass, as her soul was in departing, (for she died) that she called his name Ben-oni: but his father called him Benjamin." The writer parenthetically explains what he means when he says " her soul was in departing." As certainly as this teaches anything, it teaches that when she died her soul departed, when she was dying her soul was departing, as her soul was departing she was dying. In this house, gas and oil are both burning to give us light. Suddenly the lights are all extinguished. Do they depart or do they cease to be? You have a flaming torch dispelling the darkness. You dip it into the bosom of the Cumberland River. Does the light depart, or does it simply cease to exist, suddenly and forever? It is not necessary to answer that question. We all know it simply ceases to exist. The Bible teaches that when the soul departs death is the result; the Bible teaches that when the soul is departing we are dying; the Bible teaches that in death the soul departs. That settles that, if we believe the Book.

" But God said unto him, Thou fool, this night thy soul shall be required of thee: then whose shall those things be, which thou hast provided? So is he that layeth up treasure

-23-

for himself, and is not rich toward God." (Luke 12: 20, 21.) This is part of the lesson on which I based the first discourse I ever tried to deliver—the story of the rich and selfish farmer, prospering marvelously, making preparation to keep all he had and get all he could, God suddenly saying to him: "Thou fool, this night thy soul shall be required of thee: then whose shall those things be, which thou hast provided? So is he that layeth up treasure for himself, and is not rich toward God." I believed the Bible then; I believe the Bible now.

"And fear not them which kill the body, but are not able to kill the soul: but rather fear him which is able to destroy both soul and body in hell." (Matt. 10: 28.) This language fell from the lips of the loving Lord himself. He addressed it to his own disciples, whom he tenderly loved. Did he deliberately deceive them? Does not the man who kills the body destroy the life? The man who kills the body does not destroy the soul, the Bible being true. The Savior taught his disciples to be "wise as serpents and harmless as doves," dreading no danger, fearing no death, living for the good that they could do. A soul secure in the love and service of the Savior can calmly smile at the assassin's sword, and safely say: "You may kill the body in which I dwell, but you can never kill me; for my Savior says so, and whatsoever he says is true." If this does not teach that within this mortal body there is a soul that shall "survive the wreck of matter and crash of worlds," then logic, truth, reason, and revelation combined can never teach anything. God teaches, Christ teaches; patriarchs, apostles, and prophets teach; the Bible teaches, that man is not all flesh, bone, brain, and blood, but that there is

within these tenements of clay something that shall live forever—that shall plunge into eternal darkness and dread
despair, if not prepared to meet God in peace; but shall be
borne by angels to a place of rest, to dwell in God's eternal
home forever, if in harmony with his will the life lived here
has been. Well might our Savior, knowing this, ask the
question: " For what is a man profited, if he shall gain the
whole world, and lose his own soul? or what shall a man
give in exchange for his soul?"

We should all remember that " life is the time to serve
the Lord, the time to insure the great reward, the day of
grace when mortals may secure " the blessings of heaven.
In this brief period of probation we must fit ourselves for
eternal blessedness, or be wrecked and ruined forever.
How brief is life! How short the time! How long, how
limitless, is eternity! Some saintly soul has said:

> " Lo, on a narrow neck of land
> 'Twixt two unbounded seas I stand,
> Yet not insensible.
> A point of time, a moment's space,
> Removes me to yon heavenly place,
> Or shuts me up in hell."

My dying friends, pilgrims to the tomb, traveling through
sorrow and sighing and suffering and sadness and sickness
and sin, whither are you tending? Standing on this narrow strip, with the surging billows about you, are you living
for time and sense and self in the service of Satan, that at
last and forever you may reap corruption; or are you living
for God, for Christ, for humanity, for heaven? Are you
sowing to the Spirit, that of the Spirit you may reap life
everlasting; or are you sowing to the flesh, that of the flesh

you may reap corruption? "Be not deceived; God is not mocked: for whatsoever a man soweth, that shall he also reap. For he that soweth to his flesh shall of the flesh reap corruption; but he that soweth to the Spirit shall of the Spirit reap life everlasting. And let us not be weary in welldoing: for in due season we shall reap, if we faint not. As we have therefore opportunity, let us do good unto all men, especially unto them who are of the household of faith." (Gal. 6: 7-10.)

CHAPTER XXII.

SERMON—THE GOOD CONFESSION.

WHEN Jesus came into the coasts of Cesarea Philippi, he asked his disciples, saying, Whom do men say that I the Son of man am? And they said, Some say that thou art John the Baptist: some, Elias; and others, Jeremias, or one of the prophets. He saith unto them, But whom say ye that I am? And Simon Peter answered and said, Thou art the Christ, the Son of the living God. And Jesus answered and said unto him, Blessed art thou, Simon Bar-jona: for flesh and blood hath not revealed it unto thee, but my Father which is in heaven. And I say also unto thee, That thou art Peter, and upon this rock I will build my church; and the gates of hell shall not prevail against it. And I will give unto thee the keys of the kingdom of heaven: and whatsoever thou shalt bind on earth shall be bound in heaven: and whatsoever thou shalt loose on earth shall be loosed in heaven. Then charged he his disciples that they should tell no man that he was Jesus the Christ." (Matt. 16: 13-20.)

In the northeastern extremity of the land of Palestine there was, in the days of the Savior's painful pilgrimage upon the earth, a little town or village called " Dan," corresponding to Beer-sheba in the opposite extremity of the land; hence the biblical expression, " From Dan to Beer-sheba," meant from one extremity of the land to the other. Just about three miles from Dan, toward the golden, glittering gates of the morning, stood, in ages veiled in the mists of very remote antiquity, a town, named by the pagans who built it, and called by the heathens who inhabited it, " Paneas," in honor of Pan, the god of shepherds, a creature of the imagination—half brute, half human—whose favor was supposed to be essential to the success of those who watched and cared for the flocks. Long before the Star of Bethlehem twinkled over the plains of Galilee, and the Sun of Righteousness arose with healing in his wings, to flood the world with light divine, Paneas became a heap of ruins, a fit abode for owls and bats and hissing serpents. But just before the angels shouted, " Glory to God in the highest, and on earth peace, good will toward men! " over the birth of the Babe of Bethlehem, a new town was built by Herod Philip, a subordinate ruler of the Roman Empire, on the foundation once occupied by that pagan city, Paneas; and this city built by Herod Philip he named " Cesarea Philippi "—" Cesarea " for Cæsar, and " Philippi " for himself—thus uniting and welding his own name with that of his cruel, heartless, merciless, bloody master; hence the name " Cesarea Philippi " in the language we have just read. Cesarea Philippi, like Nashville, was founded upon a mass of imperishable rock. It was built of stone, from hovel to palace, from foundation to roof, and hence, like Nashville, the capital city of my own native State, might well have been called the " Rock City " and the " City of Rocks." Cesarea Philippi was surrounded by a stone wall —high, massive, strong—an effective means of protection for a town in that far-away age of the world, being situated in one of the roughest, rockiest, most picturesque and romantic spots on earth, right at the foot of towering Hermon, that cast its deep, dark shadow upon the town for hours at the beginning of every day; and just at the head of the rolling Jordan, that leaped from the bosom of the earth and flashed and sparkled and swept on until it was lost in the embrace of the deep, mysterious Dead Sea. Just about one mile toward the rising sun from Cesarea Philippi, resting upon one of the rocky spurs of rock-ribbed Hermon, was a rock fortress that was practically impregnable in that far-away age of the world antedating the use of gunpowder, dynamite, nitroglycerin, gun cotton, and other explosives that are used in the science of human butchery in this Christian age of the world.

Now it was in the coasts or suburbs or immediate presence of this rock-bounded, rock-founded, rock-builded, rock-surrounded, rock-protected, rock-shadowed city that Jesus, the Rock of Ages, the Rock for sinners cleft, said to Peter, the " rock "—to Cephas, the " stone "—in reference to that spiritual institution that had been represented by Daniel, in the then long, long ago, by the little rock cut out of the mountain without hands and subsequently filling the earth; that divine, spiritual institution, every member of which is called in the Bible a " lively stone " or a " living stone: " " Upon this rock I will build my church; and the gates of hell shall not prevail against it." There is nothing accidental about the phraseology of the Bible, nothing any more accidental about the framing of the picture that hangs upon the wall of God's eternal truth than there is about the painting of that picture by the hand of Omnipotence itself. Hence we ought to rejoice that this wonderful picture is presented to us in this wondrous phraseology, and we should appreciate not only the picture, but the very framing of that picture, shaded by towering mountains, in which the hand of God has hung the picture upon the walls of his temple of divine truth.

There be some truths that bloom in beauty upon the very bosom of the ocean of God's revelation to man, as water lilies bloom upon the bosom of the lake that gave them birth and being; while there are other precious pearls buried far down in its solemn, silent depths. The former we can gather by simply a casual glance at the surface of this ocean of truth, just as the hand of the little child can pluck the water lily as the boat is propelled over the lake by a father's strong hand; while the latter must be brought up by earnest, prayerful research, as brave men must go down into the darkest depths of the sea to bring up the pearls hidden there. There is a representative of each of these two classes of thought in the lesson I have just read. The one is the thought that suggests the question: Was the church of Jesus Christ built previous to or subsequent to the period of time occupied by the Savior when he said, a few weeks before his crucifixion, " Upon this rock I will build my church; and the gates of hell shall not prevail against it? " Now, as long as men, women, and children who can speak the English language know whether the expression " I will build " points to the past or points to the future, it will not be necessary to argue that question. But the thought representing the pearl in the depths of the sea is here the thought that suggests the question: What is the rock on which Jesus said, " I will build my church; and the gates of hell shall not prevail against it? " Jesus is called the " Rock of Ages," the " Rock for sinners cleft; " "the tried, the precious Stone;" the "chief Corner Stone."

" Cephas " means " a stone; " " Peter," " a rock; " but did Jesus refer directly or personally to either himself or to Peter when he said, " Upon this rock I will build my church; and the gates of hell shall not prevail against it? " Human opinion, now, is not to be accepted in answer to biblical questions, but we are to turn to the word of God and see what we can learn there.   The apostle Paul says: "According to the grace of God which is given unto me, as a wise master builder, I have laid the foundation, and another buildeth thereon.   But let every man take heed how he buildeth thereupon.   For other foundation can no man lay than that is laid, which is Jesus Christ."   (1 Cor. 3: 10, 11.)   It is absolutely certain that this did not refer to Peter; but a careful and critical examination of the phraseology used by the Savior shows that he did not refer personally, directly, to himself, the term translated " rock " being of a gender which shows that Jesus selected a word positively precluding the possibility that he had reference to himself or to Peter when he said: " On this rock I will build my church; and the gates of hell shall not prevail against it."   Jesus is the chief Corner Stone, the Bed Rock, the Foundation of foundations; but he did not have reference to himself, as we have already learned, the gender of the term used being one that could not admit of its being correct for us to say that he referred to himself.

" When Jesus came into the coasts of Cesarea Philippi, he asked his disciples, saying, Whom do men say that I the Son of man am? "   This conversation occurred.   Why? It was not idle curiosity.   The Savior's life was too busy, his time was of too much importance, to admit of the Savior's allowing idle curiosity to occupy his time for one single, solitary moment while he was on the earth. He said: "I must work the works of him that sent me, while it is day: the night cometh, when no man can work." (John 9: 4.) It was not pride that prompted him to ask the question, or the desire to be flattered. Had that been his desire, it had not been necessary for him to come to this earth; for yonder from all eternity he had had existence with the great I Am, had been the constant companion and bosom friend of God, and, standing by the great white throne, could look down upon innumerable worlds and claim them all for his own, while the angels cast their crowns before him and the stars were glittering dust beneath his feet. Certainly it would have been a little thing for him to be flattered by men. It was not to elicit information from them, for he had all the information on the subject. The last paragraph of John 2 (verses 23-25) settles that question. "Now when he was in Jerusalem at the passover, in the feast day, many believed in his name, when they saw the miracles which he did. But Jesus did not commit himself unto them, because he knew all men, and needed not that any should testify of man: for he knew what was in man." It follows that he could not have asked this question to elicit information as to what men said about him. Still, there was a reason for the question. Rational men do nothing without reason, and the Son of God had a reason for all he did. "When Jesus came into the coasts of Cesarea Philippi, he asked his disciples, saying, Whom do men say that I the Son of man am? And they said, Some say that thou art John the Baptist: some, Elias; and others, Jeremias, or one of the prophets. He saith unto them, But whom say ye that I am?" This shows that he was not satisfied with their first answer. Had that been what he wanted to elicit, he would have stopped when they told him what men said of him. "He saith unto them, But whom say ye that I am? And Simon Peter answered and said, Thou art the Christ, the Son of the living God." That was what he wanted to elicit, for he pressed the question no further. He went far enough to get what he wanted and then stopped. He immediately pronounced a blessing on Peter, saying: "Blessed art thou, Simon Bar-jona: for flesh and blood hath not revealed it unto thee, but my Father which is in heaven. [Hath not revealed what unto thee? That I am the Christ, the Son of the living God.] And I say also unto thee, That thou art Peter, and upon this rock I will build my church [Upon what rock? The rock that he and Peter were talking about—that I am the Christ, the Son of the living God]; and the gates of hell shall not prevail against it." The confession, "Thou art the Christ, the Son of the living God," or this truth as illustrated in that confession—the confession of which Jesus is the soul, the substance, the divinity, and the power and the glory—is the rock on which Jesus said he would build his church. The gender of the term translated "rock" is such as agrees perfectly with this expression, with this understanding. It could not have represented Peter; it could not have represented Christ personally; but it could and did represent or refer to the confession: "Thou art the Christ, the Son of the living God."

Now, in view of the importance of the foundation of the church the Savior refers to in this connection as "my church," it is perfectly natural for the human mind to ex pect to find that God has given extraordinary prominence to this confession—the confession: " Thou art the Christ, the Son of the living God." When we look into God's Book of revelation to man, we find that revelation meets this demand of the human mind.

In Matt. 3: 13-17, we find this language: " Then cometh Jesus from Galilee to Jordan unto John, to be baptized of him. But John forbade him, saying, I have need to be baptized of thee, and comest thou to me? And Jesus answering said unto him, Suffer it to be so now: for thus it becometh us to fulfill all righteousness. Then he suffered him. And Jesus, when he was baptized, went up straightway out of the water: and, lo, the heavens were opened unto him, and he saw the Spirit of God descending like a dove, and lighting upon him: and lo a voice from heaven, saying, This is my beloved Son, in whom I am well pleased." At the baptism of Jesus, then, Jehovah himself made this good confession, that all the vast multitude, standing with bowed heads, waiting hearts, and listening ears, might hear and understand that God recognized Jesus as his own divine Son.

The first five verses of Matt. 17 contain this language: "And after six days Jesus taketh Peter, James, and John his brother, and bringeth them up· into a high mountain apart, and was transfigured before them: and his face did shine as the sun, and his raiment was white as the light. And, behold, there appeared unto them Moses and Elias talking with him. Then answered Peter, and said unto Jesus, Lord, it is good for us to be here: if thou wilt, let us make here three tabernacles; one for thee, and one for Moses, and one for Elias. While he yet spake, behold, a bright cloud overshadowed them: and behold a voice out of the cloud, which said, This is my beloved Son, in whom I am well pleased; hear ye him." This was the transfiguration of the Savior on Hermon's holy height, in the presence of Peter, James, and John; Moses and Elias appeared, and in the presence of them all God himself again made the good confession: " This is my beloved Son, in whom I am well pleased; hear ye him." Fifteen hundred years before that time, Moses, from the towering summit of Pisgah, viewed the promised land spread out in grandeur and beauty before him, knew that his hour had come, lay down and died, and God buried him in some lonely spot in Moab. Fifteen hundred years have come and gone; generations have been born and buried; Jesus has come (who was typified by Moses), is transfigured on the summit of Mount Hermon, and there stands Moses by his side. Almost one thousand years before that time, Elias was taken up from the land and carried over the river of death without touching its chilling tide; Jesus is transfigured on Mount Hermon, and there stands Elias by his side. Peter, James, and John are there. Moses was called the " lawgiver," because on the summit of shaking Sinai, that was shrouded by somber clouds, rifted by livid lightnings, while the thunders rocked the earth, he received from the hand of God, written on tables of stone by the finger of God, the law that was to descend and be the foundation of civilization while time itself shall be. Elias was called the " law restorer," because when the world seemed to have forgotten law he restored the Jewish law. Now, we have Moses, the lawgiver; Elias, the law restorer; Peter, James, and John, the prospective promulgators of the new law of life, on the summit of Mount Hermon.   Jesus is the central figure there.   He is robed in the glory 'that is to be his in the home of God forever, a bright cloud overshadows the scene, and from that cloud comes the voice of God: " This is my beloved Son;   .   .   .   hear ye him "—as much as to say: " The time was when you were to hear Moses, but his day is past; the time was when you were to hear Elias, but his day is gone.   My Son has come, the patriarchal age has passed, Judaism is to be abolished, the law of my Son has come and is to be established; and therefore I say to you, Peter, James, and John, to all the sons and daughters of men, in the presence of Moses, the lawgiver, and Elias, the law restorer: Hear ye him."

Now, we would naturally suppose that there would be precious promises connected with this confession.   Looking to the Bible, we find these promises: " Whosoever therefore shall confess me before men, him will I confess also before my Father which is in heaven.   But whosoever shall deny me before men, him will I also deny before my Father which is in heaven."   (Matt. 10: 32, 33.)   " For with the heart man believeth unto righteousness; and with the mouth confession is made unto salvation."   (Rom. 10: 10.)   Having heard the gospel, believed the gospel, obeyed the gospel, and entered into the fold of Christ, God's children may then, as long as they live, confess him by doing right or deny him by doing wrong, and the Savior brings out all these thoughts in the closing paragraphs of the Sermon on the Mount: " Not every one that saith unto me, Lord, Lord, shall enter into the kingdom of heaven; but he that doeth the will of my Father which is in heaven. Many will say to me in that day, Lord, Lord, have we not prophesied in thy name? and in thy name have cast out devils? and in thy name done many wonderful works? And then will I profess unto them, I never knew you: depart from me, ye that work iniquity. Therefore whosoever heareth these sayings of mine, and doeth them, I will liken him unto a wise man, which built his house upon a rock: and the rain descended, and the floods came, and the winds blew, and beat upon that house; and it fell not: for it was founded upon a rock. And every one that heareth these sayings of mine, and doeth them not, shall be likened unto a foolish man, which built his house upon the sand: and the rain descended, and the floods came, and the winds blew, and beat upon that house; and it fell: and great was the fall of it." (Matt. 7: 21-27.) Remember, the Savior has said: " Whosoever therefore shall confess me before men, him will I confess also before my Father which is in heaven. But whosoever shall deny me before men, him will I also deny before my Father which is in heaven." We are told that he will deny before the Father and the holy angels those who do not obey him, and that he will confess before the Father and the holy angels all who live in harmony with his teachings. This shows that to obey him is to confess him, and to refuse to obey him is to deny him.

We are to confess him with the mouth. " For with the heart man believeth unto righteousness; and with the mouth confession is made unto salvation." (Rom. 10: 10.)

For making this good confession, Jesus died. In Matt. 26, the paragraph beginning with verse 57 and ending with verse 68, we have Jesus on trial for his life before the high priest. Witnesses were hired to swear away his life, but their testimony was so inconsistent that every one knew that it furnished no pretext for the premeditated butchery; and, finally, the high priest, by virtue of his official position, put Jesus on his oath. He said: "I adjure thee by the living God, that thou tell us whether thou be the Christ, the Son of God." That was the question at issue; that was the great confession. It was for making this confession they had decided to kill him. "I adjure thee by the living God, that thou tell us whether thou be the Christ, the Son of God." He gave an affirmative answer. Then the high priest said: "What further need have we of witnesses? behold, now ye have heard his blasphemy." They said, "He is worthy of death;" and a storm of passion arose in that mob—a storm that swept him to Calvary's heights, where he was nailed to the cross, and where he died for the redemption of a lost and ruined and recreant race, for making that confession. And when he died, even the pagan Roman soldiers confessed him: "Now when the centurion, and they that were with him, watching Jesus, saw the earthquake, and those things that were done, they feared greatly, saying, Truly, this was the Son of God." (Matt. 27: 54.) For making this confession, Jesus died; but we have the assurance that if we make this confession we shall live forever, provided we obey the gospel and live in harmony with God's will here on earth.

In the days of the terrible persecution of the church of God in the bloody, tearful long ago, this was the test. There is an original document in the old Roman tongue, written by a subordinate ruler of a province under the Roman Empire at the time of that terrible persecution, explaining his mode of procedure with people tried for their lives upon the charge of being Christians. He says " When people are brought before me accused of the crime of being Christians, I ask them: ' Do you believe that Jesus Christ is the Son of God?' If they answer negatively, I release them; for it is a question of faith, and they alone know what they believe; but if they deny, of course the case could not be sustained against them. If they answer affirmatively, I have them scourged and warn them of the danger of persisting in that course, and ask them the second time; if they answer negatively and renounce their faith, I discharge them; if they answer affirmatively, I have them scourged more severely and assure them that they have but one more opportunity for their lives—that if they answer affirmatively, there is no appeal. I ask them the question the third time, and if they answer affirmatively, I hurry them away to execution, to make room for the next." So, then, thousands and thousands of brave men and pure women have died for their fidelity to Christ, for making this confession when they knew that death would be the result.

Now, in view of all these things, reason almost imperatively demands that we find by searching God's truth that he requires gospel preachers—workmen working upon the walls of his temple, the spiritual Zion—to measure the material for its walls by this confession. When we come to the Scriptures, we find this demand of reason fully met; and I want to quote just one passage of scripture, though there are many others that might well be quoted, to bring out this thought that Jesus requires his preachers, gospel preachers, workmen upon the walls of this spiritual temple, to measure material for it by this foundation; or, in other

- 24 -

words, to take from penitent believers the confession that they do believe with all the heart that Jesus Christ is the Son of God. I will quote the passage and let you see how it meets the demand, and I am sure you can see this: "And the angel of the Lord spake unto Philip, saying, Arise, and go toward the south unto the way that goeth down from Jerusalem unto Gaza, which is desert. And he arose and went; and, behold, a man of Ethiopia, a eunuch of great authority under Candace queen of the Ethiopians, who had the charge of all her treasure, and had come to Jerusalem for to worship, was returning, and sitting in his chariot read Esaias the prophet. Then the Spirit said unto Philip, Go near, and join thyself to this chariot. And Philip ran thither to him, and heard him read the prophet Esaias, and said, Understandest thou what thou readest? And he said, How can I, except some man should guide me? And he desired Philip that he would come up and sit with him. The place of the scripture which he read was this, He was led as a sheep to the slaughter; and like a lamb dumb before his shearer, so opened he not his mouth: in his humiliation his judgment was taken away: and who shall declare his generation? for his life is taken from the earth. And the eunuch answered Philip, and said, I pray thee, of whom speaketh the prophet this? of himself, or of some other man? Then Philip opened his mouth, and began at the same scripture, and preached unto him Jesus. And as they went on their way, they came unto a certain water: and the eunuch said, See, here is water; what doth hinder me to be baptized? And Philip said, If thou believest with all thine heart, thou mayest. And he answered and said, I believe that Jesus Christ is the Son of

God. And he commanded the chariot to stand still; and they went down both into the water, both Philip and the eunuch; and he baptized him. And when they were come up out of the water, the Spirit of the Lord caught away Philip, that the eunuch saw him no more: and he went on his way rejoicing." (Acts 8: 26-39.)

The man who took this confession was a workman in the spiritual temple of our God. He was an inspired man, directed first by an angel, and then by the Holy Spirit. He was a skilled workman, " a workman that needeth not to be ashamed, rightly dividing the word of truth." He was a master mason, and with the gospel lever he prized up from the depths of an Abrahamic quarry a solid block of Judean marble. He applied to it the square, the compass, the level, and the rule of righteousness, and tapped it with the mallet of God's eternal truth; he found it had the right proportions and the proper ring; he slipped it into place in the wall of the temple—the spiritual temple built on the foundation of apostles and prophets, Jesus Christ himself being the chief corner stone—sealed it there by the power of God's Spirit, and went on his way to another field; while the other pursued his homeward way, rejoicing to take the glad tidings to his own country lying in the shadow of darkness and the gloom of sin.

Notwithstanding these and many other lessons in God's Book just as expressive, just as plain along these lines, there be thousands of pure, prayerful, pious, intelligent, cultured people who object to this confession, who practically ignore it—honestly and conscientiously, of course—thinking that something substituted for it, broader and more comprehensive, would fill the place better. Perhaps it is not so narrow as some broad-minded men have supposed it to be. We can sometimes judge of the breadth of a thing by what rests upon it. All that rests upon Christ rests upon this confession, from the fact that he is the soul and substance, the strength and center, of it all. It is safe to say that the whole Bible rests upon Christ and rests upon this confession. Let us go back to the beginning. We read that darkness was upon the face of the deep. "God said, Let there be light: and there was light." We have an account of the six days of creation, culminating in the creation of Eve. We are told that God planted a garden eastward in Eden, and placed Adam and Eve there to keep it. In an evil hour Satan invaded that happy home and introduced sin. Eden withered, happiness fled, and the souls there were left in despair. God entered that garden, visiting his fallen children. When he looked upon Adam, made in his own image, made to walk uprightly, and saw him bowed down with guilt and shame as if under the weight of centuries of sorrow, his soul was stirred with sympathy. But when he turned and looked upon Eve—looked upon woman, the last, best, and brightest of his created work; the rich, radiant, resplendent crown jewel of the universe, at the making of whom the morning stars together sung and the sons of God shouted for joy—when he looked upon her and saw the blush of shame mantling her cheek, and knew that she, too, was involved in the wreck and ruin wrought by sin, his soul was swept by sympathy to its deepest depths, and, realizing that without hope life would be a burden too heavy to be borne, he would not let his fallen children leave Eden without a gleam of hope. He said the seed of the woman should bruise the serpent's head—in other words, that in some far-off age a descendant of Eve should come to bless the world and crush the power of Satan. From that day God was careful to preserve enough of the history of the human race so that men could see in Jesus the fulfillment of that prophecy. For instance, we have an account of the birth of Cain and Abel. Abel might have been chosen of God as a link in the chain, but he was murdered by his brother. Then when Adam and Eve were one hundred and thirty years old, Seth was born, he being supplied or appointed to fill the place left vacant by the death of Abel. Then we have Adam, Seth, Enos, Cainan, Mahalaleel, Jared, Enoch, Methuselah, Lamech, Noah—ten of the progenitors of Christ, ten of the glittering links in the golden chain of the lineage of our Lord, reaching from the bosom of Eden to the waters of the deluge. We have an account of the deluge. Noah and his family went into the ark, and God deluged the earth to blot out sin. But the storm subsided, the dry land appeared, and Noah and his family came forth out of the ark and offered sacrifices unto the Lord, and God then confirmed to Noah the promise he had made to Eve. Of Noah's sons, Shem was chosen as the representative; and we have Shem, Arphaxad, Sala, Eber, Peleg, Reu, Serug, Nahor, Terah, Abraham—ten more of the glittering links of the golden chain, the first link fastened securely to the ark as it rests upon Mount Ararat, and the last fastened securely to the tent of Abraham. God took Abraham to the plain and told him to look to the east, to the north, to the south, to the west, to the heavens that bent in beauty above him, and the earth beneath his feet, and he said, " In blessing I will bless thee, and in multiplying I will multiply thy seed as the stars of the heaven, and as the sand which is upon the seashore; and thy seed shall possess the gate of his enemies; and in thy seed shall all the nations of the earth be blessed; because thou hast obeyed my voice; " and the apostle Paul tells us that seed was Christ.   When Abraham was eighty-six years of age, Ishmael was born, but Ishmael was not the child of promise.   When the snows of a hundred years had gathered upon the locks of Abraham, and his faithful wife was ninety years old, Isaac, the child of promise, was born. After the test of Abraham's faith by having him take his son three days' journey in the wilderness to offer him as a sacrifice, God saw that nothing could cause Abraham to waver; and then, commencing again, we have Isaac, Jacob, Judah, Phares, Esrom, Aram, Amminadab, Naasson, Salmon, Boaz, Obed, Jesse, David—thirteen more of the links in the chain of the lineage of our Lord, the first of these fastened securely to the tent of Abraham, and the last to the throne of David.   The throne of David being established, God declared that the crown, throne, and scepter should not pass from it until Shiloh should come.   This made it necessary for the line to be divided.   Remember that Jesus was to be the descendant of Eve.   The blood that flowed from his wounded side when he was crucified on Calvary was to be the same blood that coursed through the cheek of Eve when she stood blushing before the Lord in the garden of Eden, and at the same time he was to be heir to the throne, crown, and scepter of David; and Jesus could not inherit the throne from his mother, Mary, since there were kings, not queens, in Israel.   He must inherit the crown, throne, and scepter through some one.   He could not inherit from his Father, for God was not an earthly king, and therefore it had to be some one who occupied the place of his legal, but not real, father. So the line was divided in David, and through Solomon the line ran down to Joseph, the reputed father of Jesus, and the heir to the crown, throne, and scepter of David. Then through Nathan, another son of David, sprang Mary, a descendant of Eve, and four thousand years after the completion of the drama of creation Jesus was born—the seed of the woman, a literal descendant of Eve through David and Nathan; the rightful heir through Solomon and Joseph, his reputed father, of the throne, crown, and scepter of David; the literal Son of God Almighty, as divine as God himself, and the fulfillment of every prophecy, prediction, and promise made or proclaimed since God said the seed of the woman should bruise the serpent's head, until the Babe of Bethlehem was born. Jesus repeatedly, during his ministry on the earth, quoted from the various divisions of the Old Testament; gave his sanction, seal, and signature to those things, showing that he assumed the responsibility for their existence. He then commissioned men to write the two hundred and sixty chapters of the New Testament, thus assuming the responsibility of them. So he stands in the midst of the ages the fulfillment of prophecy, and reaches one arm back to the throne of David, to the tent of Abraham, to the ark of Noah, until that arm rests in Eden, and holds in that hand the thirty-nine books and nine hundred and twenty-nine chapters of the Old Testament. He reaches the other arm down through Bethlehem, by way of Calvary and Patmos, until that arm rests in the paradise of God, and in that he holds the two hundred and sixty chapters of the New Testament. And thus he stands in the midst of the ages, holding the sixty-six volumes, the eleven hundred and eighty-nine chapters, of God's eternal truth, assuming the responsibility of every sentiment, syllable, page, and paragraph of God's revelation to a lost and ruined world, saying, practically: "As the tree is divine, so also is all this fruit." All these things and many times more rest upon Jesus, and hence rest upon the foundation: "Thou art the Christ, the Son of the living God." And is it not strange to hear intelligent men and women say that this confession is too narrow? O, it is as broad, as limitless, as the universe itself! It is as deep as the very depths of creation; it is as high as the holy heights of rapture that canopy the eternal throne of God; it is as vast as eternity, and as pure as that God from whose throne it burst to flood the world with light divine and lift our souls to God. And God's church, Christ's church, rests upon this foundation, built upon the apostles and prophets, Jesus himself being the chief corner stone. It is built upon this foundation, and it is sustained by the will and power of him who said: "Upon this rock I will build my church; and the gates of hell shall not prevail against it."

We should all rejoice that it is our privilege to belong to an institution divine, resting upon a foundation so strong, so firm, so secure. We that are in this institution should rejoice. We should resolve to battle right on and on and on for the glory of God, the honor of Christ, and the salvation of souls, until God shall call us home. You that are not in this divine institution should resolve to come to Jesus without one plea, save that he died to redeem you. If any in this audience are proper subjects of the gospel call, we wait to lovingly welcome you, and pray that you may come.

EXTRACTS FROM LARIMORE'S SERMONS.

PARTISAN BIGOTRY.

A ND the governor said, Why, what evil hath he done? But they cried out the more, saying, Let him be crucified." (Matt. 27: 23.)

We have a sad and shameful scene in the life of our Savior presented for our consideration in the language quoted. We have upon the bench as judge the governor of Judea, Pontius Pilate, holding that position by the grace and favor of Tiberius Cæsar, the Roman emperor, who had been then for about twenty years occupying the throne of the great Roman empire. Before this judge stands the Savior—pale, sad, troubled, pure, self-sacrificing and ready to sacrifice life itself; a personage such as had never been upon the earth before and was never to be on the earth again—the immaculate Son of the living God—a prisoner on trial for his life before that judge, surrounded by a tumultuous mob, thirsting and clamoring for the blood of the prisoner.

As Jesus stood there before Pontius Pilate, being tried for his life, he could look back one-third of a century and almost feel the breath of heaven upon his brow—that breath laden with the perfume of flowers that bloomed in the garden of God; could remember that then every flower that bloomed in that paradise on high, every breeze that fluttered the foliage of the tree of life, every world in existence, every atom in space, belonged to him, while angels and archangels around the throne of God cast their crowns before him, and the stars were but glittering dust beneath his feet.   Yet he had sacrificed all these things; had come to this world and become the Babe of Bethlehem, born in a stable, cradled in a manger; had become the Man of sorrows, the Friend of sinners, the poorest of the poor—poorer than the foxes of the fields or the birds of the air—and stands now, without a friend beside him, on trial for his life before the Roman governor.

The governor is troubled; his wife has sent him a message: " Have thou nothing to do with that just man."   He looks over the mob and wonders what to do; he makes a proposition to release unto them a prisoner, as was the custom at that time, and he hopes they will choose Jesus to be released; but they clamor for Barabbas, the robber, to be released.   He asks them, " What shall I do then with Jesus which is called Christ?" and they cry, " Crucify him, crucify him!"   Then the governor asks the question, " Why, what evil hath he done?" but they cried again, " Let him be crucified!"

The question that Pilate propounded was a reasonable question, and one that has been recognized as such by rational, reasonable people from that day to this—reasonable that he should ask such a question when the mob clamored for the crucifixion of Christ: " Why, what evil hath he done?"   But from the bosom of that mob, swept by a storm of anger, no answer comes save the furious cry: "Away with him!"   Mobs rarely listen to the voice of reason, rarely regard reason, and especially such a mob as that—a mob filled with the blackest and bitterest thing that ever shadows the soul of human beings supposed to be respectable: the spirit of religious fanaticism, partyism, bigotry, and prejudice.

They did not reject Jesus because he was an atheist; he believed in God. They did not reject him because he did not believe the Scriptures; he quoted from them repeatedly, and said no jot or tittle of the law should pass until all should be fulfilled. They did not oppose him because he was a sectarian; for there was no sectarianism in his soul.

Why do they hate Jesus so? Who are these people composing that mob? The religious advisers, spiritual teachers, or ecclesiastical heads of the various sects, parties, and denominations in existence at that time were there, with the following of their denominations, sects, and parties, and at the bottom and back of their hatred was this reason: Jesus did not regard or respect their religious parties or partyism as such, did not sustain them in the idea that every religion is right just because it is called "religion." God had established Judaism fifteen hundred years before that time—established it in a formal way at the foot of shaking Sinai, when, from the summit of that cloud-wrapped mountain, he gave the law to Moses; but base men, desiring to be leaders, and there being no head places for them, had divided Judaism for their own base purposes and reduced it to the level of partyism; and God has never set the seal of his approbation on religious partyism. Pharisees and Sadducees and the other sects and parties of the day were perpetually striving against each other, each trying to build itself upon the wreck and ruin of the others. But they laid aside all their strife and wrangling among themselves and formed a great ecclesiastical, crazy-quilt combination to oppose the Son of God because he would not recognize their sects or parties. Upon the same principle that Herod and Pilate could make friends, though they had been foes, so in the presence of Jesus these various sects and parties of the Jews formed a crazy-quilt combination, and reared upon the mountain wave of hatred and passion a billow that lifted him to the cross on which he died.

It behooves each one of us, as we value our souls and the souls of those we might win, to think seriously, carefully, and prayerfully, to see if we are guilty along this line. Are we doing as that mob did? Do we love supremely the cause of Christ? Are we willing to do and dare and die to bring sinners away from Satan to the Savior? Are we trying to get people to be Christians, and nothing but Christians—only this and nothing more—simply to take God at his word, do what he commands, become and be what he requires, live as he directs, and lovingly trust him for what he promises till he shall call us home? Is that our mission? Is that our hope? Is that the end for which we labor? Or is it our party that we love, our denomination that we are trying to support? Is it our party, and not Christ and his cause, that we defend?

An editorial clipping from the American says: " If Christ or his cause be assailed, little notice is taken of it; but if the doctrine of some denomination be denounced or criticised, a storm is raised immediately." The American has never published a plainer truth.

A doctor of divinity may deny the divinity of Christ; he may declare the Bible not to be the word of God; he may affirm that Adam was a monkey, and, therefore, that a monkey is the image of God, since Adam was made in God's own image; he may preach whatever he wills to preach, may even deny the divinity of Christ; but *the* thing he must not do is this: utter one word or quote one passage of scripture that may tend to disturb the theological equilibrium of the crazy-quilt combination—that, *he must not do.*

CONFESSION UNTO SALVATION.

On Sunday morning, February 19, 1900, at the close of the sermon, little Jessie Gleaves confessed faith in Christ. Putting his arm around her, Brother Larimore said, " Do you, my child, believe with all your heart that Jesus Christ is the Son of God?" and she replied, "I do." He then added:

" Precious little treasure, manufacturing sunshine and gladness for some fortunate family, some favored home, where, I pray, you are loved and appreciated as you deserve to be! I rejoice that you have the moral courage to stand before this audience and so earnestly and impressively say, 'I do.' And now I pray that through all your life you may be an earnest, faithful follower of Him who, more than eighteen hundred years ago, stood before Pontius Pilate on trial for his life. I pray that the Lord may protect you, love you, lead you, and let you live long on the earth, to enjoy sweetest communion with Jesus and the saints in his service here. I pray that you may fully realize all your hallowed hopes and holy, righteous desires for body, soul, and spirit. I pray that your sorrows may be few and brief, that your joys may be many and lasting. I pray that you may realize all your hopes regarding those you love and those who love you, that they may follow your example in coming to the Savior, and that you and they together may rejoice in the blessings of this life and in the hope of blessings in the life to come. I pray that Heaven's richest blessings and sweetest joys may be yours through a long life of usefulness; that your foes may be few, your friends many, faithful, kind, and true; and that at last, full of years and full of honors, you may have a quiet hour in which, nestling in the arms of the Savior's love, to breathe your last, and that then the angels may bear you home and make you unspeakably happy in eternity, where, while the endless ages come and go, you may remember that at this hour you had the moral courage to confess your faith in Him who died that you might live."

WHAT CHRISTIANITY COST.

It is claimed that the world is burdened with the cost of Christianity. I am willing to acknowledge that Christianity is costly. It is not possible, however, for me to give you any statistics that will convey to you the remotest conception of the cost of Christianity. It cost heaven the sacrifice of the darling object of God's delight; it cost the angels the companionship of Jesus for one-third of a century; it cost Jesus the sacrifice of the wealth of the universe and all the joys of heaven for the lifetime of a generation on the earth, and at last cost him life itself on

Calvary's rugged brow. So they who speak of Christianity as being costly speak, perhaps, more correctly than they know. It may be, though, that in saying Christianity is costly, they do not understand the shade of difference in the meaning of words. They may mean to convey the idea that it is expensive. There is a difference in a thing's being costly and its being expensive. A watch that costs three hundred dollars may be said to be a costly watch; but if it does not require more than one dollar to keep it in running order for seven years, it is not an expensive watch. A watch that costs three dollars is not a costly watch; but if it takes seven dollars a year to keep it in halfway running order, it is an exceedingly expensive watch. When Miss Vanderbilt paid ten millions of dollars for a husband, she got a very costly husband. I am not able to tell you whether he is an expensive one or otherwise. If it takes another million a year to keep him dressed so that she will not be ashamed of him, he is both costly and expensive; but if he manages in some way to keep himself clothed properly without her having to pay anything more than the first installment of ten millions, he is not an expensive husband. He weighs, they say, about one hundred and fifteen pounds; and some man, figuring it out on that basis, says it is the highest price per pound ever paid for veal.

Well, Christianity is costly—not a doubt in the world of that—but it is not expensive. Think of it! Just think if you can afford to stand up before high Heaven and before the earth—if you can afford to stand up before Satan, the archenemy of the earth—and claim that Christianity has been expensive to you.   Can you do that?

There are things that are expensive, but not Christianity. Things that injure us, things that doom us, are expensive— not Christianity.

Take war, for instance.   If Christianity prevailed from the rivers to the ends of the earth, and the Christian spirit enveloped it as waters cover the sea, we would have no war. War expensive?   To say nothing of the bloodshed and the wreck and ruin and distress and desolation caused by war— leaving all these things out of consideration, war is ex- ceedinly expensive.   After our cannons have cooled, our swords have been sheathed, our muskets have been stacked for more than one-third of a century, our war debt to-day amounts to thousands and tens of thousands of dollars, and our pension list shows an expense because of that war greater than the world's contribution to Christianity. When Germany was victorious over the legions of France, after a seven-months' war, France had to pay Germany a billion dollars—five million francs—to help Germany to meet a part of the expense incurred in fighting France. In 1878 Russia whipped Turkey, and seven hundred mil- lion dollars—one hundred millions for each month of the war—was paid by the vanquished nation to the victorious. Christianity proposes to lift the pall from battlefields, clear away the smoke from places where the battle rages, blot out the war spirit, and set us free from these things; then rebuild the homes that are burned, and carry the light of joy and peace into hearts that are broken and desolate.

We can find other things that are expensive. Poor, downtrodden Ireland, with all her wit and wisdom and her noble qualities, groaning under the oppressive yoke of England, complaining of being taxed until life itself is almost a burden, pays in round numbers sixty million dollars for grog every year! Christianity would save to Ireland sixty million dollars of that taxation without shedding one drop of blood.

What is the record of Christian America? Some one who has made a study of it tells us that in round numbers our contribution for evangelizing heathen lands amounts to five million dollars a year; that we pay twenty millions a year for chewing gum, one billion for grog, seven hundred millions for tobacco, seventy or eighty millions a year to theaters that are called "high-toned" and "respectable." Think of it! Billions for unmentionable gratifications of the flesh; one billion—a thousand millions—for grog; seven hundred millions for tobacco; seventy millions to " tony " theaters, such as deacons and doctors of divinity take their wives and daughters to; uncounted millions to the darker dives and baser sort; twenty millions for chewing gum; and five millions, many windy speeches, and a few long prayers to save the heathen!

A MOTHER'S LOVE.

" When I was a child, I spake as a child, I understood as a child, I thought as a child; but when I became a man, I put away childish things." (1 Cor. 13: 11.)

Paul was a sublime man—one of the sublimest characters revealed to the world in the light of history, either sacred or profane—and still he, when a child, spoke as a child, understood as a child, thought as a child; and it was not until he became a man that he put away childish things. What folly it is, then, in the light of such a lesson as this, for us who have reached manhood and womanhood to become vexed and worried and discouraged, and even angry and enraged sometimes, because the dear, precious, sweet children, even children who are the Lord's children, lambs in the fold of the tender Shepherd, do not always act like men and women who have grown old in the service of our God; because they do not now, while they are little children, do exactly what the little child Paul did not do—put away childish things. It seems to me that as the first buds of the springtime, whose bosoms seem to be filled with joy until they burst with bliss, are the sweetest smiles of spring, coming to supplant winter and fill our souls with joy, just so the childish things that sweet little children think and say and do, welling up from their guileless hearts, ought to fill our hearts with light almost divine, and love, tender and true, every day and every hour.

I am pretty sure the apostle Paul was not scolded and abused very much when he thought as a child, spoke as a child, understood as a child, from the very fact that he made a sublime man, which he could not have done, if he had been scolded very much when he was a child. If you have children, and are afraid that they will be much or do much good in the world, this is the way to prevent it: just censure and abuse and crush them when they are little.

There have been many things in the last few days that have touched my heart and carried me back almost to my cradle. I expect to go, in a short time, to see my mother and bring her to my home to spend the summer; and this being my intention, I have thought of my mother much, and I have again been in the shadows and in the gloom under which and in the bosom of which she has dropped tears that would not stain an angel's cheek, upon my own face and head and hands. I have tried to think if she ever scolded me, and I believe that in all the days of my life she has never felt any more like scolding me than I have felt like cursing you this morning. She always told me that my childhood ought to have been brighter, that there were better days before me; for me to be a good boy, and the day would come when I could look back with joy to the dark days of my life, to the bittersweet moments, bitter with sorrow, but always sweetened and brightened by a mother's love. She sympathized with her child, did all she could for him. I might have been better if she had been bitter, but I am sure I can never believe it. Eternity alone can tell how much I am indebted to the sweet spirit of that mother who never scolded her child. May the Lord grant that I may never scold, may never censure, may never unkindly criticise a child of the living God.

My thoughts will linger with my mother this morning. I can see as plainly as if it occurred but yesterday—not once, but over and over again—when I would work in the snow or the ice or the wind until my hands were benumbed, almost frozen, how she would rub them in her hands and press them close to her bosom. I can see her get a pan of water and put my hands in it; I can feel her breath upon my brow, her lips upon my lips, as she kissed and blessed her boy that had to go out into the cold again as soon as he was warmed.

MANLINESS IN BOYS.

A boy who is ashamed of his mother, even if she does wear a homespun dress and a sunbonnet, will never make a man.   He may make something that at a distance will *look* like a man, but he will never be a *man.*

ORIGIN OF MAN.

I notice, in a sermon reported in one of our papers from a very prominent man, that when God made Adam, he was only a monkey.   If it is possible to trace our lineage back to any higher or better source, then we ought to do it; if we can manage to switch off at any point along the line and say, " We came from here; we did not come from a monkey," we ought to do it.   Well, we can do that, if we want to.   That is the doctrine of Darwin and human theology.   The Bible says God made Adam; it does not say that he was a monkey; but what does the Bible have to do with it, if human theology says otherwise?   But God made Adam, and all human beings are God's workmanship in the sense that he made them; but that does not make them akin to God.   They are akin to Adam, akin to the original monkey, provided they are his descendants; but that does not make them akin to God.   Because a man makes a house, it does not follow that the house is akin to him.   Because God made us, it does not follow that we are akin to God—only akin to the original monkey; and as such descendants of Adam, the great original monkey, we have no right to look to God as our Father. He is our Creator, but we cannot trace our lineage back to him. I suppose God would not care to have us trace our lineage back to him through a monkey. But there is a way for us to become and be children of the living God. How? By entering into Christ Jesus, our Lord, who is the only begotten of the Father, full of grace and truth, in that sense the *only* Son of God; and the apostle Peter had that in view when he said: " Thou art *the* Christ, *the* Son of the living God." We can get into Christ, be recognized by Christ as being a part of himself, being related to him, and then we have a spiritual relationship to God—through Christ, however, not through Adam. Now, if we will, we can enter into that relationship by hearing the gospel, believing the gospel, repenting of our sins; in other words, earnestly resolving by the grace of God to abandon sin and Satan and enter into the service of God, confessing our faith in Christ, being buried with him by baptism into death, in the name of the Lord Jesus Christ—into the solemn name of Father, Son, and Holy Ghost—and then we are in Christ Jesus, our Lord. We have been born again and have thus become the children of God. We are the creatures of his creation, but we thus become the children of God by faith, and can call him " Father," he being our Father in a spiritual sense.

God is the Father of his own children only, and if we are not his children, we ought to be ashamed to claim him as our Father. It is a shame and a disgrace to accuse a man of being the Father of any children except his own, and it is a greater insult to the divinity of God to accuse him of being the Father of people who have no relationship with him at all. The Savior said to certain people who claimed God as their Father: "Ye are of your father, the devil."

THE SPIRIT OF CHRIST.

It has been said that the church of Christ has been, and is, a persecuting power. This is simply an impossibility. Christians compose the church of Christ, hence the church of Christ consists of Christians; to be a Christian is to be a child of the living God, a son or daughter of the Lord Almighty, a follower of Christ; and to be a follower of Christ is to be subject to the law of Christ, which is the law of love. What is the law of Christ? "Recompense to no man evil for evil. Provide things honest in the sight of all men. If it be possible, as much as lieth in you, live peaceably with all men. Dearly beloved, avenge not yourselves, but rather give place unto wrath: for it is written, Vengeance is mine; I will repay, saith the Lord. Therefore if thine enemy hunger, feed him; if he thirst, give him drink: for in so doing thou shalt heap coals of fire on his head. Be not overcome of evil, but overcome evil with good." (Rom. 12: 17-21.) "Be not deceived; God is not mocked: for whatsoever a man soweth, that shall he also reap. For he that soweth to his flesh shall of the flesh reap corruption; but he that soweth to the Spirit shall of the Spirit reap life everlasting. And let us not be weary in welldoing: for in due season we shall reap, if we faint not. As we have therefore opportunity, let us do good unto all men, especially unto them who are of the household of faith." (Gal. 6: 7-10.) " Brethren, if a man be overtaken in a fault, ye which are spiritual, restore such a one in the spirit of meekness; considering thyself, lest thou also be tempted. Bear ye one another's burdens, and so fulfill the law of Christ." (Gal. 6: 1, 2.) These are samples of the law of Christ, and it follows, therefore, that it is utterly impossible for the church of God ever to have been or ever to be a persecuting power—as utterly impossible as it would be for a snowflake to rest upon the bosom of the noonday sun, or an icicle to fringe the mouth of a volcano in active eruption.

THE FAITH OF MOSES.

" By faith Moses, when he was come to years, refused to be called the son of Pharaoh's daughter; choosing rather to suffer affliction with the people of God, than to enjoy the pleasures of sin for a season; esteeming the reproach of Christ greater riches than the treasures in Egypt: for he had respect unto the recompense of the reward." (Heb. 11: 24-26.)

We are all, to some extent, acquainted with the history of Moses, the lawgiver of Israel. We remember that he was born when the Israelites were in bondage, when a decree was in force that many thousands of the Israelites should be killed in infancy; that he was placed in an ark by his mother and hidden on the brink of the Nile, among the rushes; that he was rescued by the daughter of Pharaoh, king of Egypt, and adopted as her own child, and, by the providence of God, his own mother, a slave, was employed by the princess to care for and watch over him.

Thus adopted into the royal family of Egypt, he had before him all the preferment, all the opportunity for attaining grandeur and glory, that would naturally come to him as the grandson of Pharaoh, the king of that great country. But we are told, in the language just quoted, that when he came to years—when he reached his majority, we would say; when he considered himself free to choose his own course—he " refused to be called the son of Pharaoh's daughter; choosing rather to suffer affliction with the people of God, than to enjoy the pleasures of sin for a season."

There was demonstrated in this refusal to be called " the son of Pharaoh's daughter " the sublime spirit of the man —his integrity; his true, genuine manhood, when he had just passed through the period of youth. He was not required to take oath that he was of royal extraction; all that was required of him was to be silent, to be submissive to the wishes of his foster mother, and occupy the position in the royal household of Egypt that would naturally be his. But he would have known, after he learned that he was the son of a slave, that the world was deceived with reference to him; that he was practicing deception by acquiescing in it; and the principle of true, genuine, sublime manhood revolted at the thought.

What did Moses reject when he refused to be called " the son of Pharaoh's daughter? " He rejected all the privileges, emoluments, and glory that would naturally attach to his position as a prince of the house royal; he rejected the wealth of the wondrous country, where constant streams of golden treasures were pouring into coffers already overflowing; he rejected the pleasures of Pharaoh's royal palace, with its ease, its elegance, its feasting, its revelry; he rejected the prospect of being sovereign of all that land. Being legally adopted, there was, of course, a prospect of his wearing the royal crown, occupying the throne of the Pharaohs, and swaying the scepter over Egypt; of being buried in the tomb of the Pharaohs, and having his name go down to posterity as an Egyptian sovereign.

What did he accept instead of this? He accepted the position of a slave—one of a nation of slaves—and finally accepted voluntary, but necessary, banishment from Egypt, and became a sojourner in the land of Midian—a stranger in a strange land. He had a checkered career. Forty years he spent in Egypt; forty years a fugitive, a laborer for others; and then forty years a wanderer in the wilderness between Egypt and the promised land.

What was his reward? What position did Moses really occupy? He was the friend and confidant of Jehovah. The God of heaven chose him to be the leader of the children of Israel, and he led three millions of people—the people to whom he really belonged—out of bondage, through the wilderness, and to the bank of the Jordan—the grandest leadership in the history of the world. He was the sublimest, the greatest, lawgiver this world has ever known. He was permitted to stand on the summit of shaking Sinai, shrouded in somber clouds that were riven by vivid lightnings, while the thunders rocked the earth, and receive from the hand of God the tables of stone on which was written the law that has been, is, and is to be, the foundation of the laws of civilization in every age, country, and clime.

God watched over Moses and cared for him to such an extent that he lived one hundred and twenty years; and though he bore great responsibility and had many cares, his one hundred and twenty years were years of uninterrupted health and strength, one hundred and twenty years of vigorous youth.

What manner of death did Moses die? God permitted him to live one hundred and twenty years—thrice forty years—then called him to Mount Pisgah's height, to Nebo's loftiest summit, and there permitted him to view the promised land. We are told that when the time arrived his eye was not dimmed, his natural force not abated. The same eagle glance before which Egypt's haughty king had quailed forty years before was his as he stood on Pisgah's height, the same noble bearing, the same strength of body and mind—a youth of one hundred and twenty summers, standing there with the world spread out beneath his feet. What unutterable thoughts were his as he looked upon that scene—at the Jordan rolling at his feet; at the sweet fields of Canaan; at the smiling valleys; the silvery streams flashing back the rays of the sun; the mountain peaks lifting their heads toward heaven; and far away, at the head of the Jordan, grand old Hermon, veiled in misty clouds! While his soul was filled with rapture at this, the sublimest sight ever granted to mortal vision, the hand of God was laid upon the heart of that youth of one hundred and twenty summers, that heart was stilled, and Moses was no more. No pain, no fever, no agony, no fear in dying, no struggle; simply a youth of one hundred and twenty years, standing on the top of that lofty mountain, with the rest of the world spread out in beauty before him—his soul is filled, his eye is satisfied—and without a moment's warning the summons comes, and he falls asleep without a quiver, without a murmur. He has the towering mountain for his couch, the bending heavens for his shroud, and the Lord Almighty for his companion, no other being there but the angels that hovered, unseen, but real, around his couch; and God himself buried Moses in some lonely spot, unmarked, unknown, that his tomb might never be desecrated; that his lonely body might sleep there in solemn silence till the trump of God shall sound.

Men thirst for glory that will linger after they are gone. Did Moses have this recompense of reward? Ten thousand people—men, women, and children—know Moses to-day as the lawgiver, the leader of Israel, the meekest man of all the earth; ten thousand people know him to-day in every sense in which he would wish to be known for every one that had known him now, had he been willing to practice the deception that would have given him the crown, throne, and scepter of Egypt; yea, millions know Moses to-day— know him in the unerring love light of God's eternal truth —whereas, had he practiced that deception, in all probability not one single, solitary soul beneath the stars in this generation would have heard of him. He had simply lived as the son of Pharaoh's daughter, had been esteemed a prince, and, perchance, had swayed the scepter over Egypt; he had gone to the tombs of the Pharaohs, and had been forgotten long ago. More than three thousand years have come and gone since his death, and yet the civilized world knows Moses; and should a thousand generations more be born upon the earth, the last generation will know him as one who preferred " to suffer affliction with the people of God, rather than to enjoy the pleasures of sin for a season."

Such was part of the earthly reward that Moses received, through the providence of God, for refusing to be called " the son of Pharaoh's daughter; " but there was something beyond this in store for him. The place assigned to him in the Scriptures is enough to assure us that there is a place assigned to him in God's eternal home. He is spoken of as being with the Savior when he was transfigured on Hermon's holy height; he is spoken of in many ways in the Bible that lead us to conclude that the end of his life on earth was but the beginning of life eternal in a world that is brighter and better than this.

The choice that confronted Moses confronts every responsible son and daughter of Adam's race—the choice between the pleasures of sin and the trials and triumphs of the people of God—and there is given us in the Book of books every assurance that if, like Moses, we esteem the reproach of Christ greater riches than the treasures and sinful pleasures of this world, we shall in no wise lose our reward, either in this life or in the life to come, but shall have the sweetest, because the purest, joys earth can give, and the unalloyed bliss of God's eternal home forever. For this let us live, labor, and pray, and God will save us all.

UNION AND UNITY.

The thought of the union and unity of the followers of Jesus is not a new thought. Read the Lord's Prayer. (John 17.) Jesus earnestly prayed that not only the disciples then with him, but all who should believe on him while time shall last, might be one, as he and the Father are one: "As thou, Father, art in me, and I in thee, that they also may be one in us: that the world may believe that thou hast sent me." In what sense can Jehovah, Jesus, and his disciples be one? Just in the sense that Jesus and Jehovah are one—one in aims, one in purpose, working harmoniously together for the same glorious results. The religious world has drifted far away from the spirit of that prayer, and division and strife have found place in the church of God; but occasionally some man arises who, in sympathy with the Savior, as expressed in this beautiful prayer, though not strong enough to stem the tide, has deplored this condition in the church. John Wesley, in his "Notes on the New Testament" (a standard work), in the ninth section or division of the introduction or preface to that work, utters this earnest prayer: "Would to God that all party names and unscriptural forms and phrases that have divided the Christian world were forgot, and that we might all agree to sit down together, like little children, at the feet of our common Master, to hear his words, to imbibe his spirit and transcribe his life into our own!" Wesley was not strong enough to successfully stem the tide, but he had sympathy in his soul for the Savior, and hence, instead of trying to establish some sect or party, and thus get the world farther away from the church of God, he deplored the divisions in the religious world and uttered the prayer just quoted, which is well worth repeating, and repeating frequently. It does not come from a divine source, but it comes from the pen of a wonderfully great man, and at least merits the consideration of every thoughtful, earnest Christian.

May the Lord so bless each and every one of us that when the books are opened it may appear that none of us have ever done one single thing to prevent the fulfillment of this prayer of our Savior.

THE BOW IN THE CLOUD.

" I do set my bow in the cloud, and it shall be for a token of a covenant between me and the earth. And it shall come to pass, when I bring a cloud over the earth, that the bow shall be seen in the cloud: and I will remember my covenant, which is between me and you and every living creature of all flesh; and the waters shall no more become a flood to destroy all flesh." (Gen. 9: 13-15.)

God's kindness, mercy, and love are universally and perpetually displayed toward the creatures of his care.

> Around, beneath, below, above—
> Wherever space extends—
> There heaven displays its boundless love,
> And power with goodness blends.

That was true when it was written, it is true to-day, and it is to be forever true. God has manifested his power and grace and goodness in giving us memorial institutions, tokens and reminders of promises, and manifestations of divine providence and wonderful power, that we, when we see these reminders, may be encouraged and lifted up and cheered as we journey to the tomb.

The world's history has not been an uneventful one, not even the brief period we now call the " antediluvian age," a period of 1,656 years, beginning with creation—a wonderful event, of course, to be remembered as such while time and eternity shall last—when God from the boundless bosom of impenetrable darkness called forth light, and in that light completed the drama of creation. Man fell, Eden withered, sin prevailed. Men multiplied and sin increased till God, who could see the end from the beginning and understand all the immediate and remote results of sin, saw it had been better that man had never been made, unless the tide of sin could be stayed, and he resolved that the deluge should come, that the earth should be renovated with water—water and fire being two of the greatest purifiers at the command of God. He resolved that this literal earth should be overwhelmed, enveloped, submerged in an ocean without a shore, for the literal remission of her literal sins. But a remnant must be saved to repeople the earth. That remnant must be the right remnant, and must be saved by the power of Almighty God. "Noah was a just man and perfect in his generations, and Noah walked with God." God selected Noah to coöperate with him in the preservation of the human race from absolute extermination. He gave him directions—plain, explicit, and simple—as to the building of the ark: its length, its breadth, its height, how and of what to make it—directions as plain and simple as if given to a little child; and Noah, walking simply and solely by faith, followed these directions implicitly.

So far as mortal man has any means of knowing, it had never rained upon the earth until the coming of the storm that brought the deluge. In Gen. 2: 5 we are told that it had never rained upon the earth up to that time, and it is reasonable to presume that the elements had never been in the proper condition to precipitate rain till the coming of the deluge.   But all things are in readiness and a change is about to come.   The people out of the ark can see far away in the distance a dark, towering mountain peak they have never seen before; they look to the north, to the south, to the east, to the west, and these living mountains of cloud are there rising higher and higher, like mighty giants lifting their heads to the heavens; livid lightnings, never seen before, play upon the bosoms of the valleys between the mountain peaks, and form a wreath of glittering, golden glory round the brows of these gloomy giants in the heavens; the earth beneath begins to tremble and quake and shiver; the deep mutterings of distant thunder are heard; the whole heavens are shrouded in gloom, the whole earth filled with darkness and despair.

Suddenly the heavens begin to weep; great tears drop down from the clouds.   Thicker they fall and faster.   The windows of heaven are opened; the fountains of the deep are broken up; the waters of sighing seas and sobbing oceans rush and roar around the globe.   The plains are covered, the hills are gone, the mountains are submerged, the earth is overwhelmed; waves sweep in triumph over an ocean without a shore.   Sin is blotted out; all sinners are destroyed.   Forty days and forty nights the heavens weep and the earth is shrouded in darkness.   The storm subsides, the waters are abated, the dry land appears.

Noah and his family come forth, bringing with them all other living creatures in the ark.   Noah builds an altar, sacrifices are offered, and he and his family bow down before that altar and pour out their souls in expressions of thankfulness and gratitude to God, the gracious Giver of all good. God gives them assurance of his continued care —divine assurance of safety from another deluge of water. He enters into a covenant with them, that while the earth remains, seed time and harvest, and cold and heat, and summer and winter, and day and night, shall not cease; that while time lasts, this earth shall never again be enveloped in the waves of a deluge of water; and as a token and sign and seal of this glorious promise, God set the bow in the cloud.

Whatever had or had not been, there had never before been a rainbow in the cloud. We have a guarantee, sealed and certified by that token, that the earth shall never again be deluged by water; but we also have a positive guarantee in God's truth that it shall one day be purified by a deluge of fire, that the earth and all therein shall be burned. So the beautiful bow of promise rises out of a flood of water, spans the arch of time, and rests in a flood of fire.

When certain events of extraordinary importance to the human race have occurred, especially events that have demonstrated God's special power, providence, and protection, he has set apart something as a token or reminder of that event. In Ex. 12 we learn of the directions God gave to the children of Israel for the preparation of the passover—as plain and simple as the directions to Noah for building the ark. The building of the ark foretold a deluge of water; the preparation for the passover foretold a deluge of death. At midnight the angel of death swept over the land of Egypt, slaying the firstborn in every family, save where the blood of the paschal lamb upon the doorposts marked the household of an obedient Israelite. The feast of the passover was instituted as a token or reminder of the day when God sent this last plague upon Egypt and caused pitiless Pharaoh to relax his grasp upon Israel and let the people go; and the Jews to this day keep the passover in memory of their escape from that visitation of death.

The Israelites kept the first passover in Egypt, and marched that night from their oppressors toward the promised land; but they were not yet delivered from the power of Egypt. The Red Sea was between them and the wilderness of their wandering; beyond the wilderness was the Jordan; and they must cross the Red Sea, the wilderness, and the Jordan to reach the land of promise. This they could do only under the care and guidance and protection of God.

In Ex. 16 we are told of another memorial institution or token established for an important purpose. God commanded that the seventh day of the week, the day we call "Saturday," should be a rest day to the Jews throughout their generations—no fire kindled in their habitations, no work, no attending to business, no congregating together; but on that day there was to be as nearly absolute and perfect rest as it was possible, and the people still survive.

Why was this? "Remember that thou wast a servant in the land of Egypt, and that the Lord thy God brought thee out thence through a mighty hand and by a stretched out arm: therefore the Lord thy God commanded thee to keep the Sabbath day." (Deut. 5: 15.)

Why had they never been commanded to keep the Sabbath day previous to this time? Because the reason for it had never before existed. God had not, previous to this time, brought the children of Israel out of Egyptian bondage by " a mighty hand and by a stretched out arm."

In the still, quiet hours of this day of perfect rest, the Jews could remember how their ancestors in the land of Egypt were delivered from slavery by the hand of Jehovah himself. The Jews who now observe the Sabbath, if any do observe it, have time, in the quiet of that day, for reflection; their minds can float back on the wings of faith and imagination to the days of slavery in Egypt; and they still have special reason to be grateful to God for his goodness and power as manifested to their ancestors in the long, long ago.

There is another memorial day, a day commemorating an event of wonderful importance, something brighter and more glorious than the covenant memorialized by the bow in the cloud—the birthday of our Savior from the tomb. We learn from the introduction to the last chapters of both Matthew and Mark that this day is the day that follows the Sabbath; hence it is the first day of the week, the secular name of which is " Sunday."

Since the establishment of the church of God, this day has been observed, not as a rest day, but as a day of spiritual activity. We should read and understand and teach our little ones exactly when the command to keep the Sabbath day came, from whom it came, why it came, to whom it came; and teach them that it was never a command to the Gentiles, and that this is the fundamental reason why we do not rest on the Sabbath day—the seventh day, or Saturday. We should also teach them why we observe the first day of the week, not as a rest day, but as a day of spiritual activity.

We should teach them that this bright, blessed first day of the week is Redemption's Day—the birthday of the Savior from the tomb. Jesus kept the Sabbath in the solemn silence of death, and just " as it began to dawn toward the first day of the week " an angel swept down from the courts of glory and rolled the stone away from the sepulcher, and the Sun of Righteousness arose with healing in his wings, to flood the world with light divine and lift our souls to God. God has thus reserved to himself the first fruits of the week, and has placed the stamp and seal and signature of Heaven's approval upon the brow of this bright, blessed day.

THE SALT OF THE EARTH.

We are bringing reproach upon the cause of Christ or honoring the name of Jesus by the way we look, by the way we think, by the way we talk, by the way we live. We should be chaste in word, thought, and deed; purer and better, more self-sacrificing, more self-denying, every day we live. If we would give heed to this one thought suggested in this beautiful verse, " Only let your conversation be as it becometh the gospel of Christ," we would bless the world wherever we may be, and show a greater fitness

than the world can otherwise see in the language of the
Savior when he called his disciples " the salt of the earth,"
" the light of the world." This is what God wishes us to
do, this is what he wishes us to be; and just to the extent
that we do and be this are we in harmony with his will,
and to the extent we do and be otherwise we are in rebellion
against him. One thing is sure: we are for Christ or
against him; we are weights or wings to this world; we are
light or darkness; our lives are blessings or curses to the
human race, so far as our influence extends, every day we
live.

PURE IN SPEECH.

" Only let your conversation be as it becometh the gospel
of Christ: that whether I come and see you, or else be absent, I may hear of your affairs, that ye stand fast in one
spirit, with one mind striving together for the faith of the
gospel." (Phil. 1: 27.)

The word " conversation " here does not mean what we
ordinarily take it to mean in our day—that is, it is not
restricted simply to a certain class or character of talk.
While it includes all that we mean by the word " conversation," it is much broader in its comprehension; it embraces
our entire life, as we find from Paul's letter to the Ephe-
sians (2: 1-3). It includes what we say, what we do, and
what we think, so far as what we think is expressed in look,
in language, or in life. Still, we should be just as careful
how we use our tongues as if " conversation " in this place
meant simply the talk that we have when we are talking
to those who talk to us in return. In the pulpit or out

of it, anywhere and everywhere, our tongues should talk nothing that is not proper to be talked by the sons and daughters of the Lord Almighty, children of the Heavenly King, followers of the sinless Son of God. While the tongues that talk for Jesus, publicly or privately, should always be chaste and pure and clean, this is especially true, under all circumstances, of tongues that talk for Christ publicly.

We that occupy the pulpit should think of this, and those who occupy the pews should bring such a pressure to bear upon us as to make it practically impossible for us to ever forget it—impossible to forget that we are talking for Heaven every moment that we talk, in the pulpit or out of it.

The tongue that talks where orange blossoms kiss the brow of beauty beneath the bridal veil, when hearts are glad and hearts are sad; the tongue that talks where truest love with tireless hand rocks the cradle, while the sinless creature of a mother's care soundly sleeps and sweetly dreams; the tongue that talks where weeping wife or mourning mother holds the hand of a loved one in the throes of death; the tongue that talks where mourners, clad in blackest black, sob and sigh around the bier and shroud; the tongue that talks beside the open grave that waits for what was dearer far than life to loved ones left behind; the tongue that talks where vacant seats in the home circle tell of joys forever gone; the tongue that talks for God to man and tells of things eternal; the tongue that talks of the tears and trials and temptations of time, and then talks of the grandeurs and glories and beauties of a world where sorrows are unknown; the tongue that talks of all that is near and dear to the human race, from the cradle to the grave and through vast eternity—that tongue should be a consecrated tongue, pure and chaste and clean, that utters neither vulgarity, obscenity, profanity, balderdash, nor slang—ever!

RACE NOT TO THE SWIFT.

We should remember that the race is not to the swift or the battle to the strong, as men count speed or estimate strength; but the Lord Almighty will give the victory, glorious and eternal, to the brave, the faithful, and the true. Gideon's army when it numbered but three hundred was a greater and stronger army than when it numbered thirty-two thousand; for when it numbered but three hundred it was the army that God would have it to be, doing the work he would have it to do, working in harmony with his will for the purpose in view. The same is true to-day, always has been true, always will be true. The Lord Almighty and one brave man or true woman that fears no danger, dreads not even death, are an overwhelming majority, an invincible host, in any contest beneath the stars.

These be times when the faithful and the true should know no division, but should stand as one man for the cause of Christ, clad in the panoply of Heaven, with hearts full of sympathy for the sorrowing, suffering, sighing sons and daughters of men, battling on from victory to victory till God shall call them home. Can we afford to be wrangling and disputing and cherishing unkind feelings toward each other, when souls all around us are living in the shadow and darkness of sin? The firemen who would stop when a home or a city is burning, the members of a life-saving station who would stop when some mother's child is drowning to discuss some little matters of difference, would be worthy of praise for fidelity to duty for all time to come, in comparison with the man who, claiming to be a Christian, would sulk in his tent in times like these. There is more than a blazing city or a drowning child involved in this work. The sweetest joys earth can give and all the bliss of heaven forever, for ourselves, our friends, our neighbors, for those that know us best and love us most, are involved in the conduct of each one of us now.

TIMES THAT TRY MEN'S SOULS.

If there has ever been a day when it was important for the friends of Jesus to rally to his cause, to stand up for God's will and word and way, that day has dawned upon us. As the great infidel, Thomas Paine, I believe it was, said: "These are times that try men's souls." That language, in various forms, has been quoted thousands of times since he wrote it long ago in reference to the Revolutionary War and the times that immediately succeeded that bloody struggle, and it applies to-day, to this generation, in reference to Nashville and the contiguous country, to the condition of the people here this very moment. These are times that tell who are on the Lord's side and who are on the other side; who are brave enough to dare and do and suffer for the cause of Christ, and who are afraid to stand up for Jesus because, so far as men count numbers, they are in a hopeless minority in the land.

THE KINGDOM OF GOD.

"And in the days of these kings shall the God of heaven set up a kingdom, which shall never be destroyed: and the kingdom shall not be left to other people, but it shall break in pieces and consume all these kingdoms, and it shall stand forever." (Dan. 2. 44.)

More than six hundred years before the establishment of Christ's kingdom upon the earth, in the days of the Babylonish captivity, Nebuchadnezzar, king of Babylon, had a wonderful prophetic dream. We have this dream and many things connected with it placed before us in Dan. 2. This dream represented the four universal empires—the Assyrian, or Babylonish; the Medo-Persian, the Grecian, and the Roman—represented in Nebuchadnezzar's dream by gold, silver, brass, and iron mixed with miry clay, respectively. They are not spoken of by name—only one of them had had existence at that time—but they are represented so clearly in this dream that there is absolutely no reason why the shadow of a doubt should fall upon the mind of any one conversant with the Bible and with profane history in reference to their identity.

From the earliest days of history, ambitious men have been struggling for power, dominion, and conquest, and rivers of blood have been shed, millions of men destroyed, and billions of hearts made sad in vain and futile efforts to establish universal empires. Centuries have come and gone, many generations have been born and buried, and this desire has been in the hearts of millions of men; yet only four empires have been recognized as universal. These lasted, according to accepted chronology, all together, in the aggregate, not much longer than the church of Christ has been in existence—the Babylonish empire lasting fourteen hundred years; the Medo-Persian, three hundred years; the Grecian, ten years; and the Roman, four hundred years.

These empires were established in blood and were shielded and supported by the sword; but none of them could stand. Daniel was a captive under Babylonish rule when the first of these four universal empires was in the very zenith of its grandeur and power and glory; yet, when he came to interpret that dream, he declared that proud Babylon should fall, that the Assyrian empire should crumble and another power arise and supplant it, which should, in its turn, be supplanted by another, and that by another, till, in the days of the fourth, the God of heaven would establish a kingdom that should never be destroyed—a kingdom that should not be left to other people, but that should break in pieces and consume all those kingdoms and should stand forever.

The kingdom that the God of heaven was to set up was to be established in the days of the Roman empire; it having been established, the Roman empire should fall, be broken in pieces, and consumed—not be turned over to a supplanting or subverting or succeeding power, but be consumed. The inference is clear that there was never to be another universal empire founded by the sword of mortal man upon the earth.

The Roman empire fell many centuries ago. Fifty generations have been born and buried since that day, but no other universal empire has arisen to take its place. Napoleon, filled with pride and ambition, hoped in the depths of his sordid, selfish soul that he would be able to subdue the nations of the earth and found a universal empire; but just when the realization of his highest hopes and proudest ambitions seemed to be almost in sight, his hopes were crushed and broken and overthrown, his lofty ambitions ended in banishment to lonely St. Helena. England seems to have breathed the same spirit, and her boast for generations has been that the sun never sets upon her possessions; yet she has never been able to establish a universal empire, and to-day such an event seems less likely than at any other time for centuries past.

What of the kingdom that Jehovah was to establish in the days of the Roman empire? Jesus, the Babe of Bethlehem, the Man of sorrows, the poorest of the poor, almost in the shadow of the cross on which he died, with no sword in his hand, no army at his command, said to his faithful followers: " Upon this rock "—this sublime confession, of which I am the soul, the substance, the all—" Upon this rock I will build my church; and the gates of hell shall not prevail against it."

A few weeks after this he died upon the cross, slumbered in the solemn silence of a borrowed tomb for three days and nights, and arose a triumphant conqueror over death and the grave. Forty days after this he ascended to glory.

Seven days after his ascension the Holy Spirit descended from heaven and took up his abode in the material prepared for this kingdom, and the kingdom of God was born, or established, then and there. It consisted of only about one hundred and twenty charter members, and they as poor as the poorest; yet back of it were the promises: "And it shall never be destroyed"—"The gates of hell shall not prevail against it."

Have the powers of darkness—"the gates of hell"—tried to prevail against the kingdom of God, the church of Christ? The sorrowful, tearful, bloody history of the world for eighteen hundred years can answer that question. The church was born, like the Babe of Bethlehem, in the depths of poverty and obscurity; in the shadow of the towering mountain of Judaism, on the one hand, and the towering mountain of paganism, on the other—Judaism backed by wealth and influence; paganism backed by political power and supremacy, by millions of money and millions of men. But the kingdom established by the God of heaven was not destroyed in the days of its infancy. It passed through fiery trials at the hands of imperial Rome in Rome's declining, dying days. It has passed through days of fiery persecution at the hands of others; it has been assailed by atheism, skepticism, infidelity—by every phase and form, shade and grade, of the power of sin and Satan for eighteen hundred years; and still it stands, unmoved and immovable, never having unsheathed a sword, fixed a bayonet, loaded a gun, lifted a battle-ax or spear to preserve its existence, extend its dominion, define or defend its rights.

No other institution has been called upon to withstand one-thousandth part of what the church of God has withstood; no other institution could have weathered the storms that have swept its bosom.   Storm after storm has arisen, lowering clouds have gathered round, livid lightnings have played about it, muttering thunders have rocked it; but it has never been destroyed, and its glory and power are destined to fill the earth as waters cover the sea.   Kingdoms may be founded, may flourish, and may fall, but the church of God shall stand forever.   Atheism may scoff, infidelity may assail, skepticism may smile, and doubting hearts may tremble for the safety of Zion; but Zion stands secure, the living fulfillment of the promise of the God of heaven that the kingdom which he was to establish should never be destroyed.

Of this divine institution it may be said, almost in the language of Byron relative to Corinth of old:

> " Many a vanished year and age
>   And tempest's breath and battle's rage
>   Have swept her bosom; still she stands,
>   A fortress formed by heaven's hands.
>
> " The whirlwind's wrath, the earthquake's shock
>   Have left untouched that sacred rock,
>   The pillars of a cause which still,
>   Though persecuted, earth shall fill."